LORDS, LAND AND LABOURERS

LORDS, LAND AND LABOURERS

THE BIG HOUSES AND LANDED ESTATES OF ROYAL MEATH

EDITED BY BRIAN CASEY

The
History
Press
Ireland

In memory of Caroline Gallagher,
1958-2016

First published 2016

The History Press Ireland
50 City Quay
Dublin 2
Ireland
www.thehistorypress.ie

The History Press Ireland is a member of Publishing Ireland,
the Irish book publishers' association.

British Library Cataloguing in Publication Data.
A catalogue record for this book is available from the British Library.

ISBN 978 1 84588 087 3

Typesetting and origination by The History Press

Contents

List of Contributors

JAMES CAFFREY is a retired farmer from Wilkinstown, Navan. He holds a BA in Local History and an MA in Irish History from Maynooth University. He is a contributor to the *Navan & District Historical Society Journal* and *Meath History and Society* edited by William Nolan.

BRIAN CASEY completed a PhD in History at Maynooth University under Professor Terence Dooley. He is the editor of *Defying the Law of the Land: Agrarian Radicals in Irish History* and his research interests generally focus upon late-Victorian rural Britain and Ireland with a particular reference to the dynamics of social radicalism in the west of Ireland.

PETER CONNELL is author of *The Land and People of County Meath, 1750–1850*, published by Four Courts Press in 2004, and editor of *Riocht na Midhe*, the journal of the Meath Archaeological and Historical Society. He was a founding member of the Meath History Workshop and is currently pursuing research on the history of public housing in Ireland.

DANNY CUSACK is a native of Perth, Western Australia, his paternal grandfather having emigrated there from Kilmainhamwood, County Meath, in 1908. Currently residing at Kells, Danny is convenor of Meath History Workshop. His interests include the Great Famine and post-Famine Irish history, Meath local studies, social and labour history and the Irish in Australia.

NOEL E. FRENCH graduated from NUI Maynooth with an MA in Local Studies. Noel has been director of the Meath Heritage Centre, Trim, since 1987. He has published a number of local histories relating to Meath and is a regular contributor to the local journal, *Riocht na Midhe*.

JIM GILLIGAN is a former principal of St Seachnall's National School, Dunshaughlin. He has published *Graziers and Grasslands* in the Maynooth Studies in Local History series, is a contributor to *Meath History and Society* and is author of *Black and Amber*, a history of the GAA in Dunshaughlin.

MALACHY HAND grew up and currently farms in the scenic area of north-west Meath near Oldcastle; he also does guided tours in this area. Malachy completed a certificate course in Local History Studies at NUI Maynooth in 2005 and later studied Oral Heritage at the University of Limerick in 2010. He is also involved in various historical projects with Moylagh Historical Society.

KEVIN LYNCH lives in Navan, County Meath, and holds an MA in Historic House Studies at Maynooth University. He has taken part in studies concerning agriculture, the aristocracy and social aspects connected to the Big Houses of Ireland. He is also a GIS Analyst and is currently combining GIS analytical practices with historical studies.

JOE MOONEY is a retired teacher and has been working and teaching in Meath for many years. His MA thesis on the Headfort estate in Kells, County Meath, was published as a volume in the Maynooth Studies in Local History as *The Changing Fortunes of the Headfort Estate, 1870–1928* (Dublin, 2012). He continues to research the landed estates in Meath and how the transfer of ownership from landlord to tenant took place.

UNA PALCIC (*née* O'Reilly) is a retired secondary-school teacher. She holds two degrees from University College Dublin (1970, 2006), the most recent in Geographical Perspectives, Local Studies and Greek and Roman Civilisation. Her main research interests are in the history of Meath, in particular the barony of Fore as she is a native of Oldcastle. She is a member of the Meath History Workshop.

MARION ROGAN holds an MA in Local History from NUI Maynooth and is currently studying for a PhD. She lives near Kells in County Meath and is a retired principal of Oristown National School. Her most recent publication is *Charles Tisdall of County Meath, 1740–51: From Spendthrift Youth to Improving Landlord* (Dublin, 2014).

Acknowledgements

Thanks are due to Tom French, librarian in Navan Library, Dr Loreto Guinan, Meath Heritage Office and Seamus MacGabhann, of the Meath Archaeological and Historical Society, for their enthusiasm and support of this collection of essays from the start. We wish to acknowledge the financial assistance of the Meath Heritage Office (Meath County Council) under the Community Heritage Grant Scheme towards the publication of this book. Thanks also to the various repositories for permission to reproduce images and quotes from their collections. Jim Gilligan suggested the title, Kevin Lynch drew up most of the maps and Ronan Colgan of The History Press Ireland has been a wonderful support and great to work with yet again. My appreciation to the contributors and the other superb members of the Meath History Workshop for their patience, ideas and enthusiasm for this project from its inception. Finally, tribute must be paid to the staff, past and present, of the Department of History at Maynooth University. Most of the contributors in this volume are graduates or have a strong associations with that department and it is a testament to the quality of the teaching and research of the department that a volume such as this has been produced.

Brian Casey

Abbreviations

IGMR	Inspector General Monthly Report
IUA	Irish Unionist Alliance
JP	Justice of the Peace
MCL	Meath County Library
MCPR	Meath County Police Reports
NAI	National Archives of Ireland
NLI	National Library of Ireland
PRONI	Public Record Office of Northern Ireland
RCB	Representative Church Body
RLFC	Famine Relief Commission Papers
UIL	United Irish League

List of Maps, Charts and Tables

Introduction

BRIAN CASEY, PETER CONNELL
AND DANNY CUSACK

The New English colonisation of Ireland from the 1530s onwards may be seen as the equivalent of a major continental invasion that transformed the island from Malin Head to Rosslare and from Fair Head to Cape Clear.[1]

The mapping of Ireland in the sixteenth and seventeenth centuries is the story of English construction and conquest. The late-medieval Ireland had been displaced and a new, modern Ireland was now on display in maps and on the ground as well. The efforts of Henry VIII at gaining influence and control in Ireland saw him direct attention towards regional kings. Land equalled power in sixteenth-century Ireland and the English government was aware of that, so gaining the loyalty of the most powerful landowners in the country meant that Ireland would be easier to govern.

Sir Anthony St Leger was Henry's lord deputy in Ireland in the 1540s and was tasked with asserting order in Ireland. He felt the best way to exact obedience amongst the Gaelic Irish was to impose feudal tenure – based on the English model – in Ireland. His political skills led to the policy of surrender and regrant. This was an effort to move away from clan and kin loyalties to a feudal system based on English common law. It was an effort to assert control over clans outside of Dublin in particular, and it brought about peace and stability. St Leger was a skilful politician as well as a competent administrator, which ensured peace and stability during his years as lord deputy. The theory of plantation was that of civilisation, and sources from the early modern period show how keen the English government was in trying to implement this in Ireland. The social geography of the country changed as a result, with new settler ethnic groups emerging.[2] Sources indicate that English government officials saw Ireland as an uncivilised backwater, and plantation was a way of changing this. The Crown was also keen to anglicise Ireland, make it a reliable and peaceful destination that would not pose any risk to the safety of England. It eventually took the form of confiscation as a punishment for involvement in rebellions and the Laois and Offaly plantations were the first of these, starting in 1556, and these counties were renamed Queen's County and King's County respectively.

In 1586 a decision was taken to settle people of English birth on confiscated land for two reasons: civility and control. It was finally proclaimed on 27 June 1586 with the lands divided into various holdings ranging from 4,000 to 12,000 acres, and no undertaker could possess more than 12,000 acres, though the Gaelic Irish were ruled out as residents on plantation estates. The theory was symmetrical and well-organised estates but the reality was quite different. Disputes flared up between impatient undertakers as there were disputes over who was entitled to what land. There were several problems that resulted in only a third of the projected 11,300 persons taking up residence in Ulster. The arbitrary recognition of Gaelic land rights or English rights presented an incoherent policy regarding land and a general uprising led to its final destruction in 1598. This inconsistency in the implementation of policies was there for generations after.[3]

By the 1620s the Old English had a clear vision of themselves as an elite within society. At this time, merchants, who had acquired wealth in the towns, retreated to the countryside after settling upon farms. They were mostly Old English and they had benefitted from the peace that existed in the countryside, the single land market that emerged because of the implementation of English law across the land. Because of an economic crisis in the 1620s, smaller landholders, squires and so on arranged for mortgages with those who had spare cash and the people to which they turned the most were merchants. This had the benefit of helping stronger landholders consolidate their own power base and influence.

Following the Cromwellian campaigns, the new regime was determined to be severe with those who had fought against it and confiscation was the main instrument used against royalists. There was severe financial pressure on those being punished, and this was coupled with the fact that many landlords had severely depressed incomes and the economy was still in a poor condition. The result was that many landlords were forced to sell land (and so a series of new landlords entered the social world of Ireland in the 1650s) and the power of landlords was severely reduced. The Act of Settlement made it clear that confiscation was happening to meet the needs of the army and adventurers and also to create a more favourable security situation. However, by June 1653, we see a more extreme example and the notion of 'to hell or to Connacht' was conceived. This was called the Act of Satisfaction and ensured that those who were transplanted were not to be settled within 4 miles of the River Shannon or the sea. Essentially it meant that Connacht was being used to contain potential resistance to social changes associated with land allocation.

In the seventeenth century, the idea of absentee landlords began to emerge. While they had massive estates, there were only modest returns from them. Plantations emerged in order to bring about physical and cultural transformations but this was not as straightforward as was hoped.

> The struggle for the ownership of land that characterised the seventeenth century was largely resolved in favour of the 'new English' and the century marked the consolidation of a Protestant Ascendancy. In county Meath, prominent Catholic 'old English' families such as Fingall, Gormanston, Dunsany and Netterville managed to retain their land and positions following the Williamite War and up to twenty per cent of land in the county was still in Catholic hands in 1700.[4]

Some planters hoped that they could begin viable agricultural enterprises, but very often they faced challenges doing this. While landlords may have been absentee, they needed agents to manage their estates, and this saw the land agent acquiring considerable power and influence. Substantial tenants also developed more influence than they might have acquired with resident landlords. The landed estate was the centre point for life in Ireland for centuries, with landlords being the kingpins in rural Ireland and owners becoming a self-perpetuating and limited class of people.[5]

These essays explore an alternative Ireland, one hidden from posterity and not explored in historiography. To quote that extraordinary geographer of early modern Ireland, W.J. Smyth, this volume is part of a collective

> enduring concern is to try to get behind and beyond the more richly documented worlds of the ruling elites (old and new), to penetrate and excavate the whole society, so as to provide some glimpses of the forces, beliefs, experiences and events that shaped the lives and localities of the ordinary men and women.[6]

That the landed class was self-perpetuating is generally accepted as a given. There were numerous layers on each estate, such as manor courts, middlemen and an evolution that shows how the estate was not a static entity, but something that evolved and changed over time: such changes are explored in this collection. While middlemen were powerful and influential figures in the countryside for a considerable period, the expiration of leases and the Famine saw them disappear from the landscape as landlords began to assert control over their estates again. Mutual respect between landlord and tenants existed on numerous estates and this ensured order and social harmony remained intact. Landlords, landlord–tenant relations and the land question are dominant themes in Irish historiography. The various case studies in this collection highlight the intricate web of relationships that existed in rural Ireland on estates.

The Big Houses assumed the evocative symbolism of representing a callous colonial oppressor, while in the United Kingdom they were seen to be part of a shared national heritage. While Big House tourism has now slowly become a feature of the Irish landscape, there is a risk of over correcting the nationalist orthodoxy of capricious evictors in order to rehabilitate the plight of the landed class. Critical engagement of the source material still needs to continue. Landlords were an elite, powerful, frequently reactionary and conservative and could be devoid of empathy with the plight of the poor as religious, cultural and class differences manifested themselves in various ways with even the most paternalistic being condescending in their endeavours to alleviate distress. Deference was a tenuous form of loyalty and as the Land War showed, it could be easily undermined and destroyed.

In recent decades, the value of estate records has become increasingly appreciated as they have played a vital role in critically assessing our past, debunking certain myths and offering many vibrant avenues for new research. There is still much to do in regards to local estate studies: local historians need to be more forthright in asserting the importance of their discipline and how the inherent skills associated with its pursuit and practice ensure that this alternative and more nuanced view of Ireland can be constructed. This scholarship has shown a rather complex picture of land transfer, conquest and confiscation in efforts to assert state control over the country.[7] Furthermore, the physical landscape, while ever evolving, leaves clues and evidence pertaining to landed estates in a myriad of ways. All these are important in highlighting how the rural countryside was not just to be consumed but also to be lived in. Progressive landlordism and the devastation wrought by the Famine saw significant changes to the landscape in the post-Famine period, with Famine villages dotting the countryside as the population collapsed, townlands disappeared and emigration became an important factor in estate life.

Local history is shaped by the community that lives within it, and the individuals that mould its environment play an important role in shaping its history. These essays explore the rich tapestry of local experiences within County Meath through the prism of the landed estate, and they all show that local history is an important element of historical enquiry.

LANDHOLDING IN MEATH

From Hugh de Lacy's effective conquest of Meath in the 1170s, and the establishment of Anglo-Norman power, through to the demise of what has been termed the 'landed aristocracy' at the beginning of the twentieth century, the county's history has been shaped by the struggle for land and the wealth and power that it confers. The system of landed estates that evolved through the eighteenth and nineteenth centuries was marked by both continuity and change. Much of the land held by the Old English families of the Pale fell into new hands by the end of the seventeenth century as the Flemings, Barnwalls, Cusacks, Darcys and Dowdalls were displaced by those who were beneficiaries of the Cromwellian settlement in the 1650s and the Jacobite defeat of the 1690s. The sixty years between 1640 and 1700 marked a fundamental break in patterns of land ownership that, in many cases, were several centuries old. And yet the extent of many of the large estates that marked the apogee of the system in Meath, such as of those of Conyngham, Naper and Darnley, was defined by old property boundaries and centred on the bailiwicks of their previous Old English owners.

At the beginning of the seventeenth century, about 80 per cent of land in the county was still under the control of the Old English families. The Civil Survey provides a snapshot of land ownership across the county in 1640 and shows that two thirds of land were still in Catholic hands at the start of that decisive decade. This included most of the north and west of the county. Among the most prominent families were the various branches of the Plunketts who held land right across the county, the Barnewalls (barons of Trimblestown, near Trim) with estates in the baronies of Lune, Navan and Morgallion and the Preston family (Viscount Gormanston) with land in Morgallion, Lune and Duleek. Together with the estates of the Cusack, Darcy and Dowdall families these tracts of land became subject to confiscation under the Cromwellian settlement as the Old English of Meath supported the king against the parliament in the 1640s. The provisions of the settlement directed that those who had 'not manifested their constant good affection to the Commonwealth' would forfeit one third of their land and be allocated the equivalent of the remaining two thirds in Connacht. Some indeed were transported to Connacht, but with the restoration of Charles II to the throne in 1660 a partially successful rearguard action was fought by those who had been dispossessed. By 1670, however, just under a quarter of the land in the county remained in Catholic hands. Amongst the beneficiaries were Sir William Petty, chief organiser of the Down Survey and one of the period's most successful adventurers, who acquired over 12,000 acres in Meath, in addition to extensive estates in south Kerry and in five other counties. Viscount Gormanston was restored to most of his lands in the north of the county and the Plunketts of Killeen and Dunsany retained most of their property. The outcome of the Jacobean Wars resulted in further confiscations and, at the behest of William III in 1703, the sale of lands to exclusively Protestant buyers. It was in these circumstances that the Conynghams acquired the Fleming land at Slane. Through the early years of the eighteenth century the exigencies of the penal laws saw a number of families, including the Plunketts of Dunsany, Nettervilles and Alymers, conform to the established Church so that by the 1720s a new settlement, in terms of power and land, was securely in place. From this time, a group of Protestant landowning families who were resident in the county came to dominate its politics. These included the Taylours (Headfort), Nicholsons (Balrath), Wallers (Allenstown), Gerrards (Gibbstown) and Rothwells (Rockfield, Kells). In the decades that followed, the Ascendancy's most prominent architects were employed building great houses that gave expression to the wealth and confidence of their class. Richard Castle was responsible for the design of a number of the county's great houses in the 1730s through to 1750. These included both Headfort House and the Preston family's Bellinter House near Navan. Across the county, particularly in the valleys of the Boyne and Blackwater rivers, demesnes of gardens, rolling parklands and plantations were carved out by landlords expressing their power and wealth in the landscape.

While the great estates referred to above represent the most tangible manifestation of the new elites who assumed such a dominant position in Meath's economy and society in the 200 years after 1700, it is important to recognise that most of the county's land was in the ownership of 'middling' landlords and strong farmers. Indeed the Civil Survey shows quite fractured patterns of land ownership in 1640. In the two relatively small baronies of Dunboyne and Ratoath, for example, there were over seventy separate Catholic proprietors and a further thirteen Protestant ones. The barony of Skreen had thirty-five Catholic landed families and six Protestant. The acquisition of forfeited land by adventurers and other forms of speculation in land in the subsequent sixty years did not fundamentally alter that pattern. The detailed land surveys of the nineteenth century, such as Griffith's Valuation, confirm that the typical owner of land in the county held hundreds, as opposed to thousands, of acres. Bateman's *Great Landowners of Britain and Ireland*, published in 1883, shows that only four Meath estates exceeded 10,000 acres – Darnley, Naper, Lansdowne and Athlumney – while a further twelve exceeded 5,000 acres. In all, these estates occupied about 150,000 acres or just over a quarter of the county's land area. Meath, then, was not a county of great estates. On the other hand, there were fifty-six estates of between 1,000 and 5,000 acres occupying a further quarter of the county. The remaining 280,000 acres were owned by hundreds of proprietors, from absentees based in Dublin or Britain to graziers whose families had occupied the land for several generations. Bateman also shows that the definition of the 'Meath landlord' is not quite as straightforward as it might appear. Most landlords who owned land in the county also held estates elsewhere in Ireland. This was true of sixty-one of the seventy-one landlords with more than 1,000 acres in Meath. In the case of the Conyngham and Lansdowne estates, the land in Meath was but a small portion of what were very extensive property portfolios in counties Donegal and Clare, in the case of the former, and Kerry, Laois, Dublin and Limerick, in the case of the latter. In addition, many landlords, of course, were absentee. This was particularly true of those owning smaller estates in the county. Bateman shows that sixteen out of twenty-seven landlords owning between 1,000 and 2,500 acres were absentees. All of this suggests that the Napers, permanent residents of Loughcrew and owners of almost 20,000 acres surrounding their stately home, were far from the typical Meath landlord. Bateman's list of land-owners was published just as the era of Irish landlordism was coming to a close. The passing of the Land Act of 1881 started the reframing of the relationship between landlord and tenant in Ireland and, ultimately, the dismantling of the landed-estate system in Meath and beyond.

GENESIS OF MEATH HISTORY WORKSHOP
BY DANNY CUSACK, CONVENOR

In early 2009 two historian friends, Peter Connell and Eamon Clarke, and myself established the Meath History Workshop. The three of us had worked together previously in the mid-1990s when we had set up the self-styled Meath Famine Forum during the commemoration of the 150th anniversary of the Great Famine. In 1997 we organised two public seminars in Navan.

The workshop was motivated by a desire to provide an opportunity for practising historians in Meath to network, and to help break down isolation (particularly for those of us working alone and not attached to any academic institution). Geared primarily towards people actively engaged in research, the workshop began meeting quarterly on a Saturday afternoon (first in the Navan Library and then in the Kells Peoples' Resource Centre). As well as providing a forum for the exchange of information and ideas, the workshop also supplied an opportunity for discussion, debate and critical analysis (something not always catered for by local historical societies).

Over the six years of its existence the workshop has had a fluctuating and floating membership with a core group of about six; attendance averaging about ten and as high as eighteen. Approximately thirty people have participated at some stage or other. Topics of discussion have varied: from the folklore and oral history of Meath to 1916 to the utilisation of sources (such as the Registry of Deeds and Griffith's Valuation) for the purposes of research.

Along with our regular workshops we decided that we would try to organise one public seminar each year. Three such seminars have been held to date: the first, in 2010, had as its topic Parnell and Meath; the second, in 2011, the estates of Meath, while the third, in 2013, considered Meath and the Decade of Commemoration. In 2010 the keynote speakers were Myles Dungan and David Lawlor;[8] in 2011 the four speakers were drawn exclusively from our workshop membership[9] and in 2014 the keynote speaker was labour historian Pádraig Yeates.

At the outset we set ourselves the task of identifying areas of research relating to the history of Meath in which there were obvious gaps, gaps which we might help to fill. It was decided further that we would make our own distinctive contribution to the history of the county by producing a publication that would share the fruits of our research in one of these areas.

Map 1: Main towns and villages of County Meath.

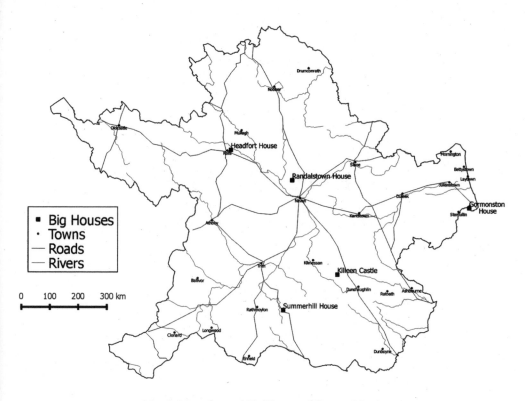

Map 2: Map of several Big Houses of County Meath.

Based on the success of our 2011 seminar and the fact that we had a cohort of about half a dozen within our group with some kind of expertise in the area of landed estates, we decided that we would compile a selection of commissioned essays on the estates of Meath. Rather than aiming for comprehensivity, it was intended that such a collection be a representative sample of the largest estates from the seventeenth to the twentieth century. Along with workshop members, a number of outsiders were invited to contribute. The focus of the collection would not be the Big Houses and the landed families alone, but what the estate records could teach us about the lives of ordinary people (estate workers, tenants, and so on) viewed in the context of the times.

As the number of participants in the workshop has grown and people have got to know one another better, so a strong spirit of collegiality and solidarity has developed. This has served to enrich the experience of Meath historians and, hopefully, the researching and writing of Meath history itself. This publication will underline and highlight that experience, and serve as a model for others.

Bective 1147–2006:
From Monastic to Landed Estate

NOEL E. FRENCH

INTRODUCTION

This study will examine the elements of continuity between the Cistercian monastery of Bective and the later landed estate. The buildings at the centre of the monastic estate were re-used as the centre for the new landed estate in the sixteenth century. Many estates were centred at dissolved monasteries as at nearby Lismullin. As the land continued to be vested in one controlling entity or person, there was a continuity of boundaries with the civil parish of Bective emerging from the dissolution of the monasteries and its continuance as a landed estate. The development of the house and demesne in the nineteenth century will be explored as will the use of the house and demesne into the twentieth century.

The main sources for the monastic period are the religious histories such as Anthony Cogan's *The Diocese of Meath: Ancient and Modern* and Archdall's *Monasticum Hibernicum*, but these only provide information on the religious aspects of the buildings and estate. It is only at the dissolution of the monasteries that a complete view of the landholdings of the monastery is set out in *Extents of Irish Monastic Possessions 1540–41*. Roger Stalley's *The Cistercian Monasteries of Ireland* provide a general overview of the development of the Cistercian movement in Ireland and a detailed survey of the development of the monastic buildings.

In the absence of estate records the development of the estate has to be traced through references in surveys such as Lewis' *A Topographical Dictionary of Ireland* and by contemporary visitors to the area such as Wilde's *The Beauties of the Boyne and its Tributary, the Blackwater.* Maps allow comparisons to be made and trace developments of the demesne and house. Ordnance Survey fieldname books provide information in relation to the tenantry of the estate in the 1830s while Griffith's Valuation provides similar information for the 1850s. From the late-nineteenth and twentieth century a number of contemporary memoirs provide details of the residents of Bective. Records at the Representative Church Body (RCB) Library provide information in relation to the church erected by Richard Bolton at Bective and its clergy, which have connections to the family. Census returns for 1821, 1901 and 1911 are useful in documenting the presence or absence of the estate's owners and the number of servants working in the house. Bective is one of the few civil parishes for which the 1821 census returns survive for County Meath. Contemporary newspapers such as the *Meath Chronicle* provide snippets of family information.

The civil parish of Bective, in the barony of Upper Navan, County Meath, is located on the north bank of the River Boyne about halfway between the towns of Navan and Trim. It contains eight townlands, comprising 3,726 acres. The Cistercian monastery of Bective was founded in the mid-twelfth century. The abbey was the landowner in the parish until the dissolution of the monasteries in the 1530s. The lands held by Bective Abbey correspond to the civil parish and with the landed estate that succeeded it. The abbey buildings were adapted to create a manor house, which served as the centre of the estate. The property passed through various owners until 1630 when the lands came into the hands of the Bolton family who were absentee landlords. The estate at Bective was developed in the nineteenth century when Richard Bolton came to live there and it was he who erected a new mansion house at Grange. The public road was altered to provide entrance avenues, the demesne was walled and trees planted. A new church was erected to serve the estate and parish by the Boltons. A village developed at one end of the parish where the Boltons provided a site for a chapel and a school. Following Richard Bolton's death the estate went through a number of different owners who preserved the demesne, but the estate was purchased by the tenants at the turn of the twentieth century.

Both the monastic and landed estate have left an enduring legacy in the landscape through houses, ruins, buildings, walls and trees. The abbey ruins remain as a mark of the medieval estate while the church, demesne walls, plantations and Big House represent the development of the landed estate in the nineteenth century. Continuity in boundaries and name is evident in the development of the landed estate from 1147 to the twentieth century. Bolton's walls and church remain a visible legacy of a landlord's vision and the integrity of the house and demesne continue to impact on the local landscape.

THE MONASTIC ESTATE AT BECTIVE

Bective, on the banks of the River Boyne, was a significant site as it was a crossing point on the river, possibly on a route from Tara to the west of the country. An enclosed settlement to the west of the river crossing may have been a high-status site within the local kingdom. The presence of a number of souterrains within Bective townland suggests the presence of settlements.[1] Bective was the site chosen for the first daughter house of Mellifont. The first Cistercian monastery in Ireland was founded at Mellifont in 1142 and within a decade there were four daughter houses. Each community consisted of an abbot with at least twelve monks and a number of lay brothers. Bective was founded on 14 January 1147 and endowed by Murchad Ua Maelechlainn, King of Mide. Cistercian monasteries were usually located in isolated rural settings and situated alongside rivers. The site on the north bank of the River Boyne provided a good water supply, a source of fish and power for a mill. The abbey was endowed with good, arable, fertile lands on the banks of the Boyne. Located near a ford there was also a route along the river with boats that made it possible to travel from Trim to Drogheda.[2]

Dedicated to the Virgin Mary, the monastery was given the name 'Bective' from *De Beatitudine* or *Beatitudo Dei*, meaning the blessedness of God. Another derivation is from the Irish *beag teach*, meaning little house, contrasting with the Big House at nearby Tara, but this derivation is unlikely.[3] Bective was located in the centre of the territory of Mide, which was granted to Hugh de Lacy following the arrival of the Anglo-Normans. Gradually the Irish monks were replaced by monks of English extraction. The abbots sat in the Irish Parliament in Dublin as one of the fifteen spiritual lords.

In 1195 Hugh de Lacy's body was interred at Bective while his head was buried at St Thomas' Abbey, Dublin. Communities were anxious to acquire the bodies of their founders or distinguished benefactors. Endowment and burial place were closely intertwined. Further controversy over his remains ended in 1205 with a papal judgment in favour of removal of the body to St Thomas', where it was buried alongside that of his first wife. The feud may have had more to do with the lands conferred to Bective than with the mortal remains of Hugh himself.[4]

Nothing of the twelfth-century building remains. In the early thirteenth century, Bective became involved in a struggle between the Irish monasteries and the chapter general of the order. In 1227 all the Irish abbots were deposed. Bective was then described as a strongly fortified place to which visitors could come in security. Following its restoration to the care of Mellifont, Bective underwent rebuilding. Five bays of the south elevation dating from 1274–1300 survive. This design is closely related to that of Hore Abbey. Bective arcades are similar to those at the Benedictine Abbey of Fore. Leask suggested that the same masons were responsible for both. Fore was a monastery founded by the de Lacys.[5]

The Cistercians were industrious farmers who grew cereals and owned cattle and sheep. Fisheries were developed and mills, bakeries and other local industries initiated. It is probable that this land was laid out in farms, which were rented to lay people or farmed by lay brothers of the monastery. Each Cistercian abbey had a number of granges or out farms, which were farmed by lay brothers. When a grange was over 6 miles from the abbey, sometimes a small monastery was constructed with a hall, dormitory, kitchen and chapel as well as farm buildings and barns. A grange could be described as an arable farm inclusive of land and buildings. 'Grange' still occurs as a townland name, but the grange buildings rarely survive into the present landscape. The townland of Grange is the furthest in the parish from Bective Abbey, but the term 'grange' was used in some legal document to describe each of the townlands of the parish. Granges may have been rented out to lay tenants in the later medieval period.[6]

The Black Death resulted in the number of monks being halved, and lay numbers were also greatly reduced. The abbeys were forced to employ paid labour or lease out their granges to lay tenants. The communities dwindled and the greatly decreased population resulted in alterations to the buildings to reduce costs. The rebuilding at Bective c. 1450–1500 was prompted by the need to adapt the buildings for the smaller numbers of monks. The south aisles of the church were demolished and the adjoining arcades were blocked off. The nave was truncated by the construction of a fortified tower. Another tower was erected at the south-west end of the cloister, which dominated the abbey buildings. A large fortified tower was constructed for protection from attacks into the Pale. [7]

The abbey continued to accumulate land and offer religious services in return. About 1488 Ismaena, widow of Jorel Comyn, brought a writ against the abbot for a third of a messuage and 66 acres of land at Ballybret (Balbrigh), at which time she paid a fine of 1 marc, whereupon the abbot agreed that a chaplain would celebrate a constant service for the repose of her soul and the souls of her ancestors. [8] A regular monastic life continued into the early sixteenth century. An abbot of Bective attended the general chapter of Citreaux in 1512 and was also one of four appointed to investigate the affairs of the Cistercian nunnery in Derry in 1512. [9]

By royal commission, dated 6 May 1536, Bective and four other Cistercian houses, all within the Pale, were ordered to be dissolved. The order was delayed in September to allow the monks to sow their winter corn. In October 1637 the deputy forced the parliament to assent to the dissolution of a number of monasteries including Bective. The monastery thus became the property of the king. [10] In 1538 the abbot, John English, was provided with a pension of £15 for life. Abbot English had removed chattels worth £35 but these were recovered by the accounting officer as well as two bells weighing 180lbs, valued at 35 shillings. [11]

At an extent court in 1540 a survey of the abbey's property was carried out. The roofing of the church and the chancel were thrown down, and the timber was used for repairs of the king's mills at Trim. There were a hall, a cloister roofed with tiles, certain chambers, and other buildings that would be of use to a new resident landowner. At Bective there were 250 acres of demesne lands, a water mill and fishing weir. The abbey owned 4,400 acres of land with the vast majority of it centred around Bective. A list of tenants, their holdings and value of such holdings was compiled. The lands were broken down into arable, pasture, waste and commonage. There were small commonages of approximately 20 acres each at the grange of Bective, Balgill, Balbraddagh and Cloncullen, and 12-acre commons at Balbrigh. The tenants of messuages were required to provide certain services in return for their landholdings. They were bound to cart all manner of grain and hay in the demesne. Each tenant holding a whole plough had to give five days ploughing and cart four loads of turf; he who had half a plough, two days of each labour. Each tenant, whether of a messuage or a cottage, had to give five hokes and ten hens. The abbey also held land at Monktown, near Trim, and also the rectory of Balsoon. The tithes of the parish were granted to the abbey and therefore to the new landowner.[12] The abbey had an annual income of £83, which can be compared with that of the smaller English houses such as Buildwas and Croxden. The goods and chattels were sold off, yielding £108. The profit from most Cistercian houses in Ireland yielded between £10 and £20, so it appears that Bective was quite wealthy.

FROM MONASTERY TO LANDED ESTATE

Following the dissolution of the monastery the estate passed through the hands of various civil servants, none of whom had the time to pay any great attention to its development, but the abbey was converted into a mansion. In December 1537 Bective was leased to Thomas Agard. Bective was a valuable property as it was within the Pale and within easy distance of Dublin. Many of the confiscated monasteries were granted to the New English, civil servants and professional soldiers who had recently entered Ireland. Agard arrived in Ireland as a supporter of Thomas Cromwell in the 1530s and became vice-treasurer of the Mint, becoming known as 'Agard of the Mint'. As vice-treasurer of the Mint, Agard presided over a debasement of the coinage resulting in massive profit for the Crown. Thomas Agard also benefited from the confiscation of St Peter's in Newtown Trim and St Mary's also of Trim. Within three months of acquiring Bective, Agard was making plans for a cloth-weaving enterprise which would employ over 100 people. The monastery buildings were converted to a fortified mansion. The residence was designed around the cloister. The fifteenth-century tower acted as a pivot for two wings. The main approach to the building was beside the tower and a flight of steps led up to the entrance on the first floor. This opened onto the main hall, previously the refectory, which was lit by five new windows. A fireplace was installed to heat the room. From the hall, a wooden staircase led up to a solar or private chamber in the south-west corner on the second storey of the tower. A door at the other end of the hall led to the old dormitory where Agard added an extra storey, which was lit by a dormer window in the gable. This may have been used for accommodating the servants. New fireplaces were installed. Stalley described the result of the adaptations as 'a sprawling mansion offering plenty of space, but not much architectural coherence'. The main living areas were on the first floor and below each wing were vaulted basements from the monastic era. These may have been used as cellars or kitchens. In the same range there is a large baking oven. A stone staircase leading from the hall to the basement was installed. The elevations were very irregular but a degree of visual continuity was provided by the repetitive use of the Tudor mullioned windows. The building was not designed to provide a strong defensive position as attackers could gain entry through the first-floor windows.[13]

In 1544 the abbey was held by John Alen, lord chancellor.[14] It was purchased in 1552 by Andrew Wyse, vice-treasurer of Ireland. The grant sets out the lands, which are identical to those given in the extents of 1540. There is also mention of the Church of Cladaghe (Clady). This small church, located near the Boyne, was a short distance downstream from the abbey buildings.[15] On 22 February 1553 licence was granted to Andrew Wyse to alienate to Richard Dillon of Preseston, John Wycombe and Richard Cox, all of the possessions of this abbey, which he had purchased. In 1558 Jacques Wingfelde was farming the lands at Bective for the queen.[16] Bective was conveyed by Wyse to Gregory Cole, citizen of London.[17] There was quite an amount of litigation between the queen and Wyse's widow until the property passed to Wyse's son-in-law, Sir Alexander Fitton. Fitton's daughter and heiress, Catherine, married Sir Bartholomew Dillon of Riverston.[18]

The Bolton family acquired Bective in 1630. The transfer of the manor of Bective from Bartholomew Dillon to Edward Bolton probably took place on 10 August 1630 but other sources suggest a date of 1639 with the purchaser being Edward's father, Richard Bolton.[19] Sir Richard Bolton was lord chancellor of Ireland in 1639 and established himself at Brazeel in north County Dublin. His son Edward became the owner of Bective in the 1630s and is listed as its owner in the Civil Survey 1654–6. The family seem to have resided at Brazeel, near Swords. The building at Bective may have suffered damage during the wars of the 1640s and been allowed to fall into ruin. The Civil Survey listed a castle, an abbey, a church, two mills and two weirs in the townland of Bective. There was a bridge and a weir in the townland of Balbrigh so perhaps this townland extended to the Boyne at this time. There is also a record of a weir at Dunlough, which is some distance from any significant river. Sir Edward Bolton is listed as proprietor of the parish and of Balsoon townland on the opposite side of the river.[20]

There appears to have been a castle at Bective on the opposite side of the river to the abbey, which was taken by Irish rebels in the early 1640s. In the Civil Survey 1654–6 there was a stone house in the townland of Balreask, parish of Balsoon, the property of Sir Edward Bolton. According to Moore the castle was situated where the village of Bective existed on the south side of the river. A stone house said to date to the seventeenth century stood at Bective crossroads.[21] The townland of Ballina or Bective is in the parish of Balsoon and was the site of small hamlet of houses. Fairs were held on 16 May for dry cows and young heifers and on 1 November for cattle and pigs. There was a village of thirty houses and 142 inhabitants in 1836. The villagers called the road through the village towards Navan 'the Street'.[22]

In 1654–6 Bective/Ballina was the property of General Taylor and by the mid-1850s it had become the property of one of his descendants, Thomas Edward Taylor of Ardgillan, Dublin. There was a connection between the Boltons of Bective and the Taylors of Headfort. Thomas Taylor took the title Earl Bective of Bective Castle in 1766. In 1767 and 1770 Bective Castle was listed as the abode of Thomas Taylor. According to the Ordnance Survey field name books for Ballina or Bective 'from this townland the Marquess of Headfort takes his second title'. Richard Bolton from Bective is listed as 'of Headfort' in his marriage settlement of December 1827.[23]

ESTATE DEVELOPMENT IN THE NINETEENTH CENTURY

Richard Bolton was born about 1802 and inherited the manor of Bective after the death of his father. Robert Compton Bolton married twice and by his second wife, Charlotte, whom he married in 1800, he had a daughter, Anne, and two sons, Richard and Robert.[24] Richard was under nine when his father died.[25] The family home at Brazeel was destroyed by fire in 1810.[26] Bolton did not live at Bective until the late 1820s as there was no record of a Bolton in the 1821 census for the parish of Bective nor were there any houses with large numbers of servants. In the 1820s Bolton established himself at Bective. Richard married his cousin, Frances Georgina Bomford of Rahinstown, in November 1827, probably in Dublin. She was a member of the local landed class. These marriage patterns were replicated by other members of the landed class in Ireland and Britain and succeeded in creating a self-perpetuating and limited class of landowners. Frances Georgina had turned 21 and had received £1,800 on 18 April 1827 out of her £3,000 through a mortgage on the Bomford estate at Rahinstown. A final marriage settlement payment to Frances Georgina Bomford was agreed on 8 December 1827. Her sister, Jemima Letitia, married a man of the same name, Richard Bolton of Monkstown Castle. In the same year of 1827 Dr Robert Logan, brother of a tenant of Bolton, became Roman Catholic bishop of Meath. Due to high debts Rahinstown was sold in 1852 through the Encumbered Estates Court.

The ownership of land provided wealth, which gave this class influence in local and national politics and administration. As a member of this class, Bolton took a prominent role on the local political, judicial and religious stage. He was high sheriff of County Meath in 1828. As such, he was the principal representative of central government in the county in relation to the execution of the law in both civil and criminal actions issuing from the courts. Bolton was appointed by the lord lieutenant. He was expected to be resident in the county and possess ample dispos-able income as the position involved meeting the expenses incurred during the year in office.[27] Richard Bolton was also a JP, a position reserved for the established active gentry of the county.[28] Furthermore, he was a member of the Grand Jury, which possessed a wide range of administrative functions. Bolton's membership would have assisted him in re-routing the road away from his mansion.[29] As a leading landowner, Bolton was a subscriber to Samuel Lewis' *Topographical Dictionary of Ireland* in 1837 and in 1838 he subscribed to D'Alton's *Memoirs of the Archbishops of Dublin*.

Richard Bolton provided the site for a new national school at Robinstown, Balbradagh townland, in 1840 and became patron of the new school. His father, Robert, had provided a site for a chapel and school in 1800. In the mid-1850s, a dispute arose between Mr Bolton and the local priest as to the right to visitation and the appointment of teachers. This became a bitter dispute, which was finally resolved in 1861 when Bective School at Robinstown became a non-vested school and Bolton's influence ceased.[30] Bolton was a resident landlord: he lived close to his tenants and took an active interest in the development of his estate. In 1800 approximately one third of landlords did not even reside in Ireland and in the 1870s only half the landlords resided on their estates. Bolton employed an agent to supervise the collection of rents. Mr Justice from Dublin was the agent in 1836 and Mr Tisdall, who resided locally, was agent in 1861. The agent's duty was to collect the rent on gale days in May and November, keep accounts, draw up leases and manage the estate. Bolton erected a house for the estate, walled in the demesne and erected a parish church. He was determined to stamp his footprint on his estate at Bective, becoming a landscape architect through the creation of a demesne. These improvements to the landscape were largely carried out for aesthetic rather than economic reasons. The construction of a suitable house and demesne may have been carried out to establish Bolton as a landowner of substance to his peers, particularly as the family had not been resident in the county. Bolton must have had considerable disposable income available for these improvements. Presumably, monies accumulated during his minority were used to erect the house and the demesne, while economic growth from the mid-1850s facilitated the continued development of the estate. Arrears that had accumulated during the Famine were paid off, which provided landlords with an additional boost of income.[31] Richard Bolton died on 27 February 1868 and was buried in his church at Bective on 4 March with the service being conducted by the bishop of Meath, Samuel Butcher. His widow, Frances Georgina, lived on for another sixteen years. In the surveys of landowners in the 1870s she is listed as owning Bective. Mrs Bolton died, aged 80, on 23 June 1884 at Suffolk House, Cheltenham.[32]

In 1836 Richard Bolton was recorded as the owner of Bective parish of 3,385 acres. His agent was Mr Justice from Dublin and the lands were let at rents from 25s to 40s per Irish acre on leases for one life or 21 years to three lives or 31 years. These types of shorter leases became the norm in the early nineteenth century. Farms were from 4 to 100 acres. The entire townland of Cloncullen and part of Dunlough were rented to Mr Jones who resided at Cloncullen Cottage. Mr Jones kept a 2-horse-power threshing machine. Most of the parish was under cultivation with the main crops being wheat, potatoes, oats and flax.[33] In Griffith's Valuation of 1854 Bolton was the landlord of the entire parish of Bective and also held lands nearby at Shanbo, in the parish of Rataine. Half of the farms are larger than 10 acres with all the small holdings in the village of Robinstown or in the townland of Gillstown.[34]

Farm size for parish of Bective from Griffith's Valuation, 1854	
In excess of 300 acres	1
100–299 acres	8
50–100 acres	8
11–50 acres	22
5–10 acres	11
Less than 5 acres	28

Table 1.

Bolton erected a new house in Grange townland downstream from the abbey, making the most of the local scenery. Described as 'a cottage' in 1836 and 'a handsome modern residence' in 1837, the house is linked to the river and also to the abbey. Named 'Bective House' to emphasise the continuity of the estate, it was also occasionally recorded as 'Bective Abbey' or 'Bective Lodge'. The house is in an understated architectural style in the spirit of Francis Johnston. The front is seven bays with a side elevation of five bays. Indoors the plan was simple. The main house is two rooms' deep on a tripartite plan with a large and restrained central stair hall. It has been ascribed to earlier dates of 1790 and 1800 but no house appears on Larkin's map of 1812, and it is more likely that it was erected for Richard Bolton's marriage.[35]

Bolton created a demesne at Bective as a focal point of the estate. Sizes of demesnes varied. In a sample of 100 landed estates, Dooley found seventy-three were below 600 acres in size. Features of demesnes included walls, gate lodges, plantations, open parkland, ornate gardens, lawns and kitchen gardens.[36] Plantations and woodlands were created to provide shelter and privacy and also to cater for shooting. Bective House was surrounded by a wide expanse of parkland, dotted with clumps of trees and secluded from the outside world by perimeter belts of trees. The plantation of these trees and creation of parkland led to the walling in of the demesne and the re-routing of the Trim-Navan Road. By 1836 Bolton had planted larch and scotch pine trees at Balgill, Gillstown and Grange as part of his proposed demesne.[37] Trees were used to screen the house and were planted in a design as features on the landscape.[38] It took a number of decades for the trees to mature. The plantation was still being recorded as 'young' in 1849.[39] In 1854 there was a plantation of approximately 12 acres in his demesne of 202 acres and there were smaller plantations on the gravelly hills in six townlands of the parish including Balbrigh, Balbradagh, Balgill, Bective, Gillstown and Grange.[40] The planting of trees marked the confidence of the landed class.[41]

The old road from Navan to Trim passed through Balbrigh in the north of the parish, but the new road passed though Bective townland and Grange townland. As Bolton created his demesne he decided to re-route the road away from his house and parkland. By 1849 the estate was completely walled in and had a band of perimeter plantations. These walls, stretching over 2 miles in length, made Bective a conspicuous feature on the local landscape. Gate lodges monitored visitors to the estate, preserving the landlord's privacy and emphasising the status differential between landlord and tenant. Impressive ashlar gateways were erected at each entrance to the estate with gate lodges at each and an additional number of houses to cater for workers on the estate. The gate lodge at the Trim entrance was erected in 1852 and is adorned by the Bolton crest. Bolton acquired his own coat of arms and crest. He adopted the motto *Deus providebit*, meaning 'God will provide'.[42] A walled garden was constructed near the house and provided produce for the family and household. Later the garden produced roses and vegetables for sale.[43] In 1852 Bolton removed the baptismal font from the Clady ruins and erected it in his garden as an ornamental bird bath.[44]

The relocation of the road and the creation of parkland obviously involved the removal of various houses. A poem published in 1926 entitled 'The corpse at Clady gate – an epic of 62' described Bolton as 'a landlord of the vilest type' who levelled the cottages at the Clady on 'Bolton's vast demesne'. A funeral cortège arrived at the demesne gates to go to Clady Graveyard but was barred from entering by a chain. Shaun O'Reilly stepped forward and urged the people to take action. The chains were broken and the funeral proceeded. An accompanying newspaper article in 1926 described Bolton as a bigot noted for his oppression, evictions and demolition of Clady village. According to the article, Bolton was marked for assassination during the Fenian period but died from a broken neck following a fall.[45] Memories recorded in the 1930s suggest that only two families were removed when the new gates were constructed: one went to a smaller farm while the other family were evicted. Another person recalled that Bolton provided a lot of employment but he never showed any kindness to his employees or tenants.[46] An overtly nationalist ideology provides the general view of all landlords as being capable of evictions on a whim as part of popular history right up to the present day.[47]

When Richard Bolton inherited Bective the local Protestant parishioners attended church at Trim or Kilmessan. As the patron of the parish and the owner of the tithes, Bolton decided to erect a church for his tenants and servants. The Church of Ireland was associated with the Ascendancy and Bolton was linking his estate and his family firmly to the Church of Ireland and thus religion created a gulf between the Protestant landlord and Catholic tenant. Designed by Joseph Welland, the church was erected on lands provided by Bolton and the cost of construction was also met by him. The laying of the foundation of the new church at Bective was attended by a number of Bolton's friends and a strong muster of tenantry. A fine cut-stone building with crypt and bell-tower, the church was designed in a plain gothic style and dedicated to St Mary. The church bears a plaque: 'To promote the worship of God, Richard Bolton Esq. of Bective Abbey erected this church at his sole expense for his tenants and neighbours in the year of Our Lord MDCCCLI'. The church was consecrated on 15 June 1853 and enlarged in 1858. A glebe house was also erected in 1853. Mrs Bolton left a substantial amount of money and property to the church. When these funds had been exhausted, the parish fell into poor financial state and this continued until its union with Trim parish in 1934. In 1953, when the centenary of the church was celebrated, the old font was taken from the gardens of Bective House and erected in the church. The Birds, later owners of Bective House, left a bequest to the church at Bective. The church closed in 1990 and was purchased in 1994 by artist John Ryan, who converted it to a studio and living quarters. Bolton's remains were removed from the vault under the church and re-interred in the graveyard.[48]

A railway line was laid from Dublin to Navan by the Dublin and Meath Railway and opened in 1862. The station at Bective, on the Clonsilla to Navan line, became a component of the estate. In 1892 Bective Station was described as a thriving station.[49] A post office was established near the church. It is possible that Bolton was considering the establishment of an estate village on the main Trim–Navan Road, which might have replaced the chapel village at Robinstown.

On her death in 1884, Francis Georgina Bolton bequeathed

Bective to her nephew, Revd George Henry Martin. He resigned his position as rector of Agher in that year and became resident at Trinity College, settling at Palmerston Park, Rathgar. Bective House was leased by him for a number of years to General Sir Charles Fraser, a bachelor and a cavalry-man. He held house parties there and hunted with the Meath Hunt.[50]

In 1889, a public meeting to be held at Bective Abbey to raise funds for the support of tenants evicted due to the Plan of Campaign was prohibited by the government.[51] A number of Martin's tenants sought a reduction in rents through the judicial rents system of the Irish Land Commission. Rents were fixed for Patrick McCann, John Sheridan, both Bective, and Thomas Clerkin, Balbradagh in 1890–91, and the amounts were reduced by between 30 and 40 per cent.[52] Bective Abbey ruins were vested in the Board of Works in 1894.[53] Martin's daughter, Frances Georgina Martin, was born on 24 April 1874 and was named after her great-aunt, Frances Georgina Bolton of Bective. Together with her brothers and sisters lived at Bective during her teenage years. In 1898 she married her cousin, Revd Richard Frederick Mant Clifford, who went to Bective as curate and then as rector from 1902 to 1903. Clifford then spent three years as curate at Castleknock, Dublin, before returning to Bective where he was installed as rector in 1910. He stayed at Bective until 1917. The Boltons and their immediate successors had considerable influence in church matters relating to Bective.[54] George Henry Martin died on 12 December 1896, aged 63. Bective was bequeathed to his fourth child, Mary Louisa, who lived there from perhaps as early as 1895. She farmed Bective for a period but later sold the house to John Watson, and the majority of the estate to the Land Commission. She retained a small portion, which was named the 'Abbey Farm', being located near the ruins of the abbey.[55]

In 1906 a survey of untenanted lands was carried out throughout Ireland. This usually illustrated the state of demesnes, and in the townland of Bective there were 104 untenanted acres, presumably part of the demesne of Bective. There were smaller portions of untenanted lands in the townlands of Balbradagh, Balgill, Bective, Gillstown and Grange, all recorded as the property of the representative of F.G. Bolton.[56]

HOUSE AND DEMESNE IN THE TWENTIETH CENTURY

John Watson purchased Bective House and demesne after retiring from the army. He was master of the Meath Hunt from 1891 until 1908, when he died. Watson erected kennels for the Meath Hunt at Bective. He was highly regarded as a huntsman and well known for his temper. Neighbouring landowners such as Lady Fingall and Lord Dunsany make considerable reference to him in their memoirs. An active polo player, he created a team at Bective and introduced the game to America. The hunt and the house created a great deal of employment. Servants brought their own difficulties, especially if the owner was as short-tempered as Watson. In 1902 Kate Lawlor, parlour maid, took Watson to court for wrongful dismissal after working at Bective for two weeks. She left her employment because Watson let out a curse after she dropped a plate. Watson was absent on the night of the census in 1901. He died at Bective House 14 November 1908 after which the estate was put up for sale.[57]

Following Watson's death Bective was acquired by Captain Henry Stern, late of the 13th Hussars. He and his wife Constance made a home at Bective. The 1911 census show the family in residence. A house of Bective's size required an adequate number of servants. In 1911 Stern, his wife and three children were present at Bective House in addition to one nurse, one nursery maid, two housemaids, two lady's maids, two footmen, two laundresses, one between maid, one kitchen maid, one scullery maid and a cook. Six of the fourteen servants were from outside Ireland and all the others were from Ireland with just one from Meath. In 1911 only 14 per cent of domestic servants in Ireland were born in the county in which they worked, 47 per cent were born elsewhere in Ireland and 39 per cent born in England.[58] Like other Protestant employers Stern employed Protestants in preference to Catholics. Only five out of the fourteen were Roman Catholic.[59] In 1911 71 per cent of servants in big houses in Ireland were Protestant.[60] Twenty-one per cent of all males working in domestic service in Meath in 1911 were Protestant.[61] In 1912 Bective house was altered for Captain Stern.[62] James, the captain's son, went on to have a career as a writer and used Bective as a house name. The Sterns were unsettled by the troubled times in the early 1920s. In February 1921 the public house at Robinstown, although owned by a Protestant family, was plundered by the Auxiliaries.[63]

An American paper manufacturer, Charles Bird, came to Meath to hunt in the early part of the twentieth century. In 1926 Bird with two friends put in a bid of £3,000 for Bective only to be amazed when a telegram arrived in the States saying 'Congratulations, you own Bective'. The syndicate wished to become involved in hunting in Ireland. When the friends sold their shares, the Birds owned the place outright and the couple rejuvenated the house and gardens. The estate's most famous horse, Heartbreak Hill, came sixth in the 1932 Grand National at Aintree and won steeplechases all over Ireland.[64] The steward at Bective was Tom Lavin whose daughter was Mary Lavin, the short-story writer. In September 1942 Mary married William Walsh, a lawyer, who later entered politics. They took over the management of Bective estate on the death of her father. Following her husband's premature death, Mary Lavin devoted her energies to running Abbey Farm, beside ruined Bective Abbey, rearing her children, and continuing her writing. Her first collection of short stories, entitled *Tales from Bective Bridge* was published in 1943.

George Briscoe, who had sold the neighbouring estate and house at Bellinter, took over the management of Bective in 1952. Briscoe and his wife moved into the wing at Bective. The Tara Harrier kennels and Briscoe's horse were relocated to Bective. Bird became the joint master of the Meath Hunt so there were two hunts centred at Bective. The cost of upkeep of the house and hunts was considerable.[65] In 1960 the Birds and the Briscoes moved across the river to Assigh, and Bective House became home to Norman Wachman until the mid-1970s. Wachman allowed the Tara Harriers to continue using the kennels at Bective and began to develop a stud farm. [66]

Bective was purchased by Michael Wymes in 1975. He developed a pheasant shoot on the property.[67] In 1986 the demesne was described as having 140 acres in permanent pasture, 130 in tillage and the remaining 105 in mature woodland and amenity grounds. There were twenty-six loose boxes and six estate houses. The house had an enclosed porch, reception hall with doric columns, study, drawing room, family room, breakfast room, modern kitchen, old kitchen with flagstone floor, pantry, back kitchen, games room, master bedroom, five further bedrooms, staff quarters and domestic offices. In 2008 a new road was constructed which cut through the demesne, isolating the church building from the house. In July 2006 the property was sold.

CONCLUSION

Continuity is demonstrated in Bective with the landed estate succeeding the monastic estate. Landlord residences were often located at the centre of pre-Reformation parishes.[68] Bective estate was based on the territorial divisions of parish. The core of Bective estate had roots going back to medieval times with the foundation of a Cistercian monastery in the twelfth century. This monastery and its holdings were confiscated in the sixteenth century and became the centre of an estate held by the Boltons from the seventeenth century. Many country houses in England also originated as confiscated monasteries.

There were a number of major changes. The monastic building served as the centre of the estate until the sixteenth century, after which it fell into ruins. Richard Bolton erected a new mansion in the nineteenth century to serve as the new centre for the estate. Bolton moulded the landscape to his own vision and he possessed the power and resources to carry out his vision. The legacy of the Boltons' nineteenth-century developments is ingrained on the local landscape. Hunting and outdoor pursuits were popular among the landlord class, and these continued to be the basis of the use of Bective for the twentieth century. The settlement, landholding and buildings of Bective are a metaphor for the history of Ireland over the last 900 years, from the introduction of continental orders in the twelfth century to the businessman of the late twentieth century.

The Creation of a New Landscape in the Barony of Demifore in Post-Cromwellian Settlement

UNA PALCIC

INTRODUCTION

The barony of Demifore is situated in the north-western corner of county Meath with the other half located in neighbouring Westmeath. The dramatic events of the mid-seventeenth century brought about considerable change in the barony. These changes are most notice-able in the areas of land ownership, settlement, economy and religion. However, some elements of continuity can be observed in spite of these great changes. The aim of this essay is to illustrate these changes through an analysis of the barony of Demifore in the seventeenth century. This half-barony was completely dominated in the pre-Crom-wellian period by Old English landowning families. It was granted to a New English family – Naper – as part of the Cromwellian settlement. This essay traces this period in order to highlight the transition that occurred and its extensive impact on land ownership, settlement and the people of the barony.

BACKGROUND: THE CROMWELLIAN PLANTATION

In seventeenth-century Ireland, the ownership of land signified both wealth and power. Land ownership was the main generator of wealth and any significant changes in its ownership would ultimately lead to an important shift in the power base for the country's people. The Cromwellian plantation, which took place in the middle of the seventeenth century in Ireland, had a profound effect on the socio-economic geography of this island. The influx of a large new wave of settlers from England changed the old order of control from that of Anglo-Norman lordships to a New English grouping. It has often been said that the Anglo-Normans became 'more Irish than the Irish them-selves' but this is never said of the 'New English'. The new settlers formed alliances and intermarried with the old order but came to be seen by both the native Irish and Old English as a distinctly 'English' order.

The Cromwellian settlement came about as a result of the Rebellion of 1641. The lands of those who had taken part were confiscated and then granted to the soldiers and adventurers who had supported Oliver Cromwell. The policy of plantation was not new and had been pursued by successive English governments as a means of placing loyal subjects in recalcitrant areas such as Ulster and Munster. After the Reformation, many New English settlers had come to live in Ireland. As a result, by 1641 this group had already established a strong foothold and some 25 per cent of Irish land was in Protestant ownership.[1] Under Cromwell's Act for the Settlement of Ireland of 1652, confiscated lands were assigned not only to the adventurers but also to the soldiers of Cromwell's large army. Parts of certain counties were used to pay the soldiers' arrears and in this way the half-barony of Demifore was assigned to Captain Naper of Colonel Ingolsby's regiment.[2] Following the Restoration of 1660, many who had lost land in the 1650s petitioned Charles II to have their lands restored. Few were successful and in the 1690s, as a result of the Williamite victory, more land was confiscated and granted to New English. Consequently the political power that the Protestant grouping had held prior to 1641 increased dramatically and was reinforced by their control of even more land. Whereas 75 per cent of land in Ireland was in Catholic ownership in 1641,[3] this share had fallen dramatically to 22 per cent by 1688; and by 1703, as a result of the Williamite settle-ment, it stood at just 14 per cent.[4]

METHODOLOGY

The primary source material in this study consists of three major seventeenth-century government documents that are concerned with land ownership, namely the Civil Survey,[5] the Down Survey,[6] and the Books of Survey and Distribution.[7] Limited use was also made of the 1641 Depositions.[8] In addition, Church records provided some useful data, in particular for the latter part of the century. The Civil and Down surveys came about as a result of the 1652 Act for the Settlement of Ireland. The aim of the surveys was to determine the amount of confiscated land that resulted from the Rebellion of 1641. The Civil Survey focused on obtaining data on land ownership, acreage, and land quality. The data was collated into 'terriers' (lists of lands). This information was of assistance to the surveyors in the subsequent Down Survey led by Sir William Petty, where the data collected was mapped by parish and barony. Terriers were also produced as in the Civil Survey. Significantly, the maps document townlands, rivers, roads, churches and other important material. The barony map of Demifore provided the starting point for this research and is used to illustrate land ownership and settlement in the pre-Cromwellian and post-Cromwellian periods.

The Books of Survey and Distribution illustrate what actually happened to the confiscated lands. These books record the changes in land ownership that occurred as a result of the Cromwellian, Restoration and Williamite settlements. The material is arranged into county, barony, parish and townland divisions. The books also record the acreage, calculated in profitable and unprofitable measurements, as well as the religion of the original proprietors, in a similar fashion to the Civil and Down surveys which preceded them. In addition, some records of the Fingal branch of the Plunkett family are also consulted. The Plunkett family and its various branches were the dominant land-owning group in the pre-Cromwellian period. In order to illustrate the objectives of this research, three parishes, Loughcrew, Oldcastle and Killalon, were selected as case studies. These are analysed in greater detail using the records available in order to examine this transition.

A number of difficulties arose in the course of this research. The Civil Survey for the barony sometimes uses an old land measurement, the cartran, and its fractional subdivisions along with the plantation acre. This use of the cartran, which is difficult to quantify in modern terms, makes it hard to compare the acreage figures for the Civil Survey with those of the Down Survey. It is important to note that all of the acreages given in this chapter are in plantation or Irish acres, which are equivalent to approximately 1.62 of a statute acre (often called an English acre).[9]

THE BARONY OF DEMIFORE

The barony of Demifore in north-west Meath is a half-barony, the other half being located in County Westmeath. Presumably the barony is named after the Abbey of Fore, situated just across the border in Westmeath. The pre-Cromwellian landowning group in Ireland consisted of both Old English and Gaelic Irish. In the barony of Demifore, it was the Old English who completely dominated the area. As a consequence of the Cromwellian settlement, the Old English lost much of their land to a new group of mainly English Protestant settlers. The barony contained eight civil parishes and comprised a total of almost 23,000 acres (Down Survey figure). To the north the barony borders on County Cavan, to the west County Westmeath and to the east, County Meath itself (see Map 3, below, the Down Survey map of the barony).

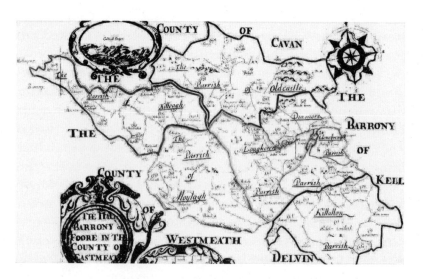

Map 3: Down Survey map of the Barony. (TCD.ie)

The topography of Demifore is dominated by a range of hills, Slieve na Calliaghe, also known as the Loughcrew Hills, which rise at their highest point to approximately 300 metres. The Barony is drained by the river Inny, which rises in the eastern part of the district and flows westwards on its long journey to the River Shannon. The barony is strategically located on the watershed between the Boyne basin to the east and the Shannon basin to the west. The river and its tributaries were important to the area in earlier times as they provided power for numerous mills and contributed in a significant way to the economy of the area. Over the centuries, the barony has always been an attractive place to live as evidenced by the numerous archaeological sites dating from the Neolithic era. In their turn, the Anglo-Normans deemed the land of the barony as worthy of ownership. The Norman invasion of Ireland in the twelfth century left an indelible mark on County Meath. Not only are there visible remains such as mottes and baileys, castles and church foundations, but also evidence of land ownership and the control that this group came to exercise in the succeeding centuries. The Anglo-Normans, or Old English as they came to be known, eventually lost power to the new force that arrived in the seventeenth century, the Cromwellians, who unsurprisingly also saw the barony as desirable.

Hugh de Lacy was granted the kingdom of Meath by Henry II in March 1172 and given complete control over the area. He, in turn, parcelled it out amongst his followers. He granted an area stretching from Granard, County Longford to Oldcastle, County Meath to Richard Tuite.[10] The barony of Demifore forms part of the Tuite grant. This area was on the borders of the Pale and there were frequent battles with the neighbouring clansmen of Breifne. Later, the Anglo-Norman Plunkett and Nugent families established themselves in the area. The arrival of the Anglo-Normans and their subsequent control of the area led to significant changes in the landscape. The extensive Norman influence in the barony is clearly illustrated in Sweetman's (1987) *Archaeological Inventory of County Meath* where the motte and bailey at Castlecor is one of nine recorded sites that point to the importance of defence in this borderland between Ulster and Leinster. According to Graham,[11] approximately forty mottes have survived in County Meath into the present day with an additional nine destroyed or replaced with stone castles during the medieval period. This would suggest that the barony contained a significant percentage of such sites compared to the rest of the county, particularly when one considers that there were six castles or 'sites of' also listed for the area in the inventory. In order to consolidate their colonisation of an area, the Normans often sited stone castles on or near the original mottes. Other reputed sites such as Oldcastle, Castlecor and Newcastle, which all retain the word 'castle' in their townland names, demonstrate the multiplicity of fortified sites in the area. By way of illustration, the ruins of the castle in Moylagh are still visible today surmounting the Norman motte. The Civil Survey lists no less than sixteen castles, four of which were in repair and four in ruin (see table 4). The Down Survey lists thirteen, five of which were in a ruinous condition.

OVERVIEW OF THE BARONY-CIVIL AND DOWN SURVEY

To learn more about Demifore in the early seventeenth century, reliance must be placed on the Civil and Down surveys as important repositories of primary-source material. These surveys provide a snapshot of the area in the middle decades of the century prior to the adjustments caused by the land settlements. The tumultuous events of the 1640s and 1650s brought about considerable change to land ownership, settlement, religion and the economy of the barony. Consequently, by the end of the century, much had changed in Demifore, although in some areas continuity had been maintained. Three parishes will be used as a means of illustrating the developments that occurred.

PRE-CROMWELLIAN LAND OWNERSHIP

The most important aspect of the surveys was that data became available on the landlords, the holders of power in the barony. The Down and Civil surveys record the owners of lands confiscated as a result of participation in the Rebellion of 1641. Twenty-five landlords are identified by the Down Survey and twenty-four by the Civil Survey. According to the Down Survey, total acreage in the barony amounted to 22,968 acres of both profitable and unprofitable land. Table 2 provides evidence of land ownership in the barony prior to 1641. It would appear that the Anglo-Normans, or Old English as they came to be known, controlled land ownership in the area. All of the names with the exception of Thomas Kearnan are of Old English origin. In addition, table 2 includes the place of residence of the landowners, and most are residents of County

Meath. Significantly, the largest landowners, Lord Dunsany, the Earl of Fingal, Robert Lord Dillon of Kilkenny West and Sir Richard Barnewall, are not residents of the barony. Some of the smaller proprietors are also non-residents, for example Walter Dowdall of Athboy.

Name	Cartrans	Profitable acres	Unprofitable acres
Patrick Lord Baron of Dunsany	22	1414	334
Christopher Earl of Fingal	14.667	988	201
Robert Lord Dillon of Kilkenny	12.083	821	146
John Plunkett of Loughcrew	14	715	139
Christopher Plunkett of Clonebreny	5	440	85
Oliver Balfe of Corrstowne	4	278	7
Henry Plunkett of Hartstowne	3.1667	230	6
Sir Richard Barnewall of Crickstowne	3	205	87
Theobald Tuite of Baltrasney	3	190	87
Thomas Nugent of Rosse	4	180	100
Richard Nugent Earl of Westmeath	2	160	20
Richard Plunkett of Irishtowne	2	155	18
William Golding of Peirstowne Lundy	1.333	110	5
Christopher Plunkett of Ballimacad	2	105	15
Thomas Plunkett of Drumsaury	1	90	20
Richard Plunkett of Loughcrew	1.5	90	30
Thomas Fleming of Cabrah	2	84	25
Gerard Plunkett & Edmund Tuite	1.667	70	15
Walter Nugent of Portluman	1	70	24
Sir John Hoey of Cottlandstowne	0.667	55	10
James Nugent of Ballenah	1	54	25
Thomas Kearnan of Thomasbridstowne	1	50	15
Christopher Nugent of Ballinah	1	44	10
Walter Dowdall of Athboy	0.667	40	20
Total	103.75	6,638	1,444

Table 2

Note: This table uses the old form of land measurement, cartrans, as well as the normal acres. A cartran can vary from 30 to 120 acres, which makes it difficult to quantify real totals. If a measurement of 120 acres was used for a cartran the total would come to approximately 20,500 acres which is within 2,000 acres of the Down Survey total acreage for the area. This anomaly could be explained by the inclusion of 453 acres of Church lands and unknown lands of 810 acres included in the Down Survey and not in the Civil Survey, but this is really a matter of conjecture.

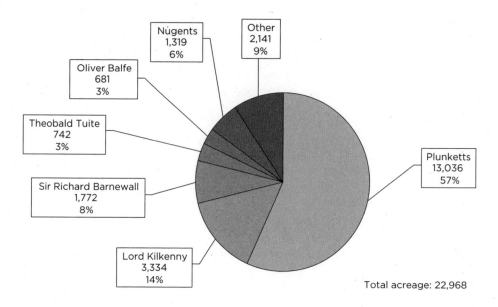

Chart 1. Dominant Landholders in the Barony
Source: author's calculations from Down Survey figures.

The Civil and Down surveys show that the barony was dominated by the extended Plunkett family in the 1640s. Both Lord Dunsany and the Earl of Fingal are members of the Plunkett family. The Plunketts were also related by marriage to the Barnewalls and the Dillons, both notable proprietors in the barony. (The Anglo-Norman families often intermarried in order to retain land ownership and control.) Major Plunkett landowners residing in the barony were John Plunkett of Loughcrew, Thomas of Drumsawry, Christopher of Ballymacad, Henry of Hartstown and Christopher of Clonebreny. In all, according to the Down Survey, the extended Plunkett family owned some 57 per cent of the land in the barony (see chart 1).

Map 4, based on the Down Survey map, also serves to illustrate the dominance of the Plunketts and how their influence spread throughout the barony. Lord Dunsany, the major Plunkett proprietor, occupied some of the best lands in the area around Oldcastle, whereas his cousin the Earl of Fingal occupied the higher land in the south-eastern area of the barony. John Plunkett's holding in Loughcrew is strategically placed in the centre of the barony, whereas Christopher Plunkett's holdings are scattered throughout the area. Map 5 illustrates the holdings of the major non-Plunkett landowners. The size of Lord Dillon's (Kilkenny West) landholding demonstrates his control of a substantial area in the eastern part of Demifore. The Dillons were

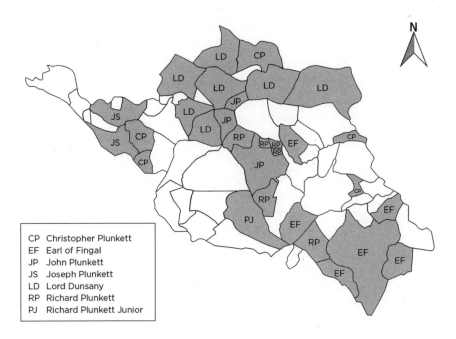

CP   Christopher Plunkett
EF   Earl of Fingal
JP   John Plunkett
JS   Joseph Plunkett
LD   Lord Dunsany
RP   Richard Plunkett
PJ   Richard Plunkett Junior

Map 4: Plunkett lands, *c.* 1640.

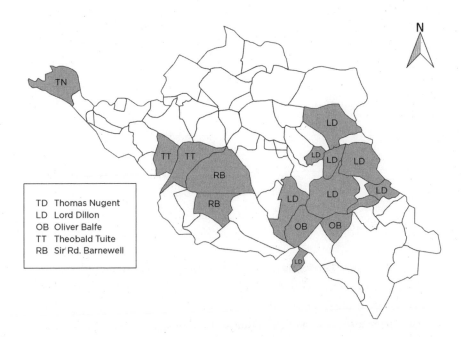

TD   Thomas Nugent
LD   Lord Dillon
OB   Oliver Balfe
TT   Theobald Tuite
RB   Sir Rd. Barnewell

Map 5: Non-Plunkett Proprietors, c. 1640.

an important Old English family who owned considerable sections of Roscommon and Westmeath bordering the River Shannon. Sir Richard Barnewall owned large areas in the centre of the barony. A notable feature of the landholdings in the barony is that all of the landholdings were grouped in substantial blocks of land with the exception of one townland, Chunacon, belonging to Lord Dillon.

Table 3 illustrates the breakdown of the barony into profitable and unprofitable land by parish. Almost 6 per cent is classified as unprofitable, usually denoted as bog, heath and mountain pasture. The parishes of Oldcastle, Killeagh, and Loughcrew in the central and northern areas have a low percentage of unprofitable land, whereas the parishes of Moylagh and Diamor and Clonebreny in the hillier southern area of the barony contain a much higher proportion of unprofitable land (the exception being Killalon). A related point is the location of a corn mill (see table 4) in each of the four parishes containing a higher percentage of profitable land, namely Loughcrew, Oldcastle, Killeagh and Killalon, which demonstrates the importance of tillage to the local economy in these areas.

Land classification by parish		
Parish	*Profitable acres*	*Unprofitable acres*
Oldcastle	5,037	108
Moylagh	3,627	419
Killeagh	3,690	81
Loughcrew	2,599	175
Diamor & Clonebreny	2,565	384
Killalon	4,135	144
Total	21,653	1,311

Table 3. Source: author's calculation from Down Survey figures.

SETTLEMENT

The settlement pattern in the barony in the early seventeenth century can be deduced from the Civil Survey. This survey yielded more information than the later Down Survey terriers and was therefore more suitable as a source for this material. Table 4 lists the data relating to built structures according to the Civil Survey by parish. A number of village sites were spread throughout the parishes of the barony. Castle sites were often the foci of nucleated settlements and the Civil Survey terriers note twenty cabins at Castlecor, thirty at Loughcrew, twenty at Moylagh, thirty at Baltrasna in Moylagh parish and thirty at Ballymacad in Killeagh parish. At all of these locations a castle was recorded pointing to a village settlement in all instances. In addition, twenty cabins and an old chapel are recorded in Diamor parish, with ten cabins beside a church and 'ruinate castle' recorded in neighbouring Clonebreny, indicating some form of village settlement. Oldcastle parish is revealed as the exception to the other parishes with only four cabins listed, which gives the impression of a lack of settlement. Yet the Down Survey lists five castles in the parish, three in association with 'divers cabbins', therefore indicating a denser settlement here. The nucleated settlement sites occur in all of the parishes and demonstrate the strong Anglo-Norman impact on the barony. All of the villages were located near a castle, castle and church or a church, and this was the normal pattern.[12]

	Buildings present in parishes							
	Killalon	Diamor & Clonebreny	Loughcrew	Moylagh	Oldcastle	Castlecor	Killeagh	Totals
Castles	1		1	2		1	3	8
Ruinate Castle	1	2		2	1			6
Unroofed Castle					1		1	2
Churches				1				1
Ruinate Church	1	1			1			3
Unroofed Church						1		1
Old Chapel		1	1					2
Mill	1							1
Corn Mill	1		1		1		1	4
Tuck Mill	1				1			2
Cabins	10	30	30	57	4	20	74	225
Stone house			1					1
Unroofed House	1							1
Fishing Weare	1						1	2

Table 4: Source: author's calculations from figures included in the Civil Survey.

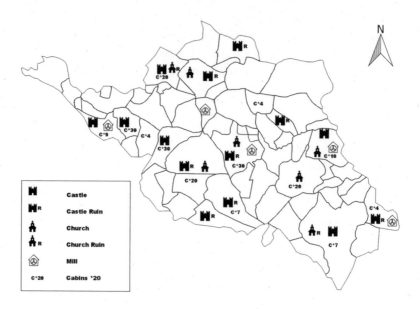

Map 6: Civil Survey buildings present in parishes.

The Down Survey barony map (p.42) was used as a template for visually illustrating the Civil Survey data. Map 6, based on the afore-mentioned map, shows in graphic format the high density of housing and population in parts of Killeagh parish (as illustrated in table 4 where seventy-four cabins are recorded for the parish). The settlements in Loughcrew and Moylagh located in the centre of the barony are a significant feature. The choice of Loughcrew as a later centre of influence may have been dictated by its strategic location. The village sites are dispersed fairly evenly throughout the barony as illustrated in map 3. The number of cabins listed for Oldcastle at a very low figure of four is not borne out by the data from the Down Survey. Oldcastle was the market centre for the barony and the two mills recorded in the parish would corroborate this data.

The obvious lack of settlement in the north-eastern section of the barony is very evident and may be due to the topography of this area, which contains some of the higher ground. The townland of Booleyes, its name indicating the practice of booleying (where livestock were moved away from the home farms to fresh pastures) during summer months, might also explain the lack of housing in this area. The overall number of 225 cabins recorded for the barony may not be a true reflection of the real figure. Unfortunately it is not possible to compare this total with the Down Survey, which does not provide information on cabin numbers. Instead, the Down Survey generally uses the term 'divers cabbins', indicating that an accurate listing of the number of cabins was not a priority for surveyors.

ECONOMY

Information contained within the surveys provides a useful insight into the economy of the barony. Table 4 highlights the differentiation between the various types of buildings as recorded by the enumerators. The condition of the buildings was an important factor as evidenced by, for example, the classification of castles into three categories and the churches into four. Twelve years of warfare had preceded the survey and this is evidenced by the number of buildings identified as being in poor condition. An evaluation of land quality was most important and the surveyors categorised the land into arable, meadow, pasture and unprofitable acreages. This categorisation would seem to demonstrate that mixed farming was practised. The importance of agriculture to the economy is also evident from the listing of mills in the barony. There were seven mills recorded, four of which are shown as corn mills, illustrating the significance of arable farming in the area. Much of the land was classified as arable, indicating the necessity for these corn mills in the area. Two mills were listed as tuck mills. These were used for processing wool and indicate the prevalence of sheep rearing in order to manufacture woollen cloth. Two fishing weirs were also listed, which demonstrates that they may have formed a significant part of the local economy. Their presence may also indicate that fish constituted an important part of the people's diet.

COMMUNICATIONS

It is difficult to provide a clear view of the road network existing in the barony when the Down Survey maps were drawn, because the emphasis was placed on indicating main roads. Only one road was shown on the Down Survey map of the barony and none were indicated on the parish maps. The road was labelled as the road from Finea to Kells. Finea, in neighbouring Westmeath, was an important bridging point on the River Inny. Significantly, it was a communication point for both Cavan town, leading north into Ulster and west towards Granard, County Longford. The Down Survey map indicates its significance. The bridge is illustrated, along with a castle and six houses, one of which would appear to have a symbol attached indicating that it was an inn. A significant battle took place there in the 1640s, when the Cromwellian forces under Munro were forced to retreat to Cavan by the Confederate forces under Myles the Slasher O'Reilly. The Civil Survey does not document any roads but lists in the townland of Ballinah, 'a bridge goeing into the couenty of Cavan'. It would appear that this bridge still exists today in the modern townland of Ballinrink and links to Castlecor, Oldcastle and Mountnugent. Other roads must have existed linking the settlements and presumably the seven mills in the barony. Traces of these roads may possibly be deduced using the Down and Civil surveys and the road network that still exists today.

THE CHURCH

Nine church sites listed in the Meath Archaeological Inventory give their name in most cases to the parishes listed in the barony for the Civil Survey: Oldcastle, Moylagh, Loughcrew, Diamor, Clonebreny and Castlecor.[13] Killalon is the exception without a church listed. On the other hand, Killalon is mentioned in both the Civil and Down surveys as having a church in ruins, the remains of which are still there today. Seven churches are listed in the Civil Survey and six in the Down Survey. The churches not listed are one in Drumsawry (near Loughcrew) and one in Moat townland, which is situated in the old parish of Killeagh where an extensive churchyard remains today. This location is reputed to be the site of the original parish church of Killeagh.

Only three church buildings were intact according to the Civil Survey. These were located in Loughcrew and Moylagh, with an old chapel recorded in Diamor. The fact that only three were in use may demonstrate the poor state of the Catholic Church in the post-Reformation period. It may also illustrate a population decline leading to insufficient funds for the upkeep of these churches. Local tradition places Loughcrew and Moylagh as Plunkett churches because members of the family resided nearby. The family were also reputed to be patrons of the church in Drumsawry not far from Loughcrew. Tradition tells a tale of a falling out between Plunkett wives resulting in a separate church so that they would not have to worship together.

PRE-CROMWELLIAN CASE STUDIES: KILLALON, OLDCASTLE AND LOUGHCREW

This section examines the pre-Cromwellian landscape in three separate parishes of Demifore in order to demonstrate the typical Anglo-Norman settlement with a village centred on a castle and church. These same parishes are re-examined in the post-Cromwellian period later in the essay as a means of illustrating the impact of the Cromwellian and Williamite settlements.

Killalon

There is a very large motte located here and nearby is a graveyard that includes the remains of an early church. This would appear to retain the features of a typical Norman manorial settlement, namely a motte and castle with church nearby. According to Graham, this motte lacked a bailey and was built on an earlier ringfort.[14] Killalon along with Castlecor was one of Richard De Tuite's manors, and he is noted in 1271 as holding land in both areas for three services and twenty-four carucates according to the Gormanstown register. Both places are mentioned in Piperoll of 11/12 John. He also held manors in Diamor in Demifore barony and Kilskyre just outside the barony and quite near Diamor. According to the same, a castle was built beside the motte.[15]

The Civil Survey records 'a castle with a Bawne' in Killalon, whereas the Down Survey terriers note a 'ruined castle'. Healy's *History of the Diocese of Meath* mentions a castle taken by rebels in 1642 and destroyed'.[16] The Down Survey records the Earl of Fingal as the major landowner in the parish and two other members of the Plunkett family held large farms there. The Plunkett connection in Killalon can be traced back to Joan De Tuite who married Sir Walter De Cusack, who in her right became the eighth Lord of Killeen. Joan's granddaughter Joan was inheritor of Killeen and married Sir Charles Plunkett in 1403. This established the Plunketts at Killeen, which went on to become

the House of Dunsany. The title Baron of Killeen went on to become
the earls of Fingal. The Killalon lands came to the Plunketts through
Joan de Cusack.[17]

Oldcastle

Oldcastle, the only town in Demifore, is said to derive its name
from a castle located there in medieval times. The Down Survey
terriers list five castles in the parish suggesting a spread of population, whereas the Civil Survey describes a 'ruinous castle and
church'. No mention is made of the number of cabins in the Civil
Survey with the exception of Oldcastle, but the Down Survey notes
'divers cabbins' in parts of the parish. The Down Survey map shows
Oldcastle located on hilly ground with a castle and three substantial
houses indicated. No visible remains of the castle exist today with
the exception of the reputed steps and part of a wall. The Church of
Ireland was allegedly built on the site of an earlier church mentioned
in the Civil Survey terriers and is situated near the reputed castle
site on the highest point of the hill on which the town is located.
The association of reputed castle and church sites would indicate
a sizeable settlement. Oldcastle was also the market centre for the
area. In 1619, Lord Dunsany, the landlord for the area, was granted
a patent by James I to hold a weekly market there as well as two
annual fairs.[18] Earlier evidence of Oldcastle as a market centre comes
from a complaint made to parliament in 1480 that new markets in
counties Cavan and Longford were adversely affecting the existing
ones in towns such as Oldcastle, Fore and Kells.[19]

Loughcrew

The Civil Survey records at Loughcrew 'a castle in indifferent good
repair one stone house adjoining thereto but defaced, a bawne an
old church with a steeple thirty cabins a corne mill'. This description
implies the presence of a village in Loughcrew. The Down Survey map
shows a church, what may be a castle or tower house, and three other
substantial houses. In Loughcrew today the remains of a tower house
with church attached are still to be seen. A very substantial motte
is located near the tower house and indicates the Anglo-Norman
presence on this site since the twelfth century. An archaeological

Norman Motte at Loughcrew. (Ciaran O'Reilly)

Tower house at Loughcrew (now part of the church). (Ciaran O'Reilly)

survey carried out on behalf of the Naper family in 1997 by Marshall and Sharpe describes a rectangular tower house of three stories.[20] A fourth storey at roof level incorporates a walk with turret above. A date of the early fifteenth century is tentatively ascribed for the tower house. The adjoining church appears to be of a later date, probably late-seventeenth century. This would imply that it was built by the Naper family but traditionally the church is associated with St Oliver Plunkett.

PLANTATION AND SETTLEMENT

As noted earlier, the Cromwellian settlement came about as a result of the Rebellion of 1641. Parts of certain counties were used to pay the soldiers' arrears and, in this way, all of Demifore in County Meath was assigned to Captain Naper of Colonel Ingolsby's regiment. The soldiers had to draw lots for provinces and counties and land was initially valued under the Gross and Civil surveys into profitable and unprofitable lands (also summed per 1,000 acres). The Down Survey in turn superseded these two surveys and was carried out by Sir William Petty. Maps were an important part of this later survey and the barony map produced in this survey is an invaluable source for the period, showing the parishes, townlands, settlements, churches, and so on. The Civil and Down surveys denote the initial stages of the settlement. The subsequent Restoration and Williamite settlements were contributory elements to both change and continuity in Demifore.

CHANGES IN LAND OWNERSHIP

The most significant change resulting from the Cromwellian plantation was the transfer of large areas of the barony to new ownership. Some of the larger Old English landowners had their lands restored during the Restoration period while others, such as Lord Dunsany, did not. Also, some smaller transfers took place as part of the Williamite settlement which continued into the new century. Adjustments had to be made by all who lived in the barony. A new order had taken control of the land and would set out to impose its imprint on the area and its people.

The Books of Survey and Distribution are the primary source used here to detail the change in land ownership that occurred as a result of the confiscation of lands. These books record the changes, if any, which occurred as a result of forfeiture. Lands were forfeited due to participation in the Rebellion of 1641 and the later Jacobite rebellion, which in turn led to what became known as the Williamite settlements. Some landowners were transplanted to Connacht and Clare and compensated with land there. The Books also record the Restoration settlement, which occurred as a result of the restoration of the throne in England in 1660. Proprietors of forfeited lands applied to have them restored; some were successful, but others were not as illustrated through analysis of the data contained in the Books of Survey and Distribution. In addition, data obtained from the estate records of the Naper and Plunkett families is also used to illustrate the post-Cromwellian landscape.

Table 5 provides data from the Books of Survey and Distribution on the proprietorial landscape after the Cromwellian plantation. Lord Dunsany no longer heads the table, losing all of his 4,163 acres in the barony. Sir Richard Barnewall, whose family were substantial landowners in Meath and Dublin, suffers a similar fate losing all of the 1,772 acres he previously held in the barony. James Naper, the captain in Colonel Ingolsby's regiment who was granted the barony, now heads the table and has possession of nearly 15 per cent of the land. More than 70 per cent of the total shown in this table is now seen to be in the hands of new owners. Eight are shown as joint ownerships, most of these showing old and new together, for example Fingal/ Naper. These have been excluded from the 70-per-cent figure but in themselves amount to a not-inconsiderable 16 per cent.

Chart 2 serves to illustrate the dramatic changes in land ownership, already outlined in table 5, in graphic format. It can be seen immediately that land ownership is more fragmented with James Naper dominating at 15 per cent. The other new proprietors hold smaller acreages, for example Thomas Newman at 8 per cent and Richard and Henry Ingolsby at 7 per cent along with many others coming in at 3 per cent or less. Twenty landowners held less than 500 acres and eight landholdings are shown as joint ownerships, whereas only one was recorded in this way in the Down Survey. The earls of Roscommon and Fingal are clearly seen as substantial landholders who successfully petitioned in the Restoration settlement. Sir William Petty, who took

Post-Cromwellian Landholdings (Books of Survey & Distribution)			
Name	Acres	Roods	Perches
James Naper	3,428	2	30
Earl of Fingal★	2,368	1	0
Earl of Roscommon	2,005	1	36
Thomas Newman	1,825	3	4
R. & H. Ingolsbye	1,688	0	0
William Cambell	1,450	0	11
Edward Baines	1,084	0	21
Sir W. Petty	762	2	0
Thomas Baker	719	3	0
Henry Wade	721	1	22
John Wade	693	0	0
John Jeffreys	645	2	20
Lance Sands	638	0	0
Walter Burgh	502	1	10
Fingal / Naper	454	0	0
A. Plunkett / P. Tuite	421	0	13
R. Balfe / J. Blennerhasset	416	0	0
A. Plunkett / H. Wade	404	0	0
James Nugent	397	2	0
W. Usher	359	0	0
Humphrey Rogers	313	0	33
John Asgill	248	0	0
Richard Younge	234	3	3
William Hoy	175	0	0
R. Balfe / Roscommon / E. Moore	127	0	0
Charles Wade	122	0	0
R. Balfe / W. Petty	109	0	0
John Blennerhasset	104	0	34
Fingal / Bishop Dublin	99	3	36
Andrew Ram	80	0	0
Edward Plunkett	78	0	0
D. Hignett / S. Wrotham	59	0	0
Charles Campbell	22	0	0
Church	14	0	0
Total	22,770	3	33

Table 5.

★ The Earl of Fingal's total acreage includes 1,600 acres listed
with the Earl of Anglesey in the Books of Survey

charge of the Down Survey, is a notable name here. He had local connections; his sister was married to Captain James Naper who gained the highest acreage of landholding in the post-Cromwellian settlement. The Napers went on to consolidate and increase their holdings and became the biggest landowners in the barony. The Wade family went on to build an estate in the eastern part of the barony centring on Clonebreny House, previously belonging to Christopher Plunkett. The landholdings of the Wade family extended into the neighbouring parish of Kilskyre in the barony of Kells, which borders the barony of Demifore.

As illustrated in table 5 and chart 2, there is no doubt that the new proprietors dominate the landscape, but some pre-Cromwellian owners did manage to hold on to their land as illustrated in table 6. The earls of Fingal and Roscommon (who was Lord of Kilkenny West in the Down Survey) lost 3.3 and 5 per cent of their land-holdings respectively. Both received pardons from King William,[21] which helped their position, whereas Lord Dunsany did not and the 1641 Depositions also help to illustrate his position clearly.[22] He was the only one of the landowners in the barony called before

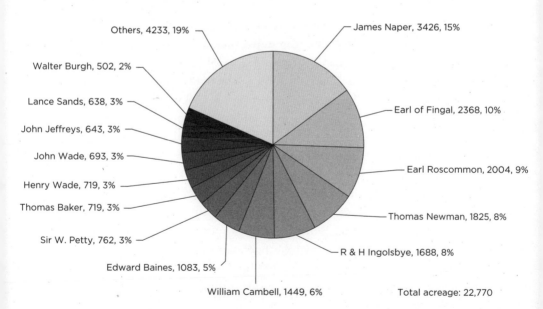

Chart 2: Dominant Landholders in the Barony - Books of Survey & Distribution
(holdings over 500 acres)

the commissioners for County Meath to state his case, yet numerous depositions mention the Earl of Fingal, Sir Richard Barnewall, and Lord Dillon of Kilkenny West, even though they were not called to testify in person. The smaller landholdings belonging to the Plunketts who resided in the barony were reduced dramatically, falling from over 22 per cent to just 4 per cent of the barony lands (table 6). These landowners were unable to hold on to their lands, presumably because of their lack of influence. The more fragmented nature of their landholdings was a possible factor contributing to their significant losses.

Percentage of land held by Pre-Cromwellian landowners in the Barony		
	Down Survey	Books of Survey & Distribution
Lord Dunsany	18.4%	0%
Earl of Fingal	13.7%	10.4%
Lord of Kilkenny West	14.8%	8.8%
Plunketts★	22.5%	4.0%
Sir Richard Barnewall	8.0%	0%

Table 6: Source: Author's calculations from figures included in the Down Survey
★ Plunkett families excluding Lord Dunsany and the Earl of Fingal

Map 8, based on the Down Survey map, serves to illustrate some of the changes in ownership. The map shows the 3,250 acres of land held by the Naper family according to the Books of Survey and Distribution. Their landholding was located in the centre of the barony. The decision of the Napers to live at the Plunkett house in Loughcrew may have been influenced by their desire to see its continued use as a landlord base plus the fact that its tower house was inhabitable. The strategic location of these lands may have helped the family to go on to consolidate their position as the dominant landowners in the barony. Map 8 also illustrates the holdings of the other new proprietors with over 700 acres according to the Books of Survey and Distribution (where parts of townlands are shown indicates joint ownership). The holdings of the Wades (grouped together) are shown in the east where they centred themselves on the Plunkett holding in Clonebreny. The Wade family were granted most of the surrounding lands and 1,490 acres elsewhere in Meath.[23]

William Petty, who undertook the Down Survey, obtained some of the better land in the northern part of the barony. Edward Baines

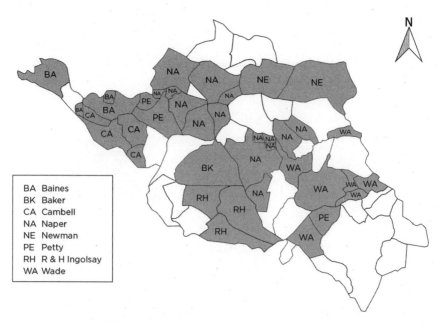

Map 7: New Proprietors over 700 acres.

and William Cambell received lands in the north-west section but further research is needed in order to indicate whether any of the aforementioned actually took up residence in the barony. It may be that they sold their lands on as was commonly done at the time. Richard and Henry Ingolsby obtained grants of land in the area to the south-west of Loughcrew. They also received lands in County Clare and Limerick city and appear to have settled there. A grandson of the original Captain James Naper and Dorothy Petty married an Ingolsby so there may have been some prior connection between the families.

The landholdings retained by other Old English proprietors, for instance those of Alexander Plunkett and Oliver Balfe, were quite small and shown in joint ownership, which indicates a dispute as to their ownership. The map clearly demonstrates the losses suffered by many of the pre-1641 landowners such as Christopher Plunkett, Thomas Nugent, Lord Dunsany, Theobald Tuite and Sir Richard Barnewall (Sir Richard Barnewall may have concentrated on consolidating his lands in Dublin where he gained 966 acres).[24] Their holdings are now too small, or have disappeared altogether, to even feature on the map. Map 7 illustrates clearly the changing power base from Old English to New English.

Map 8, based on the Books of Survey and Distribution, illustrates the holdings of the only two Old English proprietors to retain over

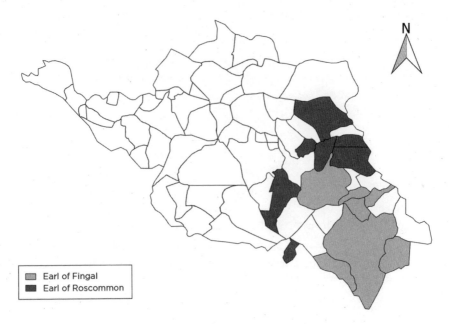

N

Earl of Fingal
Earl of Roscommon

Map 8: Old English Proprietors over 500 acres. Post Settlement.

500 acres. These lands were located in the eastern and south-eastern section of the barony. The Earl of Fingal's lands are shown with the townland of Killalon as the dominant feature. The townland of Seraghstown is not included as part of his lands but is shown as in his ownership on the Fingal papers from 1692.[25] The Earl of Roscommon (previously known as Lord Dillon of Kilkenny West) is shown as losing two of his townlands to the Wade family as part of the Williamite settlement, thus reducing his holdings considerably. Diamor, comprising nearly 700 acres, went to John Wade and Martinstown, comprising 159 acres, went to Henry Wade.

CHANGES IN LAND OWNERSHIP

While there is no doubt that great changes occurred as a result of the Cromwellian and subsequent settlements, there is also evidence of continuity. In order to better illustrate the impact of the plantations on the barony, the next section re-examines the three parishes used earlier as case studies to help describe the pre-Cromwellian landscape. The main sources used include terriers from both the Civil and the Down surveys, Church records, the Fingall Papers held in the National

Library, and memorials from the Registry of Deeds for the Naper family. The maps included in the Down Survey were also invaluable as they are the only surviving maps for the barony from the seventeenth century (a gap of 100 years exists between those maps and the next available set dating from 1778).

Loughcrew

Loughcrew serves as a perfect example of the process of change brought about by the Cromwellian settlement. The Naper family developed their home base here and built up an extensive demesne centring on a new long house built in the late-seventeenth century. The earliest available map of the Naper demesne[26] from 1778 provides clues to the changes that occurred there in the latter half of the seventeenth century. The long house and formal gardens are clearly depicted. The doorcase of this house survives to this day, incorporated into the walled garden. The old tower house of the Plunketts is shown as a church. Presumably, the choice of Loughcrew as his base by James Naper may have been due to the fact that it had 'A Castle in Indifferent good Repair One stone house Adjoynening thereto but Defaced A Bawne and old Church with a Steeple 30 Cabbins a Corne Mill'.[27] The Down Survey map depicts a castle, a church and three other substantial houses. John Plunkett of Loughcrew is listed as the owner according to the Civil Survey and was presumably resident there. Here was a readymade village settlement, ideally located in the centre of the barony and already in use as a landlord base.

The Atlas of the Irish Rural Landscape uses the 1778 demesne map and the earlier Down Survey maps to reconstruct the development of Loughcrew. The first map, dated circa 1640, shows what the village may have been like. It depicts a typical manorial settlement based around castle and church and tenants' cottages as indicated by the Civil and Down surveys. The second map illustrates what might have changed by 1720, showing the creation of the demesne area around the Big House with its formal gardens. The village settlement has disappeared, the cottiers shown living some distance away on the lower slopes of the nearby hills. Here is clearly illustrated the most significant change, the removal of the tenants' dwellings away from the vicinity of the landlord's house. The creation of a demesne and formal gardens around the landlord's house necessitated this relocation of the

Doorcase from long house with date stone above – 1693
(now incorporated into later walled garden). (Ciaran O'Reilly)

cottiers. This marks the new trend away from the nucleated manorial settlement towards the landlord living in 'the Big House', isolated from his tenants by the surrounding demesne. These maps indicate the radical changes in the landscape from the old manorial settlement grouped around the castle and church to the new demesne where no trace of the village remains.

Church records from the seventeenth century also help to reveal the changes that took place in Loughcrew. Bishop Dopping's visitations of 1682–85 and 1693 provide an overview of the area.[28] The parish church was in good repair with a slated roof and glazed windows. The parish had been united with the parishes of Diamor, Killeagh and Moylagh, and also with Clonabraney *pro tem* in 1682. This may have been because the visitation revealed that very few Protestant families lived in the adjoining parishes. In Loughcrew, on the other hand, a vibrant Protestant community had been established. Two ministers resided in the parish and religious services were provided once a week for the around 100 Protestants recorded as living there. There was a Protestant schoolmaster listed, which attests to an increasing population of children. The availability of these vital services would attract Protestant families to the area. The impact of a resident landlord intent on building up a power base is very evident here. A Catholic priest was listed for the parish, nevertheless the change from control by the Plunkett family earlier in the century to that of the New English Naper family is apparent in the parish.

The parish of Killalon serves as a useful example of an area with little change in land ownership post-settlement. The Books of Survey and Distribution record the Earl of Fingal as holding Killalon townland in joint ownership with Lord Anglesey, but Fingal successfully petitioned to have his lands restored during the Restoration.[29] The Fingall papers in the National Library, containing various rentals and miscellaneous papers from 1668 to 1793, prove that this was indeed the case. The townlands in Killalon parish owned by Fingal are the same as those recorded in the Books of Survey and Distribution, namely Killalon, Ghecanstown, Seraghstown and Galboystown.[30]

Table 7, based on the Fingall papers, illustrates that the Reilly family were the principal tenants and held the largest townland, Killalon, which consisted of 1,650 acres. The earlier figures from 1692 to 1722 are based on a document setting out a 31-year lease to Mr James Reilly. The annual rent increased gradually over the period, presumably as it was considered that the income from the tenant would increase due to improvements. This is apparent in table 7, where the rent in years one to three is low at £60/80, while in the middle period of the lease there is a substantial increase of 66 per cent over the starting rent. During the full time period of the lease the rent increased by 300 per cent in order to generate income and influence the tenant to utilise the land more productively.

J. Reilly Rent (Killalon)		
Year	No. years	Rent (£)
1692	1	60
1693	2	80
1695	4	100
1699	7	140
1705	6	180
1711	6	200
1717	5	220
1722	31	275

Table 7. Source: Fingall Papers MS8024.

The Books of Survey and Distribution record the townlands of Ghecanstown, Gallogestown (Galboystown) and Seraghstown as belonging to the Earl of Fingal. He is also the recorded owner of the same property in the Civil Survey and the Down Survey. There is a difference in the spelling of Galboystown, which appears as 'Gallogestown' in the Books of Survey and Distribution and as 'Galboystown' in the Civil Survey and Down Survey and in the Fingal papers. There are no figures available for these townlands prior to 1709. Table 8 shows that the townland of Geighanstown, with the highest percentage of unprofitable land, commanded a very low rent per acre of 8 pence whereas the other townlands averaged around 2 shillings.

Church records further illustrate the parish of Killalon in the later seventeenth century. Ussher's Visitation of 1622 valued the parish at £40.[31] This value had not changed according to Dopping's visitations later in the century.[32] The church was recorded in these documents as being in ruins. Similarly, it was recorded in the earlier Civil and Down surveys as being out of repair. Yet it was a functioning parish as a service was held once a month in a private house by the minister, who also held services in Oldcastle. There were a house and garden provided and 7 acres of glebe land, an increase of 3 acres from that recorded in the Civil Survey. This may explain the viability of the parish even though only three Protestant families are recorded.

Rents paid in other townlands	
Galboystown: Chapman Rent (351 Profitable; 48 Unprofitable)	
Year	Rent paid
1709	£49 7s 0d
Geighanstown: Hogan Rent (211 Profitable; 111 Unprofitable)	
Year	Rent paid
1709	£13 6s 11d
Seraghstown: B. Reilly (235 Profitable; 24 Unprofitable)	
Year	Rent paid
1709	£27 14s 7d

Table 8. Source: Fingall Papers MS8024.

Dopping's Visitation provided some evidence of the parish having an active Catholic population. A Catholic priest and Catholic school-master were listed, which illustrates that not only were religious services provided but that there was a school available for the parish.[33] The provision of a school is significant because only one other Catholic school is recorded in the barony, in the parish of Oldcastle. The Earl of Fingal had these lands restored to him as mentioned earlier in the text. As the Fingal Plunketts were a prominent Catholic family, this may have been a factor here. This family provided continuity for its tenants through their retention of these lands and demonstrates that not all areas of the barony underwent dramatic change.

Oldcastle town continued its role as the only market centre in the barony. The Dunsany Plunketts encouraged this development as illus-trated earlier. The only available data from the 1778 map of Oldcastle townland[34] provide evidence for its further development, showing a market house in the central square and a fair green on the edge of the town. The Naper family were the major landowners in the town, and it must be presumed that the family promoted and facilitated this continuing development. The earlier Civil and Down surveys demonstrate that mixed farming was practised. Tillage was important as evidenced by the four corn mills listed in the barony. Another mill, use unspecified, was also listed and may have been a corn mill. Two tuck mills indicate that sheep farming was prevalent. The presence of these mills illustrate that a market centre was necessary as a focus of trade for the people living in the area.

Church records provide valuable data on the population of the town. The Dopping visitations from the 1680s and 1693 demonstrate that the Protestant community was composed of sixteen families.[35] If each family had two children, this would amount to sixty-five people approximately. These numbers indicate that it came second to Loughcrew in the size of its Protestant population. The church was out of repair and services were held once a week in a private house. Dopping's Visitation mentioned that some of the Protestant families were Quakers and there is further evidence of this from Quaker records analysed by Cassidy.[36] Cassidy details how as early as 1659 a Quaker meeting had been established in Oldcastle, and was attached to the Cavan monthly meeting. In 1699 the Quakers had leased a burial ground demonstrating that they maintained a strong presence in the area. Their records suggest that perhaps seven families belonged to the meeting in 1699. Some emigrated in the early eighteenth century, one of whom was a linen draper. The Quakers were known for their industry and their departure would likely have been a loss to the town. The Catholic population was also in evidence from the Church records. A Catholic priest was listed and also a schoolmaster, indicating that there were sufficient people living there who needed these services. In the 1680s, Owen Grady is recorded as the Catholic priest according to Dopping's Visitation.[37] There is a priest listed in all the parishes of the barony, which points to a functioning Catholic community.

CONCLUSION

In summary, this essay has outlined the profound changes that occurred in the seventeenth century in Demifore. The primary source materials were drawn upon in an attempt to capture the change in land ownership from the pre-Cromwellian period dominated by the Old English families to the post-Cromwellian period dominated by the New English. Focusing on the chosen parish examples helped to demonstrate the various effects of the Cromwellian and Williamite settlements. In particular, the use of estate records helped to create a picture of the barony during this period, the maps illustrated the landscape while the rent rolls provided important economic data.

The Cromwellian and Williamite settlements effected profound changes in the landscape and population of Ireland in the seventeenth century. The old Anglo-Norman manorial settlement grouped around castle and church was replaced by the new landlord system centred on a demesne cutting the landlord off from his tenants. This was in stark contrast to the Anglo-Norman system where the landlord or his agent lived in close proximity to his tenants. During the pre-Cromwellian period in the barony of Demifore, the Anglo-Norman system was well established with Old English families dominating the area. All of the parishes exhibit the structures of the Anglo-Norman period, that is, manorial settlements based on castle and church. The churches had suffered in the post-Reformation period but the study demonstrates that three churches were still in use in the barony, which indicates the strength of the church in this area. There also existed a pattern of nucleated settlements in many parts of the barony as was illustrated in this study.

The Old English proprietors who lost their lands did so because of their participation in the Rebellion of 1641 and the debts accrued due to wars waged by both the Cromwellian and Williamite administrations. The barony of Demifore was used therefore to pay arrears of soldiers' pay. It was granted in this way to Captain James Naper, who received 15 per cent of the land according to the Books of Survey and Distribution. The study demonstrates that many others, such as Sir William Petty himself, were granted lands. There is no evidence to indicate how many of those who received patents actually took up residence in the barony. It was common practice for many soldiers to sell their debentures and return to England.

The family of the original Captain James Naper went on to become the dominant landowners in the area. The Naper family brought about many changes in the landscape. The establishment of their demesne at Loughcrew meant that the village settlement that had existed there prior to their arrival was dispersed. Continuity of landlord residence was maintained by the Napers by their choice of Loughcrew as a residence, having taken it over from the Plunketts. The only other New English family to establish a large estate in the barony was the Wade family. Their estate was based on the Plunkett holding in Clonebreny in the eastern part of the barony. The continued development of Oldcastle as a market town is another notable feature. The Naper family owned the town and lands of Oldcastle and chose to centre the local economy there.

The Old English proprietors who survived the dramatic changes in land ownership found that their landholdings were greatly reduced. The Earl of Fingal and the Earl of Roscommon were the only Old English landowners to retain holdings of over 500 acres. The Plunkett families who owned some 57 per cent of the barony in 1640 were now left with just over 14.4 per cent. The Plunketts residing in the barony who previously held 25 per cent of the land saw their holdings decrease substantially to a mere 4 per cent.

In conclusion, it is obvious that the barony of Demifore changed substantially during the seventeenth century. The old Anglo–Norman system based on medieval manorial settlements was generally replaced with a new landlord system focussed on the Big House and its associated demesne. Replacing the old castle and church settlements, the introduction of the demesne wrought many changes to the landscape and isolated the landlord from his tenants. In addition, the New English Protestant landlords introduced settlers of the same religious persuasion, a factor that helped to further alienate them from their native Irish tenants. Profound changes in land ownership came about as a result of the Cromwellian and Williamite settlements. The old order controlled by the Old English gave way to a new order dominated by the New English settlers and their membership of the established Church. The ownership of land provided this new grouping with the wealth and power previously enjoyed by the old order.

The Manor Courts of Martry in County Meath: Law and Order on the Tisdall Estate 1789 to 1792

MARION ROGAN

The manorial system was introduced into Ireland with the coming of the Normans in the twelfth century. In 1172, in a bid to curb the power of Richard de Clare (Strongbow) in Leinster, Henry II, King of England, granted the liberty of Meath to Hugh de Lacy, a powerful magnate with property in Normandy, Wales and England. Meath was one of the major landholdings granted by the Crown during the initial attempt at colonisation of Ireland by the Anglo-Normans. Hugh held Meath by the service of fifty knights.[1] Not all of Meath was directly occupied and controlled by the de Lacy family themselves. Some was granted to their followers in what was known as subinfeudation. Within the barony, so called since it was the land occupied by the baron, the primary unit of landholding was the manor. A manor was a composition of different settlement components interacting within a defined area. Essentially a local institution, the manor was a self-sufficient landed estate together with a number of rights, such as its right to hold local courts and control mills, under the authority of the lord of the manor. John Norden's 1607 description of it as 'a little commonwealth, whereof the tenants are the members, the Lord the body, and the law the head,' neatly captures its essence.[2]

The first reference to the granting of the manor of Martry occurs in 1318. For some time prior to that date, the manor had been held by Walter Saye. Walter, however, forfeited his possessions, including the manor of Martry, by rising with Robert and Edward Bruce against the Crown. On 1 February 1318, King Edward II of England (1307–26) granted the manor to a knight named Hugh Turpelton 'with appurtenances, both in lordships and demesnes with the reversions of dowers and advowson of the church of that manor, and liberties, homages, services of free tenants, wards, marriages, reliefs, escheats, and other appurtenances'. The annual render was 'one unmewed sparrow-hawk'.[3] Hugh was killed in 1330 in defence of Roger Mortimer (1287–1330) at Nottingham Castle, when Roger was seized by Edward III.[4]

The justiciar was the chief governor of Ireland in the pre-Tudor period. Between the years 1323 and 1337, John Darcy, an unimportant household knight, was justiciar of Ireland on three separate occasions for a total of twelve years.[5] The first Lord Darcy de Knayth and his mother Joan (widow of the 2nd Earl of Kildare and third daughter of the 2nd Earl of Ulster) were granted lands for their services to King Edward II at the battle of Crécy 1346.[6] Their grandson, John Darcy of Plattin in County Meath, while still a minor, inherited the manor of Martry in 1362 from his grandmother.[7] Martry remained in the Darcy family possession for over 300 years until Nicholas Darcy the elder, an Irish papist, had his estates confiscated following the 1641 Rebellion.[8] They were partially restored to his grandson, Nicholas the younger, in 1666 following an appeal to the court of claims. The Darcys never lived in the manor of Martry; their family seat was in Plattin, near Duleek in County Meath.

Sometime in the early seventeenth century the first of the Tisdall family in Ireland, Michael Tisdall I, arrived in Castleblaney, County Monaghan from England, probably from Teesdale in northern England.[9] In 1668, his eldest son Michael Tisdall II leased the manor of Martry in County Meath from Nicholas Darcy, an Irish papist, who appeared to have been in financial difficulties.[10] The extent of the manor in 1669 was 1,900 acres. Its jurisdiction extended to the townlands of Phoenixtown, Jakestown (alias Bloomsbury), Athgaine Little, Volvenstown, Nugentstown and Martry.[11] Four years later, in 1672, Michael purchased the manor. He now held the title of lord of the manor and all rights pertaining to it. His elder son, William, inherited the estate on his father's death. During William's minority, the estate was managed by his uncle James Tisdall, later MP for Ardee. In 1689, William's elder son, Michael III, succeeded to the manor. He died aged 33 and the estate passed to his elder son, Charles, who was then only 7 years of age. Charles came into his inheritance in 1740 and managed the estate until his premature death in 1757.[12] He left two sons, Michael IV, born December 1755, and Charles, born ten months later in June 1757.[13] Michael Tisdall IV was 2 years old when his father died and he came into his inheritance in 1776. Like the Darcys, the Tisdalls owned Martry for almost 300 years until its eventual sale to the Land Commission in 1968.[14]

Manor of Martry holders <1318 to 1968		
< 1318	Walter Saye	Granted by Edward II
1318 –	Hugh Turpelton	Granted by Edward II
1346	Lord Darcy of Knayth and his mother Joan	Granted by Edward II
1362	John Darcy of Plattin	Inherited
1362–1672	Darcy family	
1672	Michael Tisdall II	Purchased
1672–1968	Tisdall family	

Table 9. Source: Antiquissime roll, 1 February 1318
(http://chancery.tcd.ie/document/Other/antiquissime-roll/61) (23 April 2013);
Bernard Burke, *Burke's Irish Family Records* (London, 1976), pp 1104-9.

The manor of Martry was a small, rural County Meath manor straddling the banks of the River Blackwater, midway between Navan and Kells, in the baronies of Upper Kells and Lower Navan. Martry's unique location may mean that the site was deliberately chosen as the manorial centre. Martry lay at the intersection of two routeways; the Navan–Kells Road ran along its southern boundary and the old road to the north across the River Blackwater passed through it at the ford of Martry.

Some topographical features and physical remains, still evident in the landscape today, suggest the existence of a manorial centre at Martry. A hill, known locally as Castle Hill, may have been the site of a motte-and-bailey castle. Castles were erected to consolidate the newly granted lands; it was there that the lord of the manor would have lived. An Edward II coin was found there some years ago.

A placename nearby, referred to as Moatroe in 1740s by Charles Tisdall, further suggests the possible existence of a castle.[15] Close by on the south-eastern side of Castle Hill was the medieval parish church and graveyard of Martry. By the time of Bishop Dopping's visit to the area in the 1680s, the church had been wholly demolished, but he recorded a house, possibly the glebe house, in 15 acres of glebe land; glebe land was the land held by the Church to maintain it.[16] A holy

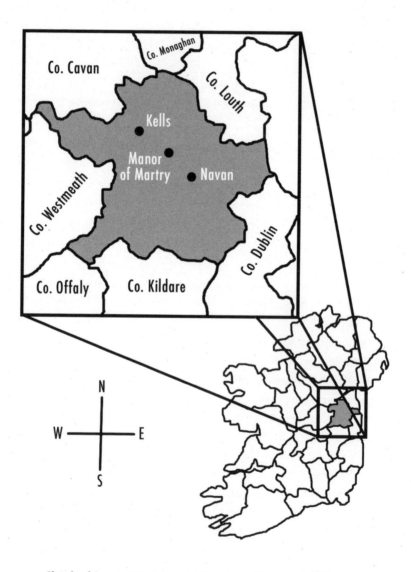

Sketch of County Meath showing location of the manor of Martry.

Martry Mill. (Photograph courtesy of Tallon family, present owners of Marty Mill)

well, dedicated to St Brigid, is nearby. A mill was another salient feature of the manor and the Civil Survey of 1641 records a mill in the parish of Martry; this has survived as a working mill to the present day.[17]

A 1669 document, no longer extant, but transcribed by John Ainsworth in the 1950s, records that the manor of Martry contained 1,900 acres with 100 cottages, ten messuages and ten tofts (table 10). A messuage consisted of a house with outbuildings, and a parcel of land or a yard. A toft appears to have been slightly different. It may have been a messuage, or rather a place or piece of ground where a house formerly stood, but was in ruins. It had two windmills and a pigeon house. Pigeons and doves were an important food source and were used to provide meat and eggs for the lord of the manor's table. They were also a source of dung.

Manor of Martry features in 1669						
Messuages	Tofts	Windmills	Cottages	Pigeon houses	Gardens	Land
10	10	2	100	1	20	1, 900 acres

Table 10. Source: John Ainsworth (ed.), *Report on private collections*, p. 2284.

MANOR COURTS

Another constituent of manor life was the manor court, the lowest court of law during the feudal period. The manor and court could not exist independently of each other; the one was conditional on the other.[18] The jurisdiction of the Martry court extended to those who resided in the manor or who held lands within it, and tenants, such as Edmund Gibney of Volvenstown in 1696, were expected to do 'suit and service at the manor court of Martry'.[19] Part of the manor court book for the years 1789 to 1792 is preserved on microfilm in the NLI among a small collection of Tisdall papers.[20] It is the main primary source for this study. The court book consists of seventy-six pages of court records, four of which are duplicate pages, and is a rarity as few such records are still extant.[21] Fortunately, also surviving for the same period, and thus complementing the court book, is a rent roll of Michael Tisdall, lord of the manor of Martry at the time, relating to his property c. 1792.[22] This gives the names of twenty-nine tenants, the acreage and location of the lands they leased, the terms of their leases and the half-yearly rents due each May and November, helping to establish a profile of those tenants who sought redress in the manor courts. The study is further supplemented by scattered miscellaneous material from the Tisdall family's private possession.

In 1714, William Scroggs published a manual on the operation of manor courts.[23] Whether these guidelines were closely adhered to or not in the manor courts is not clear. However, the appraiser's oath used in the Martry courts appears to be a copy of that in the Scroggs manual.[24] In 1837 a select committee was appointed to enquire into the operation of the manor courts in Ireland.[25] Thousands of questions were posed of court officials, barristers and jurors in order to ascertain the efficacy or otherwise of the manor courts, to identify their weaknesses and their strengths, the abuses that existed in them and to propose remedial action. The report revealed that there were 204 of these 'small debt recovery courts' still functioning at the time, from Malin in County Donegal to Ballydehob in County Cork, but mainly in Ulster and Munster. There were some in Leinster but none in Meath. The enquiry elicited much factual information, but also much that was hearsay and rumour. While cognisant of the biased and conflicting nature of many of the opinions offered, this comprehensive report has been used as a backdrop in order to place the manor courts of Martry in the national context and to flesh out the surviving meagre documentation preserved in the Martry court records. What happened to the rest of the court records in Martry is not known. George McDonagh was the seneschal throughout the period under study here. Seneschals varied in professionalism. Perhaps George McDonagh was a better record keeper and custodian of documents than the previous or later appointees to the position. Perhaps he was the only seneschal who preserved any records at all. Perhaps it was the then-lord of the manor and lawyer Michael Tisdall IV, high sheriff of Meath in 1781, who ensured their preservation.

Chris Briggs' essay, 'Manor court procedures, debt litigation levels, and rural credit provision in England *c.* 1290–*c.* 1380', adds considerably to the understanding of procedure in the manor courts, albeit in England and in the fourteenth century, four centuries earlier than the period under study in this essay. Raymond Gillespie's article, 'A manor court in seventeenth century Ireland', emphasises the paucity of surviving evidence describing the essence and operation of the courts. His article includes the text of instructions given to the jury at a manor court in County Clare *circa* 1670.[26]

The pages of the Martry court book present a number of challenges for the historian. Although it is written in English, deciphering the handwriting is the first difficulty. However, since all of the court records were written in the same seneschal's hand, one becomes familiar with the style. An additional help is that much of the language is formulaic, and so is found repeatedly. On the negative side, this repetition means that the actual information on the court cases is quite scant. Some prior knowledge of the expected information that the records are most likely to contain is useful in extracting names of tenants, jurors, those owing suit of court, court officials and those involved in lawsuits. The survival of the rent roll of the tenants on the Tisdall estate for the period facilitates this.

The microfilmed pages are not paginated, neither are they in chronological order, so it is difficult to decode the cases, though the jury lists provide some answer. The seneschal recorded the names of the jurors empanelled for a case towards the beginning of the court record of the day, in his own handwriting. At the conclusion of the case, the jurors then signed their names, confirming the verdict. In the microfilmed records, these two lists of jurors do not appear in sequence. Sometimes a number of pages separate them. When compared, however, the jurors'

signatures are always in the exact same order as the seneschal wrote
them. Thus, by cross-referencing the two lists of the jury, some
semblance of order and sequencing can be put on the pages of the
court book and some court cases can be extrapolated, although few
can be followed through from their initial presentment in court to
the verdict delivered by the jury. The first page of the court book lists
sixty-three inhabitants who held an acre of land or more and who
were obliged to pay leet monies to the lord of the manor. The rest of
the court book contains the names of those who attended the courts
as jurors, plaintiffs, defendants, witnesses or court officials.

There were two different types of manorial courts, the court
baron and the court leet. In *The Court Keepers Guide*, published in
1650, William Sheppard states that the court baron was incident to
every manor, the court leet was not. A man could 'not be ousted
of his court baron unless he be ousted of his manor'.[27] The courts
were administered according to the set of rules and regulations
known as the custom of the manor, which governed the relations of
tenants to each other and to the lord. These regulations differed from
manor to manor. In Martry, they were 'according to the constant and
uninterrupted custom observed at all times in this manor within our
memory'.[28] It was the court leet that made these bye-laws, which
were formally confirmed annually at a court leet held in the manor
for that purpose. Unlike the court baron, the court leet required a
special prescription or patent.[29] This writer has not seen any indication of the patent that instituted a court leet in the manor of Martry,
so perhaps it was held by prescription. The court leet was usually
held twice a year within a month of both Easter and Michaelmas
but by prescription it could be held more often. This appears to
have been the case in Martry (table 11). The courts baron in Martry
appear to have met every three weeks, usually on Mondays; on
only one occasion, 1 March 1789, was the court held on a Tuesday.
On 8 December 1789, both the court baron and the court leet met
on the same day. It is not clear what difference existed between
these two types of courts in Martry at the end of the eighteenth
century since the demarcation line is blurred in the surviving
records. The fragmentary records show that nineteen courts were
held between 16 February 1789 and 1 November 1792 (table 11).

Courts held in the manor of Martry 1789-92	
Date	Court
16 February 1789	Court leet
March 1789	Court leet
3 March 1789	Not stated
14 May 1789	Not stated
1 June 1789	Easter leet
15 June 1789	Not stated
6 July 1789	Court baron
3 August 1789	Court baron
24 August 1789	Not stated
7 September 1789	Court baron
23 November 1789	Not stated
8 December 1789	Court baron Michaelmas court leet
1 March 1790	Court baron
9 May 1791	Court baron
13 June 1791	Court leet
30 June 1791	Court baron
2 January 1792	Court leet
23 October 1792	Court baron
1 November 1792	Court baron

Table 11. Source: compiled from manor of Martry court book, 1789-92.

The courts served the interests of the tenants, lord and community alike. They resolved inter-tenant disputes in a speedy, cheap administration of justice, under rules and regulations understood by all from time immemorial. They supplemented the lord's income through fines and charges levied and maintained his rights and prerogatives over his manor. A court leet held at Castletowne, Athboy in County Meath, not far from the manor of Martry, on 10 November 1664 gives some idea as to the nature of these privileges. The court found that, by the ancient custom of its manor, the lord was entitled to twenty geese yearly at Michaelmas from the corporation of the town for allowing free passage to the bog for turf and six gallons of aquavite (whiskey) yearly at Christmas. Every house and castle had to supply the lord with a reaper with his hook upon demand. At the same court, it was decided that a pinfold should be made within the manor, probably for impounding straying animals, an issue which would have concerned and benefitted the whole community.[30]

The custom of the manor determined where the courts sat. In the period 1789 to 1792, during Michael Tisdall IV's tenure, the manor court was held in Charlesfort, probably Charlesfort House, where no place in the manor was further than 4 miles distant. Charlesfort House had been built in the 1740s by Michael's father, Charles Tisdall.[31] Prior to the construction of Charlesfort House, they may have been held in Mount Tisdall alias Bloomsbury, the first Tisdall residence built in 1672. In earlier times still, the court may have been held at Martry Cross or under the tree at St Brigid's Well in Martry.

Lords of the manor sometimes requested their tenants to provide facilities for holding the courts in their houses. On one occasion, in 1748, it is likely that a court was held in John McKartney's house. Perhaps, Charles Tisdall directed John McKartney to hold the courts in a room in his house as Lord Glengall did in Rehill in County Tipperary.[32] John was a tenant on the Tisdall estate, holding 25 acres. In some manors it was customary for the jury to enjoy a meal and drinks after the courts. On 12 April 1748, Charles Tisdall paid a bill of £1 4s 'to John McKartney for a dinner at his house at the first mannour court'.[33] Does the reference to the 'first' manor court perhaps suggest that this was the Easter court leet and therefore the first of the court leets to be held that year? Not all manor courts were held in the manor house. Many, such as the court in Macroom in County Cork, were held in public houses. In Bray, County Wicklow, the courts were held in the schoolhouse, while in the seaside town of Kilkee in County Clare, they were held in bathing houses that were empty during wintertime. In Listowel, in County Kerry, a granary was the court location for a period.[34]

The seneschal was the most senior manorial official and presided over the manor courts. He was appointed by the lord of the manor. Qualifications of seneschals varied. In Clonakilty, County Cork, the seneschal was a respectable man who had been in the navy, but was blind. In Bantry, County Cork, he was a tanner. In Belfast, the seneschal was bred to the profession of attorney, while in the County Antrim court of Bucknaw, he was a JP.[35] No evidence has come to light as to George McDonagh's qualifications. For the duration of the three years under study here, the seneschal was assisted in his work by a bailiff/ constable. Since the manor was small, the duties of bailiff and constable were amalgamated and held by one man, Philip Lynch. This office was unsalaried and part-time, so in addition Philip farmed 10 acres in the townland of Martry. Before each court the seneschal instructed the bailiff of the court to notify the public of the date, time and location of each court sitting six days beforehand, unless the custom of the manor differed, and advise the tenants, who owed suit and service, to attend under penalty of a 3s 4d fine, unless they were excused. The fine for non-attendance at a court leet survives. This was a substantial fine, being the equivalent of five days' wages at 8d per day in 1789.[36]

> every person who resides within this manor and holds an acre of land and who does not attend the court leets held in and for said manor after being duly summoned by the Bailiff of said Manor six days before the court leet is held such person so and absenting himself without a proper cause assigned on oath if required and approved of by the seneschal of said Manor for the time being shall be subject and liable to a fine or penalty of three shillings and four pence sterling to be levied in case of non payment by distress to be taken up by said bailiff and sold by auction by him after due notice and a precept from the seneschal to said bailiff for that purpose.

Any attempt to understand law in the manor courts must consider how business was brought to the court, how cases proceeded and how they were resolved. The proceedings were initiated by summons by a plaintiff for any debt or damages arising within the jurisdiction of the court, returnable at the next court, three weeks later. The first business of the manor court was the selection of the jury and a jury foreman. The juries in the manor courts of Martry varied in number from twelve to the largest recorded jury of twenty-four. This latter number served at a court leet held on 3 January 1791 when the rules and regulations of the manor, and the court officials for the following year, were confirmed. The largest juries seem to have been in attendance at these courts leet. The following year, on 2 January 1792, again at a court leet, twenty jurors approved the manor's rules and regulations. Neither of these courts was held within a month of either Easter or Michaelmas, suggesting perhaps that the custom of the manor allowed the court leets in Martry to sit in January also. The foreman of the jury was listed first. It was the custom in Martry for a new jury to be selected each time the courts met, although some jurors' names appear more often than others. Following the selection of the jury, it was sworn in. On two occasions the oath was administered by John Singleton, who received a British half a crown (2s 6d) for this service, paid by the bailiff on one recorded occasion.[37] In these courts, British sterling was the extent of their pecuniary jurisdiction. Bringing cases to court in 1789 cost 6d for serving the process. Jurors received 6½d each for every action in the court, while the seneschal received 5s 11½d.[38] Witnesses for the plaintiff and defendant were also sworn, and gave their evidence. When all the evidence had been heard, the jurors made their final judgment, possibly based on both the evidence presented and on their personal knowledge of the accused. The jury's decision had to be unanimous. If the jury found for the plaintiff, a decree of execution was immediately issued by the seneschal for the amount of the finding. This was levied by the bailiff of the court before the next court.

A reconstruction of some cases of inter-tenant disputes that came before the courts in Martry provides some rare insight into its functioning, the procedure on court day and the verdicts delivered. The cases involved ordinary eighteenth-century people, dealing directly with the law and the courts without the assistance of professional lawyers. The courts provided quick, cheap and easy access to justice, avoiding the necessity for recourse to the higher, more expensive courts. There were some tenants whose names appeared regularly in the court book. A study of one tenant's relationship with the courts of Martry will shed some light on the nature of plaints. Walter Cavanagh was one of sixty-three tenants on the Tisdall estate who was obliged to pay leet monies in 1789. He leased 26 acres of land in the townland of Hurdlestown from Michael Tisdall IV; the lease for thirty-one years began on 1 May 1782.[39] An estate map of 1802 survives, showing Walter's holding on the southern bank of the River Blackwater along the main Navan–Kells Road at Bloomsbury Bridge, approximately 3 miles from Charlesfort, where the manor courts were held during the period under study.[40]

During the course of one year, between March 1789 and March 1790, the fragmentary court records show that Walter had recourse to the manor courts on thirteen occasions. On eight of these occasions he was the plaintiff, initiating the proceedings; on five he was the defendant. Was the frequency of Walter's court appearances due in some measure to the convenience, regularity and proximity of the local manor court? Perhaps it was because of his regular appearances there as a juror and his resulting familiarity with the law, the court and its proceedings? He was a juror on eight occasions

Court cases involving Walter Cavanagh				
Plaintiff	*Defendant*	*Action*	*Amount*	*Verdict*
Walter Cavanagh	John [Kinn]	Distringues	£1 2s 9d	
Walter Cavanagh	Sylvester Reilly	Due for hay	£2 6s 9d	
Walter Cavanagh	Valentine Nowlan	Due for cash lent	£1 2s 9d	
Walter Cavanagh	Michael Nowlan	Due for unpaid draft	£6	
Walter Cavanagh	Michael Nowlan	Due for barley	£2 0s 3d	
Walter Cavanagh	John Clarkan	Outstanding debt	£7	Found for plaintiff £2 5s with 6d costs.
Walter Cavanagh	John Clarkan			No witness to prove service of process, case dismissed
Michael Nowlan	Walter Cavanagh	Not stated	£3 4s	
Michael Nowlan	Walter Cavanagh	Rent	£8 6s ½d	
Valentine Nowlan	Walter Cavanagh			
Ann Mulherin	Walter Cavanagh	Promissory note unpaid	£2 5s 6d	
Philip Lynch	Walter Cavanagh	Corn milled	10s 9d	
Walter Cavanagh	Michael Nowlan	Silver watch, £2, draft		Not stated

Table 12. Source: compiled by Marion Rogan from manor of Martry court book, March 1789 to March 1790.

and was appointed to the office of appraiser for 1790 at a court leet held on 8 December 1789. Appraisers assessed the damages done by animals trespassing on the manor; their fees in 1789 were set at 6½d at the Easter court leet.[41] Appointed each year, they assisted the courts by valuing property and goods distrained for non-payment of rent and damage done to crops by trespass.[42] The oath sworn by them, which gives their job description, is recorded in the court book:

> that we will during our continuing appraisers of the Manor of Martry to the best of our knowledge, judgement and experience appraize and value all damages, that we shall, be brought to decide in said Manor, during our continuance in office, and a just and fair return will make to the parties when required.[43]

Only a limited number of cases are traceable from their initiation by a plaintiff to the verdict adjudged by the court. One such case was that brought by Ann Mulherin, plaintiff, the only female named in the court book. Women could not act as jurors but they could bring cases to court. On a date prior to 1 March 1790, Ann Mulherin evidently lent either money or goods to the value of £2 5s 6d to Walter Cavanagh. Walter in return gave her a promissory note, which was due for repayment on 1 June 1790. By May 1791, almost a year later, the debt had still not been paid, by which time Ann Mulherin commenced court proceedings for its recovery. Ann Mulherin approached the seneschal, George McDonagh, with her claim for debt recovery. He then put the summons into the hands of the bailiff, Philip Lynch, who served it seven days in advance of the court date of 9 May 1791, setting out the names of plaintiff and defendant, the amount of debt claimed and the cause of the action. The bailiff's fee for this service was 6d.[44]

The case was then tried at a court baron held in Charlesfort on 9 May 1791. A jury of twelve was empanelled and, in this one instance only, it is recorded that the jury was 'approved of by defendant'. Perhaps it was always the defendant's prerogative to do that, although it was not stated in the surviving records. The approved twelve-man jury was then sworn. William Cowly, having been duly sworn, gave evidence that the process had been served seven clear days before the court date on 2 May 1791, a day earlier than required, and was acknowledged by the defendant, Walter Cavanagh. Another witness, Michael Nowlan, was also sworn and gave evidence that the defendant, Walter Cavanagh, acknowledged his debt of £2 5s 6d sterling to Ann Mulherin; that he, Michael, was a subscribing witness to the transaction, and that he saw Walter Cavanagh acknowledge the said promissory note. It is not known whether or not the jury in Martry retired to another room to consider their verdict. In some courts, there was a separate room for the jury to retire to; in others there was not. In Martry, the jury returned its verdict at the court session in which it was requested. In Ann Mulherin's case, the court found for the plaintiff and awarded her £2 5s sterling damages with 6d costs. Perhaps, being the successful party, she then paid the 'drink money' as was the custom in many manor courts at the time.[45] The verdict was then signed by the jurors and confirmed by the seneschal.

More than half of all the surviving cases in the three-year court records involved Walter Cavanagh and all thirteen of them were heard during a one-year period. Six involved Walter and two members of the Nowlan family, Michael and Valentine. Both Nowlans were near neighbours of Walter; Michael Nowlan leased 8 acres in the adjoining townland of Martry. There is no record anywhere else of Valentine Nowlan and he was not included in the list of inhabitants holding 1 acre or more in 1789. He and Michael may have been sons of John Nowlan, stonemason on the Tisdall estate in the 1740s and 1750s who held over 14 acres in Hurdlestown, in the same townland as Walter Cavanagh. Much of the stonework surviving in the landscape today bears testimony to John Nowlan's handiwork.[46] By the end of the eighteenth century, the manor courts in Ireland were essentially a small debt-recovery service and the cases in Martry substantiate this. Seven of the eight cases that Walter Cavanagh brought to court were for recovery of small debts.

In a cash-strapped farming community, where income was irregular, seasonal and weather-dependant, neighbours borrowed in times of little and lent in times of plenty. The court cases represented only a fraction of the lending and borrowing ongoing. Most debts were probably paid on time without resorting to the courts, but the lenders were always secure in the knowledge that recourse to the manor courts was an option if the debtor defaulted. The cases against Michael Nowlan were for unpaid debts; one was for barrels of barley sold and delivered to him by Walter Cavanagh, another was for an unpaid draft of £6 sterling. The case against Valentine was for £1 2s 9d cash lent but unpaid. Walter Cavanagh brought John Clarkan to court on two occasions. Clarkan had a substantial holding of almost 90 acres in 1791, 70 acres in part of Nugentstown including the mill race and a further 20 acres in Athgaine, called the Rananagh.[47] He was also a regular juror at the courts. The first case was for the recovery of a debt of £7 sterling, which was the outstanding part of a larger sum of £12 12*s* lent. In this instance, the then-lord of the manor, Michael Tisdall IV, was sworn and gave evidence in the case.[48] The court found for the plaintiff and awarded Walter £2 5*s* with 6*d* costs. On the second occasion, the case was dismissed because Walter Cavanagh produced no witness to prove the service of the process.

Michael Tisdall IV (1755-1794). Michael Tisdall IV was lord of
the manor of Martry 1776-94 and High Sheriff of Meath in 1788.
(Photograph courtesy Anthony Tisdall, September 2013)

Walter Cavanagh's claims ranged from the smallest sum of £1 2s 9d to the largest sum of £7 for an outstanding debt. Small is relative, however. These amounts were substantial for the small landholders. £1 2s 9d was equal to the yearly rent that Walter paid for one acre of land on the Tisdall estate in 1789. When James Clarkan sought payment from Thomas Lee for nine days' work 'taking up manure' on 15 June 1789, he was awarded 6s wages or the equivalent of 8d a day. The largest claim for £7 corresponded to 210 days' labouring wages. The total value of cases brought by Walter Cavanagh in one year was £27 5s 6d, while cases against him amounted to £24 14s 9½d. These amounts were not far short of Walter's annual rental bill of £29 9s 6d for his 26-acre holding. In contrast, when Michael Tisdall IV was high sheriff of Meath in 1788, the awards in his court ranged from £29 3s 6d to £504 8s 6d.[49]

Two cases were returnable for trial on 1 November 1792, both involving Laurence Murray and John Mitchell. Laurence Murray leased 7 acres in part of Martry in 1782. John Mitchell held a small holding of less than 4 acres, also in Martry, which included the mill race. Were relations strained between these two neighbours? Borrowing and lending of animals was common in this rural, agricultural community. John Mitchell claimed, and Michael Horkin gave evidence on oath, that about three years previously in 1789, John Mitchell had given Laurence Murray the use of five horses and mares to plough his land. This arrangement was intended to be reciprocal. However, Laurence Murray had not returned the favour during the following three years by giving John Mitchell the service of five horses in return. The court found for the plaintiff, John Mitchell, to the sum of 7s 4d with costs. Laurence Mitchell appeared to have paid the fine on the day of the court.

In the second case, Laurence Murray was the plaintiff, and Philip Lynch, in his capacity as bailiff and constable, was the defendant. The action was dated 23 October 1792 and returnable for court eight days later on 1 November. John Mitchell's cattle had trespassed onto Laurence Murray's land, causing damage to the corn crop. The cattle were impounded, as was the practice, in the manor pound at Martry and left in the care of the bailiff, Philip Lynch. Laurence Murray claimed the sum of 14s 2d sterling. This was the amount of the appraisers' bill for damages done to Laurence Murray's corn by John Mitchell's cattle plus the cost of the court case. Laurence Murray was called by the court three times but did not 'appear in person or otherwise' and the case was dismissed as per rules and regulations of the court.[50]

Detail of the 6in Ordnance Survey Map (1836),
showing the pound at Martry located close to the corn mill.
(Reproduced by kind permission of Ordnance Survey of Ireland)

At a court baron in Charlesfort on Monday 30 June 1791, the plaintiff, Patrick Monaghan, sought compensation from John Hoey, defendant, for the sum of £2 5s 6d sterling due for cash lent. Neither Patrick Monaghan's nor John Hoey's names appear on leases or rent rolls as tenants of the head landlord, Michael Tisdall, although both appear on the list of those holding 1 acre or more of land. They were probably subtenants, leasing land from middlemen. The court heard that Patrick Monaghan, plaintiff, entered into an agreement about the lease of 2 acres of land from John Hoey, defendant, at a cost of 2 guineas, £2 2s. That the 2 guineas were paid around 17 March 1791 was acknowledged by sworn witnesses for both parties. The dispute arose regarding the ploughing of part of the land, which the plaintiff thought was part of the arrangement, but to which the defendant, John Hoey, would not agree. Consequently the plaintiff never got possession of the land and so sought recovery of the 2 guineas plus costs. Not all cases ended up being tried; some were settled out of court. A summons was issued on behalf of Owen Burn, plaintiff, against John Hoey, defendant, for the recovery of 8s 10d. This amount was for the unpaid rent for potato land and a larger unpaid sum. The case was set for trial on 1 March 1789, but was settled beforehand.[51]

TRESPASS

On a rural manor, where grass, hay and corn were critical to the livelihood of the inhabitants, trespass of animals was a serious problem. In an era when fencing was lax, even non-existent in some instances, the straying of animals into common pasture, corn and meadow was legislated for in the rules and regulations of the manor understood by all from 'time immemorial'. Negligent inhabitants who left gaps in their fences were penalised and not allowed claim for trespass of animals onto their lands.[52] There were two distinct categories of trespass recorded in the manor of Martry court book: the lesser offence was for trespass into common pasture; the greater for trespass into corn and meadow up until 24 June each year. Persistent offenders were penalised by an increased fine for the second offence of trespass and a further increased fine for the third offence. Cattle and horses trespassing onto common pasture incurred a penalty of 6d for the first transgression, 1s for the second, and a penal 1s 6d for the third occurrence. The damage done by animals straying into common pasture was much less, however, than that done by them wandering into meadows or corn, where a year's labour and expense could be undone in a short period of time. Grass would grow again; oats and barley would not, until sown the following year. The fine for trespass onto meadow and corn reflected the seriousness of the offence and was consequently much steeper. Cattle and horses incurred a penalty of 1s 6d for the first incidence of trespass, 2s for the second and 2s 6d for the third (table 13).

Of all straying animals, unrestrained pigs caused the most damage and this was reflected in the larger fines for pig trespass. Pigs used their snouts to root in the ground to forage for food and they were capable of ploughing up a field of grass or corn very quickly. Nose rings were inserted to prevent them doing this by making it painful for them to use their snout. Putting some restraint on their necks for the same purpose seems to have been another practice used to prevent rooting. If pigs had both these restraints in place, the penalty for the first offence of trespass was 2d, whereas if they were unrestrained, the penalty was £1 or 120 times greater. On one occasion, two pigs, the property of Thomas Newman, trespassed onto land held by Thomas and Patrick Reilly. The pigs were seized and impounded in the pound in Martry by Patrick Reilly.[53] They were replevined by Thomas Newman. Replevin was an action taken to seek recovery of specific items of property in dispute; in this instance it was the recovery of two pigs. Common trespass was claimed by Patrick Reilly for 2s 2d and was awarded by the court. Apart from the rules on trespass, no other rules or principles governing law and order in the manor survive.

Fines for trespass			
Pigs	1st time	2nd time	3rd time
Pigs rung or neck sp[a]ked	2d	4d	6d
Pigs not rung or neck sp[a]ked	£1	£1 6s 3d	£2
Black cattle or horses	1st time	2nd time	3rd time
Common pasture	6d	1s	1s 6d
Meadow & corn until 24 June	1s 6d	2s	2s 6d

Table 13. Source: court book, not dated.

CONCLUSION

While some physical traces of the manor of Martry survive in the landscape, the lives of those who populated it have left little trace. The majority passed unobserved, and are in the main forgotten, so the court records of Martry are important. They deal with what Walter King calls the 'daily activities of little people'.[54] It is only through the random survival of these records of 1789 to 1792, supplemented by rent rolls, that some attempt can be made to open a window onto their everyday lives, and the issues that concerned them and theirs at the close of the eighteenth century. The court records prove that the manorial system and its courts were still functioning in Martry at the close of the eighteenth century. They suggest that by 1792, though, the courts were primarily concerned with the resolution of inter-tenant disputes, confirming the contention held by others that the manor courts had deteriorated into a small-debt recovery service.

Through a detailed analysis of the fragmentary surviving court cases and by recreating a number of them, this essay has attempted to recon-struct the procedure in the courts and give some insight into how the manorial society of Martry regulated itself and effected law and order. The nature of some recorded inter-tenant disputes was investigated, demonstrating that the inhabitants operated their own credit relation-ships, and disputes were generally for outstanding debts. A picture emerges of a community that frequently lent cash, goods and services, in the sure knowledge that debts could be recovered in the small-debts courts of their local manor. This rural, agricultural community grew oats, barley and potatoes, reared pigs, cattle and horses, and penalised negligent, indolent tenants for poor fencing. Trespass was common and an ascending scale of punitive fines for persisting offenders was imposed. The courts enforced the rules and regulations of the manor. In Martry, these rules and regulations were understood by all. They were 'according to the constant and uninterrupted custom observed at all times in this manor within our memory'. Since the court was an integral component of a manor, and one could not exist without the other, it can be reasonably assumed that courts had been conducted in the manor of Martry, in some form or other, for almost 500 years from the days of Walter Saye in the early fourteenth century until the end of the eighteenth century (table 9).[55]

J.L.W. Naper's Crusade to Rid His Estate of Middlemen, 1792–1851

JAMES CAFFREY

The Naper estate is situated in the barony of Fore in north-western County Meath, bordering Westmeath and Cavan and extending into both counties. The Naper demesne is at Loughcrew, a townland and parish adjoining Oldcastle and just south of the Loughcrew Hills and their Neolithic monuments. Colonel James Naper, in recognition of his services to the Crown, was granted the lands in 1653. He was married to a sister of Cromwell's physician-general and Down Survey creator, Sir William Petty. His son, James Lennox Naper Dutton, subsequently ran the estate until his death in 1768. He was succeeded by William Naper who carried out a mapping survey of the area in the 1770s and he in turn was succeeded in 1792 by his son, James Lennox William Naper, a minor, who did not assume control until 1812.[1] Another extensive landowning family in the area in the eighteenth century were the Rotherams of Crossdrum, who became agents for Naper from the 1730s[2] with George Rotheram administering the estate from 1792 until 1812. James L.W. Naper, who assumed control in 1812, is the subject of this essay, which will set out to examine his efforts to rid his estate of middlemen and transform the poverty-stricken smallholders and labourers, products of that system, into an organised, productive labour force.

Middlemen emerged during the late-seventeenth, early eighteenth century when landlords, many of them beneficiaries of the Williamite confiscations, granted long leases during periods when long-term market prospects appeared poor. The recipients of these leases, at low rents, were subsequently in a position to take advantage of rising rents in their subletting policies. L.M. Cullen points out that those long leases, regarded in the 1720–30 period as a sign of improvement, were frowned on later by the advocates of improvement and landlords alike.[3] Kevin Whelan, in his extensive study of the origin and progression of the middleman system, identifies emerging well-off Catholics in the mid-eighteenth century as part of a second category of middleman described as, 'a large-scale speculator in leases who appeared when economic prospects were buoyant but while rents still lagged behind the market value'. Earlier middlemen, according to Whelan, tended to be substantial Protestant head tenants or dispossessed Catholic landowners.[4] There was a policy of granting long leases on the Naper estate prior to 1768.

James Naper spent his early years in both England and Scotland and returned to his estate keen to adopt what he saw as their progressive agricultural practices. In a pamphlet written in 1843 he described the situation prevailing when he took over in 1812. He says that the majority of the leases granted between 1734 and 1769 were for three lives or thirty-one years and the rents ranged from as low as 5s an English acre to, in some instances, 15s. He concludes that due to subletting to the highest bidder, neither the landlord nor the end tenant was in a position to benefit from the upturn in the economy after 1770.[5] He was referring to the middlemen who in effect were a second tier of landlordism on his estate. The study will focus in particular on middleman William Gavan who presided over some of the worst poverty on the Naper estate.

The main sources for the study are the available rent-roll books and accounts of the Naper estate. The earlier books dating from 1733 are in the NLI with those dating from 1792, when George Rotheram was managing the estate, adopting an easier-to-follow chronological order. There is one volume covering the years 1792–1811 followed by a gap to 1824–5 and a further gap to 1846. The books from 1846 are available at Meath County Library apart from 1855 and 1865, which are in the NLI. Other sources include Tithe Applotment Books, census returns, evidence submitted to the Poor Law and Devon commissions and Griffith's Valuation figures. These will assist efforts to deal with questions arising as a result of the gaps in the account books. The writings of James Naper, which give an insight into his thinking, are another key source for this work. They are in pamphlet form: twelve of them are available in the NLI and just two online through Jstor.

THE 1792–1810 RENT ROLL AND
THE SIGNIFICANCE OF THE MIDDLEMEN

James Naper took over the estate at a time when the agricultural economy was still booming. In the period 1793–1815 the volume of exports from Ireland rose by 40 per cent, but even more crucial was the increase in prices with the value of goods exported rising by as much as 120 per cent.[6] This was reflected in rent increases on the Naper estate in the first decade of the new century. As the Industrial Revolution took hold in England during the latter half of the eighteenth century, leading to high food prices and an increased demand for land, the middlemen, aided by an expanding population, took the opportunity to acquire large farms on long leases and subdivide them for tillage, exploiting small tenants while themselves availing of low rents. This led to further subdivision and poverty. Peter Connell in his review of County Meath at that time puts it very well when he says, 'in areas where middlemen held land on long leases or where estate management was lax, demography and economics combined to produce a patchwork of farms and their attendant labourers' cabins'.[7] The resulting miserable cabins and potato patches in townlands such as Springhall, Milltown and Old Tully were to become an irritant to James Naper, who felt that their occupants could be more usefully employed in ventures such as land reclamation and road building.

The number of townlands on the estate leased to single tenants in 1792 clearly indicates the presence of middlemen. Among these are five (Balgree, Crossdrum, Drewstown, Glanboy and Tubride) leased by Edward Rotheram, five (Balrath, Dromone Mill, Springhall, Milltown and Old Tully) leased by Luke Gavan and one (Annagh) leased by George Rotheram. In these eleven townlands the rent remains the same from before 1792 right up until the 1840s. In fact, they benefit further from an across-the-board 7.5 per cent reduction in 1825.

The rent per acre is not readily available as the half-yearly rent roll shows total rent paid with no reference to the area leased.[8] The earliest indications of areas for these townlands are the Tithe Applotment books. The books for Oldcastle and Moylagh, the parishes concerned here, were drawn up in 1829 and they contain a list of landholders with the area farmed in Irish acres in each townland. They were not mapping-based and often relied on inadequate estimates of areas.[9] While accepting their limitations, it is possible to get from them some indication of the rent per acre and the quality of the land.

The townland of Annagh, containing just over 532 Irish acres, was all second- and third-quality land, and by converting the acreage to statute measure the rent works out at 5s per acre.[10] The tenant was George Rotheram, one of the largest landowners in the area. The most notorious of the subletting middlemen was William Gavan, whose tenants in the townlands of Milltown and Springhall were described by John O' Donovan in the 1830s as being in poor circumstances. He had long leases in five townlands paying rents as low as 5s 7d, which also benefitted from the already mentioned 1825 reduction. He was not resident in the area and his leases were apparently for more than one life as he inherited from his father Luke in the early nineteenth century without a rent increase. It is also evident by comparing the tithe records and census records that there was a third layer of leasing in the townlands he occupied. In Springhall for example the tithe figures show just four landholders, two of whom hold just over 30 Irish acres, one 25 acres and one (Gavan himself) just over 8 acres. Even if an above-average of, say, six people per family is calculated, the population would be no more than twenty-four, but the earliest townland census for Springhall in 1841 shows a population of 166, suggesting that there were up to thirty families in the townland. This third layer of leasing is referred to by Naper in a pamphlet published in 1837, in which he states that the middleman is taking as high a rent as he can for the land 'thus creating a third landlord as the tenant, unable to pay the high rent and make a profit, subdivides the land amongst a set of labourers letting perhaps half the farm for the same rent he pays the middleman'.[11] A sizeable portion of this was likely to be on the conacre or eleven-month system of leasing that commanded the highest rents. Old Tully, which is near Oldcastle town, contained 129 Irish acres and apart from 10 acres of bog was all first-quality land. It was originally leased to Luke Gavan for 5s 7d a statute acre. He also held the lease for Milltown townland at 7s 8d a statute acre in 1792. No tithe figures were available for Balrath or Dromone Mill (see table 14 and table 15). The Gavan rents were unchanged in 1810 and were still the same in 1824, although by 1810 the name had changed from Luke to William Gavan.[12]

Rents in townlands leased to Luke and later William Gavan 1792-1846				
Townland	Annual Rent 1792	Rent per acre (Statute)	Tithe acreage converted to Statute	
Balrath	£146 0s 0d		No tithe figures available	
Milltown	£243 0s 0d	7s 8d	Tithe acreage uncertain (Griffith used)	630.0
Springhall	£43 16s 0d	5s 7d	Tithe acreage uncertain (Griffith used)	150.4
Old Tully	£60 0s 0d	5s 7d	Tithe acreage uncertain (Griffith used)	206.4
Dromone Mill	£7 10s 0d		No tithe figures available	

Table 14.

Rent reductions on Gavan lands in 1825		
Balrath	£138 9s 2d	–5.0%
Milltown	£224 6s 2d	–7.6%
Springhall	£40 8s 6d	–7.6%
Old Tully	£55 7s 8d	–7.6%
Dromone Mill	£6 18s 4d	–7.6%

Table 15.

The extent of the middleman problem can be gauged when the total of 110 tenants shown on the 1792 rent books rising to 144 in 1799 is compared with the 311 on the 1825 books as Naper was gradually ridding the estate of middlemen and taking tenants directly on to his own rent roll. An idea of the financial loss to the landlord can also be gauged from a comparison of rents collected over these years. In 1792 the total rent and arrears collected was £5,365.[13] This appears to be the only income as the books for the period show no farming income. By 1810 when J.L.W. Naper was about to take over the estate, the rent figure had risen to £9,617, a 79 per cent increase, and by 1825 this had risen dramatically again to £13,590.[14] An example of the type of increase being imposed as long leases fell in was the townland of Belgree, held by Edward Rotheram in 1792 at a rent of £230. In 1810, the tenant had changed from Edward to George Rotheram and the rent had increased by 81 per cent to £418. Even more dramatic increases are recorded at Newtown where the rent take increased more than sixfold, Knockmacooney where the increase was fivefold and Oldcastle and Fennor where a threefold increase was experienced as the land passed from middlemen. A notable long lease that fell in in 1807 was that of Alexander Moriarty, described as Doctor Moriarty. The rent almost doubled to £600 per annum. The new tenant was William Battersby, a substantial landowner in the area and later a contributor to the Poor Law Commission. The number of tenants in Oldcastle town increased over this period (1792–1810) from twenty-two to seventy-one, an indication of a drift to the town of displaced landholders and labourers as subdivision was being phased out. The process of direct leasing to tenants was well in hand when James Naper took over the estate, but it was to take him another forty years to complete the process. Despite the lost rent opportunities associated with the minority of middlemen who survived post-1810, the overall buoyancy of rents on the estate meant that their low rents had minimal impact on the wealth of James Naper, who from 1824, according to that year's accounts, was also deriving an income from farming. In the meantime the poverty and wretchedness associated with tenants over whom he had no control was to become a source of embarrassment which led him on a crusade for change not only on his own estate but countrywide.

THE ECONOMIC DOWNTURN
AND NAPER'S EFFORTS FOR CHANGE

In a pamphlet published in 1831 entitled *Relief and Employment of the Poor of Ireland*, James Naper set out his own ideas for change while at the same time acknowledging that there could be no radical altera-tion without legislation.[15] He saw the labourer with a miserable cabin and a rood of ground as the problem. He envisaged a situation where able-bodied peasantry, rather than attempting to exist and feed their families on small plots of potato ground along with seasonal farm work, would come under the control of the landlord, who would supply them with comfortable housing and, during periods when they were not required for farm work, would arrange employment on a parish basis on works such as land reclamation and road building and maintenance. To finance this he proposed a rate of 2 per cent on rents received by landlords and 1 per cent on rent payments by tenants. He envisaged that the scheme would be administered by a parish committee made up of the clergy and ratepayers who would decide on the projects to be undertaken. He felt that this would not only offer fuller employment and a better lifestyle to the labourers, but would also help to provide extra resources in the form of reclaimed land and more and better roads. Another outcome he foresaw was that the labourer in such a situation would be in a position to pay a fair rent for a decent house and garden directly to the head landlord, who would then be in a position to maintain it. Naper in this situation was probably anticipating the introduction of the Poor Law, which was already enforced in England, and saw the weaning of the labourer from reliance on fragmented land outside the control of the landlord as a major part of the solution. He also anticipated an enhancement of the landscape with the replacement of miserable cabins by landlord-maintained, decent slated housing. Given his strong views and the need for legislation to implement them, it is no surprise that he was a candidate in the 1831 general elections in Meath. His subsequent withdrawal, however, was to cause controversy. The *Freeman's Journal* was particularly critical, calling his withdrawal obnoxious as it felt it would lead to the defeat of the popular candidate.[16] To get his message across, Naper had no need to run for parliamentary politics again as he succeeded in becoming a member of the Poor Law Commission in 1835 and was one of the landlords selected to give evidence at the later Devon Commission, which inquired into the occupation of land in Ireland. In addition, he continued to have pamphlets published and was an occasional letter-writer to the newspapers.

The problems of poverty and wretchedness that were driving Naper's agenda in the period post-1820 were a consequence of the downturn after 1815, when the French wars ended and the agricultural economy went into decline. Matters were compounded further by the collapse of the linen industry, which had been a lifeline for poorer families struggling to pay high rents to middlemen. The extent of flax spinning in the area can be gauged from the applications for grants for spinning wheels in 1796. The parishes on the Naper estate along with neighbouring Killalon and Kilskyre accounted for 45 per cent of all applicants in County Meath with Oldcastle and Loughcrew parishes alone accounting for 206 applications.[17] A first glance at the 1821 and 1831 census figures for occupations and particularly the section for those employed in trade, manufactures and handicraft is an indicator of the sharp decline in the linen industry in that period. Accurate comparison is not possible here as the figures for 1821 are compiled to show individuals working in the industry whereas the figures for 1831 show families. Nevertheless, taking Oldcastle parish alone, the number of individuals employed in trade in 1821 is 842 whereas in 1831 the number of families employed is just thirty-three. Considering the population in the parish decreased by 3 per cent over the period and the average number of people per family in 1831 was 5.56, this was a catastrophic collapse. The figures for Moylagh parish show 581 people employed in this sector in 1821 decreasing to thirty-four families in 1831, not quite as stark as Oldcastle but significant nevertheless, as is Loughcrew parish with 327 employed in 1821 dropping to twenty-seven families in 1831. The figure for those employed in agriculture indicates that few of these people transferred to that sector. In 1821 in Oldcastle parish there were 718 people employed in agriculture compared to 481 families in 1831. If we assume that there were 1.5 persons per family engaged in agriculture the result would be virtually no change. The figures for employment in agriculture in Moylagh and Loughcrew, like in Oldcastle, remain much the same.[18] Serious economic depressions in the periods 1819–20 and 1825–6 together with the removal of tariffs on textiles contributed to the collapse of the cottage spinning industries and the removal of an important income source from the tenants on the Naper estate.

In an 1831 pamphlet, James Naper responded to the crisis with his ideas for the useful employment of labourers. It is evident too from the pamphlet that he took advantage of the situation to clear out some of the poverty-stricken smallholders from townlands where he was regaining control from the middlemen. The available evidence suggests that this was done in a compassionate way. In the pamphlet he gives details of how he paid for the passage of forty-four persons, who with children came to over fifty, to Québec in May 1830. The total cost including groceries and blankets for the journey as well as clothes for women and children was £89 4s 0d.[19] The 1824 half-yearly accounts show further evidence of Naper's compassion with a rent allowance to tenants amounting to £1,631 18s 2d for the six-month period and a contribution of £103 10s 10d to a widow's pension as well as a sum of £115 5s 0d spent on road making in the town of Oldcastle and river-drainage works in Old Tully, Knockmacooney and Drumsavey. He followed this in 1825 with a permanent reduction in rents and a further contribution to widows, which remained a feature into the 1860s. Although a member of the established Church, he supported the Catholic cause, making a contribution of £104 16s 3d in 1824 to the building of Ballinacree church.[20] He is also known to have donated £1,000 and the site for Oldcastle church in 1815.[21] At a Civil and Religious Liberty dinner in 1829 he is quoted as saying, 'I think any measure for the improvement of Ireland until Catholic Emancipation is first granted must prove abortive'.[22]

Naper's concern for the poor and needy also emerges in evidence given to the Poor Law Commission in 1835. Quantifying the entry in the 1824 accounts the report states that, 'Mr Naper supports between twenty five and thirty widows on his estate by an annual pension of six shillings Irish currency to each'. It was also stated that Mr Naper supplied blankets and clothing to the poor at half the prime cost. Other relevant evidence given to the commission indicated that rents per acre for both arable and pasture were about 30s, that there were 542 labourers in the parish, 380 of which were in constant employment at a rate of 10d per day in the summer and 8d in the winter.[23] James Naper was one of nine commissioners on the Poor Law Inquiry; he did not therefore give evidence himself. Evidence for the Oldcastle area was given by his tenant, the already-mentioned Thomas Battersby Esq. JP, and Church of Ireland clergyman Revd Nicholas J. Halpin.

Despite his direct involvement with its commission, James Naper failed to have his proposals for the Poor Law adopted and this led to the publication of the already-referred-to pamphlet in 1837 addressed to the landlords and landholders of County Meath, in particular, and Ireland in general where he asked all landholders to unite to consider the Poor Law, which he said 'had been forced upon the government of Ireland'. In this publication he is availing of an opportunity to vent his anger and frustration at the terms of the soon-to-be established Poor Law, which were running contrary to his recommendations and those of his fellow members of the commission. He concluded that the government of Ireland was a mere tool of the English cabinet and that, as long as that was the case, Irish commissions would continue to suffer the same fate. His main concern was the setting up of the workhouses and the ratepayer's ability to finance them. He expressed particular regret that his proposal in 1831 to absorb cottiers and labourers into locally organised labour pools was rejected. He saw this as a means of keeping what he termed 'able-bodied men' out of the workhouses. Surprisingly, he felt that the rates should be levied on the landlord only who, he said, ended up indirectly paying them anyway, adding that it would then be in his interest to see that the land was worked productively and that it would also put pressure on absentees. He used the opportunity to continue his crusade against the middlemen, who, he said, 'by allowing fragmentation for monetary gain create a situation where lack of capital leads to a diminution of the holding and the productive qualities of the soil'.[24] Naper's reservations about the Irish Poor Law were to prove well founded when less than ten years later it failed to cope with the emergency that was the Great Famine. Although disillusioned with the system, Naper, to his credit, did try to operate it becoming chairman of the Oldcastle Poor Law guardians.

THE DIFFICULT 1840S AND THE FINAL DEMISE OF MIDDLEMEN ON THE NAPER ESTATE

By the 1840s, with the exception of William Gavan, the middlemen had almost disappeared from the Naper estate, but the Gavan-held townlands of Old Tully, Milltown and Springhall with their small-holders and associated poverty were proving to be the greatest obstacle in James Naper's attempts to improve agricultural production and thus living conditions on his estate. The lack of estate accounts for the Naper lands between 1825 and 1847 is a big drawback when trying to tease out the period. This is particularly so with regard to Old Tully, where there is conflicting evidence regarding the transfer of the townland from Gavan to Thomas Battersby. Both the Tithe Applotment Books of 1829 and O'Donovan's *Ordnance Survey Field Books* of the mid-1830s show the lands in Battersby's name, O'Donovan remarking that they were devoted almost entirely to grazing.[25] On the other hand, the rent roll for 1847 for Old Tully clearly shows the representatives of William Gavan paying the old rent of £55 7s 8d. The changeover is not recorded in the Naper books until 1848 when Battersby is shown as the tenant for the first time paying a rent of £220, a fourfold increase. An 1840s clear-out of tenants is supported by census evidence, with the 1841 census showing a population of 262 in forty-nine inhabited houses in Old Tully, and the 1851 census a remarkable zero population with one uninhabited house, a complete clearance of the townland.[26] In his evidence to the Devon Commission in 1845, James Naper, replying to a question about the middleman problem, suggested that in certain cases middlemen might receive an annuity for the rest of the term of the lease, the head landlord in effect becoming the middleman's tenant.[27] A half-year rent payment of £70 by Naper to the representatives of William Gavan in the 1847 accounts would suggest some sort of arrangement where Naper recompensed Gavan to allow Battersby on to the land as sole tenant. The census evidence suggests that this clearance happened after 1841, whereas the tithes show the transfer to Battersby as early as 1829. It is possible that Battersby left the subtenants in place until after 1841, although O'Donovan's remark that it was devoted almost entirely to grazing raises unanswered questions.

The population chart (chart 3) is a good indication of what was happening on the Naper estate during the twenty-five years approaching the Famine as well as in its immediate aftermath. The dip in the Oldcastle parish figures in 1831 as a result of clearance corresponds with a rise in the town figures over the same period, indicating that some of those displaced who did not emigrate moved to the town, but that they gradually began to move back again after 1831 as the chart lines once more move in opposite directions up to 1841. Moylagh on the other hand shows a steady uninterrupted rise between

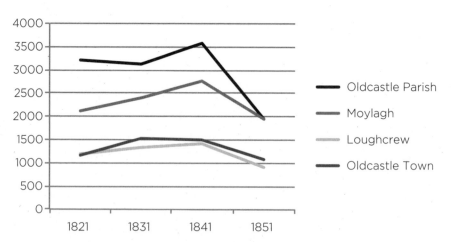

Chart 3. Population trends in the civil parishes of Oldcastle, Moylagh and Loughcrew

1821 and 1841. The less dramatic movements on the Loughcrew parish chart line are an indication of its proximity to Naper's demesne. The sharpest decline between 1841 and 1851 happened in Oldcastle parish, which can be partially explained by the gentler decline in the town indicating some movement back there and also into Oldcastle workhouse, which had a population of 1,498 in 1851. The parish of Moylagh shows the typical Famine-period curve with the population steadily increasing up to 1841 and steadily decreasing to 1851.

The poverty in Moylagh parish was largely centred on the townlands of Milltown and Springhall. James Naper's eventual successful efforts to sideline Gavan in Old Tully did not extend to the Moylagh parish townlands. Gavan's death, however, facilitated change in 1848. In that year Gavan's name is crossed off the Springhall rent roll and replaced by eleven tenants paying a total rent of £53 6s 1d rising to £58 19s 3d in 1849. The exact changeover date in Milltown is unclear but by 1851 there are fifty-four tenants paying £247 10s 0d rent to Naper.[28] These rents appear to be on the low side but they may have been part of a concession by the landlord to relieve hardship. There is also evidence of the clearance of some tenants as the census figures for 1851 show a 36 per cent population reduction in Milltown since 1841 and a 56 per cent reduction in Springhall. The wipe-out of entire families is confirmed by the complete disappearance of twenty-nine houses in Milltown and thirteen in Springhall.[29] In his evidence to a House of Lords committee on the Poor Law, James Naper revealed that he

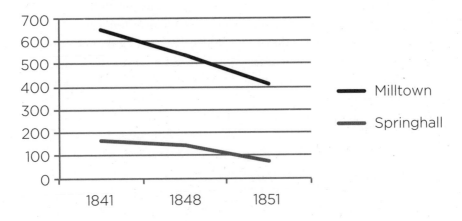

Chart 4. Population trends from 1851 census and Naper's own figures for 1848

took a census himself in 1848 to ascertain the number of labourers that might be available for a proposed labour scheme; the data in chart 4 shows that the steepest decline in Springhall was after 1848, which indicates clearance at that point.

In his evidence, James Naper went on to explain some of the circumstances surrounding the changes in Milltown and Springhall. He said that he tried and failed to buy out Gavan's interest in 1841 when the middleman was receiving a rent of about £650 but only paying £264 to him, and that within the twelve months previous to his evidence the two townlands fell out of lease and were at that stage in his hands. At the time, he said a year's rent was owed to the middleman and he informed the tenants that he expected them to pay half of that rent to him by the end of the year. Some he said were unable to pay and were served with ejectment notices. He was eager to point out that he did not serve such notices lightly and it was not his purpose to totally destroy people, but in some instances he had no other way of asserting his authority and gaining possession. He further revealed that when the tenants realised his determination to assert his authority some of them immediately surrendered about 20 acres of land in return for assistance with their passage to America. There were fifteen to twenty people involved. He said it was his intention to use spade husbandry to farm this land himself in order to improve the impoverished soil and double its output. His purpose here seemed to be to make a point to the committee about how the management of land could influence its ability to take on the burden of the Poor Law rate.[30]

In the absence of middleman rent figures it is difficult to accurately verify Naper's claim to demand half the middleman's rent when he took over in 1848. In the mid-1830s John O'Donovan indicates a rent of up to 27 shillings per acre for Milltown and 20 to 27 shillings for Springhall, whereas evidence to the Poor Law Commission quotes the rate at 30s. By taking names on the Naper lists of tenants from 1848–51 and calculating the rents paid using acreages in Griffith's Valuation we can get a breakdown per acre. Values in Milltown, apart from one as low as 7s, range from 10 to 17s per acre. In Springhall, where farms are smaller, rents are much lower, ranging from 6 to 10 shillings. Naper retained over 300 acres for himself in Milltown and 22 in Springhall.[31] These rents, which appear to be individually negotiated, seem to be well below the going rate of 27 to 30s especially in Springhall where all are less than half. While it may be difficult to reconcile the sharp drop in

population, especially in Springhall up to 1851, there is no evidence
to suggest that James Naper acted in anything other than a humane
way when dealing with his tenants. Apart from his evidence to the Poor
Law committee indicating his willingness to assist emigration where
requested and his reluctance to impose undue hardship on those he
found it necessary to eject, his accounts for 1847 and 1848 show an
allowance of £798 to tenants for loss of potatoes as well as the afore-
mentioned rent reductions.[32]

CONCLUSION

The problem of the middlemen on the Naper estate had its origins
in the eighteenth century and was well on the way to being resolved
when James Naper assumed control in 1812. The leftover business
that he inherited, however, took another forty years to conclude.
Standing between Naper and a speedy resolution was second-gener-
ation middleman William Gavan, whose underdeveloped smallholder
townlands of Old Tully, Milltown and Springhall were an embarrassment
to the progressive new landlord. The problem was finally resolved at the
end of the 1840s with the death of Gavan and the consequent expiry
of the lease. Naper was anxious to introduce to his estate methods he
had experienced in England and Scotland, and to achieve this he was
keen to lease to productive, knowledgeable farmers with capital. He saw
no hope for the smallholders created by the middlemen, who, he felt,
would be better off detached completely from the land and employed as
labourers. In his campaign for change, Naper briefly considered politics
but opted instead to get his message across through involvement in
parliamentary commissions and inquiries and publishing pamphlets.

The collapse of the cottage industries in the 1820s was a major
contributor to the poverty of that period, putting unbearable pressure on
the smallholders that depended on it to pay the rent. Naper responded
to this in a pamphlet in 1831 indicating that he had provided assisted
emigration to Canada for smallholders of cleared-out estates where
middlemen leases had fallen in. His compassion had already emerged
some years earlier when he introduced rent reductions and rebates
as well as commencing a widow's pension and organising half-price
clothing for the poor. A big disappointment for Naper was his failure
to influence the outcome of the Poor Law Inquiry in 1837, especially

since he had succeeded in becoming a member of the commission of inquiry where he hoped to influence the drafting of the bill. Undaunted, however, he again set out his ideas in pamphlet form, and although he was not in agreement with the Poor Law Bill, he contributed to the working of the new system by becoming chairman of the Oldcastle Board of Guardians. He was an advocate of high poor rates levied only on the landlord as he felt that this would encourage productivity, put pressure on absentees and ensure sufficient funds for the efficient running of the Poor Law system. It was his enthusiasm and support for the productive farmer that fuelled his rejection of the Poor Law valuations, which he felt would reward the less productive with lower valuations and penalise the progressive farmer.

In his efforts to end the middleman's role in the 1820s, when extreme poverty was emerging, James Naper attempted to buy out middleman William Gavan who oversaw most of the poverty on his estate. He eventually succeeded in negotiating a type of contra lease for the townland of Old Tully that still recognised Gavan as lawful tenant but allowed the replacement of multiple tenants with a single occupier. His efforts to regain control of the townlands of Milltown and Springhall proved more difficult, only finally succeeding in 1848 after Gavan's death. This resulted in a partial clearance with some availing of assisted emigration, some ejectments where cooperation was not forthcoming and reduced rents for the remaining tenants. Naper also availed of the opportunity to retain some of the land for his own use in an effort to demonstrate how unproductive land could be transformed.

James Naper was an advocate of agricultural improvement and supported tenants, whatever the size of holding, who raised productivity, engaged in modernisation and employed labourers. He saw no economic advantage in supporting smallholder cottiers and labourers who, he felt, would be of more financial advantage to themselves and their landlord if separated from their holdings and organised into a productive labour force. While he was forceful and single-minded in clearing out smallholders when the opportunity arose, he was also compassionate and charitable to those who cooperated with his wishes. He was at all times aware of poverty on his estate and supported the genuine needy. The study reveals how even progressive resident landlords who had compassion for their tenants were powerless to avert poverty and wretchedness where middlemen had control.

Landowners and Elections in County Meath from the Act of Union to Catholic Emancipation

JOE MOONEY

INTRODUCTION

The Act of Union not only changed political life in the whole of Ireland, it also had profound effects on the county of Meath. Prior to 1800, Meath had returned two county members and two members for each of the boroughs of Athboy, Duleek, Kells, Navan, Ratoath and Trim to the Irish Parliament in Dublin. In addition, there were ten Irish peers associated with the county: barons Aylmer, Langford, Dunboyne, Dunsany and Trimleston; earls Bective, Conyngham and Darnley; and viscounts Gormanston and Boyne, all of whom were entitled to seats in the Irish House of Lords. The premier Irish peer, the Duke of Leinster, was also associated with the county with his extensive landholding in Meath. Together these titled families held the majority of the land in the county and thus controlled the elections to the Irish House of Commons as the franchise was restricted to lease holders, most of whom were obliged to these families as tenants. In many cases these families held seats both in the Irish House of Lords and in the House of Commons. The premier Catholic Irish peer, Lord Fingall of Killeen, who was not allowed his seat in the Irish Parliament because of his religion, was also associated with the county.

Under the Act of Union all was to change. Now 100 members were returned to the (now United Kingdom) House of Commons, two members for each county and the balance from the large boroughs plus Trinity College. In addition, the 150 or so Irish peers were required to elect twenty-eight representatives from among themselves to sit in the UK House of Lords. The Marquess of Headfort (originally the Earl of Bective), together with the Marquess of Conyngham became two of the twenty-eight Irish representative peers in the UK House of Lords. The two sitting county members, Sir Marcus Somerville and Hamilton Gorges, were selected unopposed for the two new seats in the Meath constituency for the UK House of Commons.

Thus it transpired that two MPs and two peers represented Meath in the UK Parliament. Sir Marcus Somerville maintained his seat until 1830; however, Hamilton Gorges died in 1801 and the seat went subsequently to Thomas Bligh of Brittas, County Meath, a cousin of the Edward Bligh later MP for Kent (1818) and brother-in-law of John Bligh, Earl of Darnley. Thomas Bligh was supported by Headfort and in one of the few elections held in Meath beat the opposing candidate, Skeffington Thompson, by 181 votes to forty-four, while Somerville came in first with 326 votes. The Bligh family at that time had two members in Parliament as Edward Bligh's father, Lord Darnley, held a seat in the British (now UK) House of Lords. In the subsequent parliaments of 1806 and 1807, both Sir Marcus Somerville and Thomas Bligh were returned unopposed. Both supported the Catholic cause; however, Thomas Bligh was capricious in his voting in parliament and his relations with Darnley, his mentor, in parliament were difficult.

The whig/liberal position was very strong among Irish parliamentarians following from the decade of Protestant patriotic activity in what was subsequently known as 'Grattan's Parliament'. Supporters of the union had envisaged a position where some of the freedoms allowed to British subjects of the Crown would also benefit those who lived in Ireland. Among these anticipated freedoms the Catholic cause became the prominent one. This cause was taken up not only by the members for Meath, but also by many of the representative peers and other parliamentarians including prominent members of the aristocracy such as the Duke of Leinster. In the UK Parliament, the Pitt, Addington and Grenville ministries supported these views. In 1806 the king dismissed the Grenville ministry because of his refusal to stop attempts to lift Catholic disabilities. Thomas Bligh supported the new administration

of the Duke of Portland from 1807.[1] In doing so he ran into difficulties with Lord Fingall, spokesman for the Catholic committee and
subsequently Thomas Taylour the Earl of Bective was approached
by a number of people to stand in Meath to replace Thomas Bligh.
It may be these circumstances that forced the hand of those proposing
the Catholic cause and instigated the letters that are contained in the
Headfort estate papers in 1807. The majority of this correspondence
is addressed to the then twenty-year-old 2nd Earl of Bective (Thomas
Taylour, b. 1787), son of the 1st Marquess of Headfort (Thomas Taylour
1757–1829) who at that time was just coming to the age when he could
attend parliament. It was this 2nd Earl of Bective who later succeeded
to the marquisate in 1829 on the death of his father and remained as a
peer of the United Kingdom until his death in 1870.

I

The source of information for these letters is the Headfort estate collection of estate papers.[2] These papers originally consisted of approximately
300 records, each varying in size from single sheets to large volumes
of ledgers; they are on permanent loan to the NLI. The papers were
listed and partially calendared by A.P.W. Malcomson of PRONI,
and are collated in three sections: estate papers; household records and
family papers. They, together with a substantial amount of additional
material, have been recently compiled by Brian Casey into an additional catalogue, which also contains details of the letters calendared by
A.P.W. Malcomson. This calendar contains an amount of correspondence from various supporters of Bective in the period 1807–30 relating
directly to the elections in Meath and in particular to the Catholic cause.
The correspondence favours Bective as the candidate in support of this
cause. That the correspondence starts in 1807 reflects a worry among
the adherents to the Catholic cause that Thomas Bligh, in supporting
Portland, may have reneged on his previous position.

The initial letter of 1807 found among the Headfort papers
suggests that the issue of Catholic relief at that particular moment
was important enough to elicit the support of Bective. It was written
by John Pratt Winter, deputy governor and high sheriff of Meath,
a prominent Protestant supporter of the Catholic committee and an
associate of Fingall, the prominent Catholic peer:

John Pratt Winter, Agher, to Bective. 15 October 1807:

I assure your Lordship, it affords me very high gratification that the part I have taken in this county on a most interesting question, while it was dictated by my own deliberate and unbiased opinion, which I trust I shall always honestly express, has at the same time so entirely coincided with your Lordship's views and sentiments; and I feel it indeed to be a matter of congratulation to the country, and particularly this county, that sentiments so conducive to the peace and happiness of Ireland are patronised and supported by one so competent as your Lordship, from your elevated rank and powerful influence, to advance their progress with the public.

I am perfectly of the opinion that your Lordship has so forcibly expressed, that if a meeting of this county could be induced to declare itself decidedly in favour of the Catholic cause, it might be attended with the most beneficial consequences. But whether such would be the result of such a meeting to be convened at present, and of course whether it would be prudent to hazard the attempt, are points on which I can scarcely venture to offer an opinion. There appears to me, I am sorry to say, particularly among the middling order of persons, a good deal of religious prejudices still remaining, and even where that is not the case, a great reluctance to come forward and join in any public declaration on the subject. At the same time, I hope there are a considerable number sufficiently impressed with the deep importance of uniting the people at this crisis of danger, to give their cordial support to any proposition having that tendency, and there can be no doubt that the weight and influence of your Lordship's opinion would keep back many opponents, and bring forward many who are indifferent.

In the letter, Winter alludes to Catholic relief as that 'most interesting question' that was dictated 'by his own deliberate and unbiased opinion'. He suggests that Bective's support is 'to be a matter of congratulation to the country' and goes on to suggest that if a 'meeting of the county' as Bective had previously indicated 'could be induced to declare itself in favour of the Catholic cause', this would have 'beneficial consequences'. However, he cautioned Bective that the time may not have been appropriate, as there was 'a good deal of religious prejudices still remaining and even where that is not the case, a great reluctance to come forward and join in in any public declaration on the subject'.[3]

Winter's 'unbiased opinion', which he understood 'entirely coincided' with Bective's views, was possibly based on an understanding shared also by Pitt and his advisers that 'the union would be accompanied by a group of measures – Catholic Emancipation, a state provision for the Catholic clergy and a commutation of the tithe'.[4] However, the monarch, George III, 'bolstered by a strong anti-Catholic lobby among the aristocracy and by a powerful current of anti-Popery running through the various strata of British society, was an implacable opponent of full Catholic emancipation.[5] The Act was passed therefore without any reference to Catholic emancipation'.

The sentiment in the letter also suggests that Winter as well as supporting the Catholic cause had a preference for Bective over the sitting member Thomas Bligh. However, even as a landowning Protestant, his letter indicates that the pro-Catholic attitude prevailed in County Meath. Winter was not alone in expressing his views: other landowners promised their support for Bective. These included prominent members of the Catholic aristocracy such as Dunsany and Fingall as well as many small and large landholders in Meath. In parliament, the Catholic cause was unable to be promoted by the Pitt and Addington governments in compliance to the king's request. However, in a petition put forward by a small Whig opposition in 1805, it was noted that the Meath parliamentarians including Thomas Bligh voted in the minority for this bill. An 1807 petition on Catholic relief, raised by the Grenville government, was pivotal in that all it recommended was that the highest commands in the army and navy be allowed to both Catholics and dissenters. Not only did the king veto the proposal, but he required that the issue never be raised again, leading to the downfall of the government and its replacement by the Portland ministry.[6]

Prominent Catholics in Ireland regarded those who supported the new government of the Duke of Portland as being anathema to the Catholic cause. Thomas Bligh's support of the new administration became a cause for concern among those who, like Winter, supported the Catholic cause in 1807. From 1807 until 1812 Henry Grattan proposed a number of petitions in parliament for Catholic relief. Liberals who opposed the government supported these petitions but always remained a minority. Thomas Bligh, although continuing to support the government until 1810, stood with the minority on the issue of Catholic relief before returning to the opposition in

1812. His brother-in-law and mentor, Lord Darnley, had remained in opposition in the House of Lords throughout this period and supported Catholic emancipation. In a similar way Sir Marcus Somerville, the other MP for Meath, voted for Catholic emancipation and continued to oppose the government. In 1812 Darnley broke off relations with Thomas Bligh (who had actually called him out) and Bligh did not seek re-election, leaving the seat open for a new candidate. Meath had shown itself to be a liberal constituency with broad support for Catholic emancipation. The 1812 election brought about after the assassination of Perceval, the prime minister, with a vacant seat, promised to be interesting. Thomas Taylour, Earl of Bective at the age of 25, could now enter the fray. Entering the fray as well was John Naper, recommended by the Conservative government's home secretary, Sir Robert Peel.

II

Electioneering was a different process in the early 1800s. At that time, the proponents of Catholic relief were associated with the old Catholic aristocracy, such as Dunsany and Fingall, and a small group of liberal Protestants such as John Pratt Winter. The rise of the O'Connell faction did not occur until 1815. It was therefore safe to assume that the policy of Catholic relief would go down well with the Meath electorate. To ensure success at the polls it was necessary to gain the confidence of those land-owners who held land in Meath and to ensure that their tenants were registered to vote and were prepared to dispose of their votes at their landlord's discretion. It must also be noted that elections were few and far between and that, although canvassing was required, it often came down in the end to a situation where candidates withdrew prior to polling date leaving the seats available to the remaining candidates. It is thought that in some elections only 30 per cent of constituencies actually had a poll. Initially after Thomas Bligh's withdrawal, the election may have looked like a three-way split between the sitting MP Sir Marcus Somerville, the Earl of Bective and John Naper, all of whom supported Catholic relief. Knowing that an election was forthcoming, Bective had already approached a number of people in 1811. The Marquess of Lansdowne, Bowood, Wiltshire, a prominent Whig politician and supporter of Catholic Emancipation who held lands near Ratoath, gave a typical response when he stated that he 'has promised the little interest he has in county Meath to Sir Marcus Somerville, and cannot answer Bective till he has heard from Somerville'.[7]

Another answer came from Sir Thomas Chapman, Killua, County Westmeath, who held lands near Athboy and was obviously a Peelite: 'regretting that he cannot support Bective, unless doing so would assist Mr Naper, to whom he is engaged'.[8]

However, Bective had a better result from William C. Butler of Dublin, an associate of the Catholic committee, who suggested that he was:

> promising every support in his power, which he thinks will not be inconsiderable. Lord Fingall will also be a most valuable ally, and can influence, for instance, Mr. J Keogh of Mount Jerome, who has just purchased an estate on which there are many freeholders. Bective should also write to Luke Norton, an attorney with the disposal of 15 votes.[9]

Lord Fingall was the prominent Catholic peer and John Keogh was an important member of the Catholic committee. Another prominent supporter of the Catholic cause was Pierce O'Brien Butler of Dunboyne Castle, who was approached by Michael Lewis, an attorney of Kells, and promised to write to him and suggest others to whom Bective should write.[10] Others who announced their support were Mungo H. Waller of Allenstown[11] and Richard Chaloner, County Kilkenny, who promised his support and that of Mr Bligh's tenants. Richard Chaloner also suggested: 'take the trouble of writing to George Gore and Jonathan Chetwood Esq's, Portarlington. They are relations of mine and devoted for your grandfather. Archdeacon Fowler has many votes. Lady Jane Loftus must be applied to'.[12]

He also made the point that Headfort should: 'engage an attorney called Phil Smyth, who will be expensive, but who has great knowledge of the county and fifty votes in his family besides'. He urges Bective to write to the Miss Willsons co–heiresses of a large estate near Dunboyne and suggested as well that 'there is a Mr Standish, a young man who lately recovered a large property, and a Mr Hussey, heir to Lord Beaulieu. Let no one be neglected'.[13]

William Troy of Dublin offered his support.[14] Thomas Lewis O'Beirne, bishop of Meath, offered his support but suggested that his nephew, the archdeacon, would 'exert [his influence] on Bective's behalf'.[15] The bishop, although a liberal, had become disillusioned with the Irish Whigs, especially Grattan and his supporters such as Sir Marcus Somerville. He mentioned this in his letter to Bective:

> I have only one thing to observe to your Lordship. However unquali-
> fied my dislike to Sir Marcus Somerville's politics has ever been,
> and much as I condemn the principles of the party to which he has
> attached himself, yet I have that private friendship for him that I can
> never suffer my name to be employed in opposition to his interests. But
> I have great satisfaction in thinking that your Lordship's success and his,
> on the present occasion, are not incompatible.[16]

R.S. Tighe of Mitchelstown Cork, a noted writer on the Catholic Question,[17] promised his support, although his interest was small due to a defective register.[18] The Earl of Fingall, the prominent Catholic peer, referred to a meeting with Bective in which he must have had an altercation with John Pollock, who had advised Wellington in 1807 when he was chief secretary that 'Catholic emancipation was with the great body of Catholics, a cloak to cover their real object … the political power, the church estates, and the protestant property in Ireland'.[19] Fingall states that he was glad to have that meeting quite over as: 'Mr P[ollock], I daresay, as a confidential advisor of the govern-ment, thought it only his duty to join in correcting the abuses likely to arise from such dangerous measures. He goes on to advise Bective on the need to register voters:

> I have reason to think you will find your canvass everything you could
> wish. In one of Lord Headfort's last letters, he talks of registering votes
> at the quarter sessions. They are now going on, and if all yours are
> not ready for registry at Kells, you can [? surely – scarcely?] have an
> adjournment for that purpose. As I have not made up my mind to the
> parliament voting itself permanently in case of a certain event, it will be
> well to be perfectly prepared for a future day …[20]

Fingall certainly had in mind the idea that even with the change in circumstances with a new king, a free vote in parliament for Catholic relief, all occurring at that time, parliament may not have been able to permanently pass the required legislation. He suggested therefore preparation for new elections at any time.

By 7 October John Naper admitted that he had given up all thoughts of presenting himself for election: 'As I fear my intention of coming forward as a candidate for this county may have been the occasion of putting you to some inconvenience I lose no time informing you I have given up all thoughts of offering myself'.[21]

In response to this, W.B. Wade, who held lands in Diamor, asked Bective and Headfort to arrange a meeting with Sir Marcus Somerville and the electors to discuss Bective's unanimous return.[22] John Ruxton of Blackcastle in a similar vein promised his interest, but had learnt it may no longer be required.[23] Bective continued to get support from various local landowners, or as in this case from the Revd William Hamilton, who had a benefice in Meath:

> the small income of the benefice I hold in this city arises from lands in the county of Meath, which yields me only £130 a year, but to the tenants is worth nearly £2,000 a year. It will therefore be a very small compliment they could pay me to vote as I may desire them, and your Lordship may rely, no exertion shall be wanting on my part to use every influence to engage their interest. Having a very large family, and so small an income, I hope I shall be excused in mentioning that your Lordship will have no objection in defraying the expenses incurred on my going down to the election.[24]

Other supporters included Luke Norton of Dublin, promising to use his influence with his uncle Mr Eife, Walter H. Supple, Robert Wilson, Revd George Alley, and Brabazon Disney, all local landowners.[25] John Keogh of Mount Jerome informed him that he had given the disposal of his small interest to Fingall, no doubt that these would be passed on to Bective.[26] As shown above, Richard Chaloner, who had supported Bligh, had suggested to Bective a number of people who would support him. In a follow-up letter, Chaloner, as well as congratulating Bective on his unanimous election, mentioned that he had received correspondence from Naper: 'dated near three weeks ago, in which he laments his being a stranger in the county, and thinks it prudent to decline any positive declaration till he knows the inclination of the leading interests, on which consideration he requests to know how I'm inclined'.

Chaloner also reiterated the point that since there was no knowing when another election would take place, 'so they should busy themselves registering freeholders'.[27] Other recommendations came from

Viscount Gormanston, another leading Catholic peer who suggested that 'I [Gormanston] am confident your Lordship, with my friend, Sir M. Somerville, have the good wishes and confidence of the county. ... '[28] William Furlong of Dublin offered support from his son:

> Mr Richard Furlong, who is land agent to the Countess de Salis, Mrs Peckwell and Sergeant Blossett for their estates in the county of Meath, I received a letter from them directed to him, desiring him to express their united wishes to the tenantry of their estates in that county that they should give their votes, support and interest to your Lordship on the ensuing election. Their tenants are John Pollock of Mountainstown, John Smith of Newcastle and T W [?] Sheridan of Knightstown, and I have written to each of them.[29]

Although what support Bective received from Pollock, an adversary of Fingall's influence, is hard to know. Other letters of support came from Thomas Clarendon, Dublin on 19 October, and from James Carolan in Navan on 20 October mentioning that 'your highly respectable family to have always the interest of the Catholics at heart'. A letter from the Revd Blayney Irwin, Laracor, stated, 'it was my determination to have given your Lordship my vote, whether solicited or not'. Another letter from Thomas Keappock, Kells, promise the support of himself and family.[30]

Bective's initial correspondent at the time when Thomas Bligh was pulling out of the hustings, John Pratt Winter, was asked to formally propose Bective for the seat and wrote to him on 21 October thanking Bective for having chosen him.[31] In the same vein Robert Wade of Clonabreny was 'glad to hear that Bective has elected Mr Winter, an old friend of Bective's grandfather, as the person to propose him at the hustings.'[32] Even though the election was ratified on 26 October, correspondence continued to appear as if an election was forthcoming. James Johnston, an attorney, had received a copy of the registry of two of the Meath baronies, Lower Navan and Morgallion with a list of the main landlords. For Lower Navan he suggested that:

> Lord Tara has a great interest. Henry Hazelwood, I believe, would be guided by him. Catherine Taylor is, I suppose, widow of James Taylor, an attorney who lived near Trim. Thomas Hussey, the brother of the late baron of Galtrim, lives at Uxbridge, and William Thomson is a son of David Thomson of Oatlands, near Mr Waller.

In the case of Morgallion he stated that: 'Lord Fingall has eighteen, Lord Gormanston ninety and Sir James de Bathe eighteen. You see what an object it will be to get Lord Gormanston's interest'. He also mentioned that: 'The Barnewall family, I mean Bloomsberry, have considerable interest, and if they would exert themselves might register about 40. They have registered freeholders now, Mr Naper has done himself great injury by not becoming acquainted with the county on this occasion'.[33] Joseph Barnewall who lived at Bloomsbury was the person mentioned here.

Towards the end of the election, there are a number of letters of support from Conyngham-Jones of Dollardstown and Charles Hamilton of Hamwood, and a Mr Smyth pointed out that Headfort may have overlooked a Mr Canon of Daisy Hill, Duleek. John Carty of Dublin promised the support of his brother Thomas Carty 'a considerable merchant in Drogheda, and a freeholder of Meath, who on previous occasions voted for Somerville'; however, by the time Thomas Carty was approached, it was too late for this election, although he was able to thank Bective for his letter and promise his future support.[34] In the end, no election was called as Naper withdrew and Bective and Somerville were returned unanimously.

James Johnston outlined some of the problems that Mr Naper encountered: 'Mr Naper was totally ignorant of the unregistered state of the county, and acted from a consideration of his own weakness, without inquiring into your strength. I am informed that Mr Lambart declares, that if he has any information of Mr Naper's intention to decline the contest, he would have tried it'.

He went on to say that in future elections registration of voters, particularly in the towns, would be a major issue. He also noted that all of Lord Darnley's freeholders were registered, and mentioned that as a result:

> I have good reason to know that the disappointment of Lord Darnley
> and all his friends is very great on account of Mr Naper's not standing
> as a candidate for the county of Meath and contesting it to the last.

This would suggest that Mr Naper's withdrawal was not a fait accompli and that Bective would have to consider this the next time around. He also suggested that his agent, Mr Chambers: 'will from time to time be able to give you an account of the proceedings of your opponents. I am certain that every exertion that is possible will be used against the next time of election, and therefore every attention should be paid to Mr Naper's movements'.[35] Be that as it may, Bective was duly returned as the second MP for the County.

III

The correspondence with Bective, particularly in the middle of the campaign, suggested that Catholic relief was the issue that would maintain his electoral position in the county. Although Catholic relief had brought about the downfall of the parliaments of 1801 and 1807, it was the assassination of Prime Minister Spencer Perceval that led to the 1812 election. However, Catholic relief remained an issue, particularly with Irish MPs, and petitions were presented to parliament by Henry Grattan in 1808, 1810, 1811 and 1812. Irish MPs and the Whig opposition supported these petitions, but all were voted out. By 1810 the king's madness overtook him and his son, the Prince of Wales, was granted regency powers. Although this should have helped the Catholic position, the prince appeared to take on a more anti-Catholic stance. The only real change in parliament occurred with the new administration of 1812 when 'Catholic emancipation became an open question and ministers were given full freedom as individuals to vote as they wished on what was perhaps the most controversial question of the day'.[36]

The petitions themselves supported the 'veto' clause, which would have allowed payment to Catholic clergy with the proviso that the government be allowed a veto on ecclesiastical positions. This became a contentious issue by 1812 and caused the beginnings of a split in the Catholic committee between the old aristocracy, such as Fingall and Bellew, and the new merchant class represented by Daniel O'Connell and John Keogh, who sought other means to approach the problem. Reforming the Catholic committee to allow it become more representative of the population fell foul of the convention acts, which forbade any assembly that sought to challenge parliament as sole representative of public opinion. This succeeded only in creating more trouble for the Catholic cause, resulting in a need for a new approach other than the constant petitioning of parliament.

The last petition prior to the election was an inquiry proposed by Canning to look into Catholic relief, which was passed in the House of Commons and lost in the House of Lords by one vote. This established that in the new parliament in which Bective was a member the system of preparing petitions and private bills would remain as the focus for obtaining Catholic relief until new circumstances arose. The 1812 parliament had Lord Liverpool, a Tory, as prime minister. He held this position until 1826. Robert Peel was chief secretary for Ireland until 1818. Other ministries were held by talented Tory parliamentarians, such as Addington (Lord Sidmouth), the Duke of Wellington, Castlereagh and George Canning. It was the first parliament that the prince regent (later George IV) formed and was renowned for having a weak (Whig) opposition.[37] The main concern of this new parliament was progressing the war in Europe, after which the problems of expenditure and taxation and sedition were considered to be the next priorities. Due to the success of Canning's petition in 1812, Grattan proposed consideration of Catholic relief in 1813, which was passed in Commons; this was followed by a draft bill also proposed by Henry Grattan, which was also passed. However, the speaker, Charles Abbott, proposed an amendment to remove the clause allowing Catholics to sit in parliament. This was passed, and because it removed one of the main pillars of the draft bill, the bill was withdrawn. These relief bills were supported by the opposition, and although normally supporting the government, both Sir Marcus Somerville and the Earl of Bective voted with the opposition.

With regard to Lord Fingall, the prominent Catholic aristocrat, his appointment as a JP for county Meath (18 August 1803) gave rise to the publication of an exchange of correspondence with the lord chancellor, the first Lord Redesdale, in which Fingall acquitted himself with some dignity and emerged as a Catholic champion. When, on 17 November 1804, a meeting was held in Dublin to appoint a new Catholic committee to draw up a new petition for the removal of the remaining penal laws, it was Lord Fingall who took the chair. He was one of seven prominent Irish Catholics who took to London a petition for the total abolition of the penal laws (March 1805); he later took more petitions (1810, 1811, 1812 and 1813). Fingall's pamphlet, *An address to the Catholics of Ireland* (1811), increased the respect for him in Catholic circles. He faced legal prosecution after presiding over a meeting of Meath Catholics at Navan (29 August 1811), the purpose of which was to revive the Catholic Convention of 1792–3. On the issue that most divided Catholics from 1808 until 1829 – whether 'Catholic emancipation' should be conditional on a State veto being accepted on appointments of bishops and on State provision being made for the diocesan clergy – Fingall was a 'vetoist' in opposition to Daniel O'Connell. When, at a meeting held on 24 January 1815, in an attempt to reunite the Catholic Board a motion was put for 'unqualified emancipation', the earl walked out; by 1817 he was no longer prominent in Catholic politics.[38]

By 1812, the situation in Ireland had changed in a number of ways. Sir Robert Peel had intimated his intention to 'suppress … all boards, and future boards, committees and conventions'.[39] He began by taking legal action against the Catholic Board, which resulted in its disbandment as a committee. However, former members, such as Bellew, Trimleston and Fingall continued to support Grattan in his petitioning for a committee to prepare a bill for Catholic relief, qualified by allowing some security or veto to the government. These were presented to parliament in 1815, 1816 and 1819, and after Grattan's death the last petition was presented by William Conyngham Plunket (MP for Trinity) in 1821. Other members of the board now represented by Daniel O'Connell aligned themselves against supporters of the veto and were able to support a petition to parliament without securities also in 1816. This was presented by Sir Henry Parnell as Grattan refused to condone it. All of these bills were defeated except the last one presented by William Plunket, and according to the records both Marcus Somerville and the Earl of Bective voted in their favour. The majority against dwindled over the years and the 1821 submission by Plunkett was passed by nineteen votes. Again, a draft bill was prepared, and in deference to the sponsors it retained a number of securities. 'It revived the idea of government-appointed commissioners that would certify the loyalty of candidates for vacant Catholic sees and examine correspondence with Rome, and at the same time proposed a new device, a legislative explanation of the oath of supremacy that would allow Catholics to take it without compromising their religious beliefs'.[40]

This bill passed its third reading with a majority of nineteen in the House of Commons, but was defeated in the House of Lords by 159 votes to 120. Parliament was dissolved twice in the period from 1812 to 1820, in June 1818 and in February 1820. Advertisements for support in the forthcoming elections as shown here were commonplace when elections were announced. In this case, the *Freeman's Journal* noted a week later that the members for Meath would be unopposed and thus it transpired. Sir Marcus Somerville and Bective were also returned unopposed in 1820. The following Election Notice appeared in the *Freeman's Journal* in June 1818:[41]

To the Gentlemen, Clergy, and Freeholders of the County of Meath

With every feeling of gratitude for the distinguished honor I enjoyed in having sat in Parliament as one of your Representatives, allow me to offer myself again to your Notice, with the hope that my Parliamentary conduct has been such as not to render me unworthy of your future favour. Permit me, therefore, most earnestly and respectfully to solicit the honor of your Support in re-electing me to the high trust in the ensuing Parliament.

With the sincerest attachment,
I am, Gentlemen,
Your most obliged and faithful humble servant,
BECTIVE.

Headfort, June 12, 1818

However, that did not mean that Bective had not requested support prior to these elections. Letters of support did arrive from Dominick O'Reilly of Kildangan Castle, from Lord Gormanston,[42] and Claud Cole Hamilton of Beltrim, County Tyrone who wrote as follows:

I hope you will not attribute my absence from Trim at the approaching election to anything but the certainty of your being returned without opposition, and to my being detained here for the election, which will take place on the 1st, where a contest is expected, which I believe will end in the return of Sir John [Stewart] and [William] Stewart, as I assure you at all times any interest I can command in Meath shall ever be at your service.[43]

There is little mention of the 1820 elections in the *Freeman's Journal*, save as to regard the election of Sir Marcus Somerville and the Earl of Bective as a foregone conclusion. Again, people had pledged their support, including Dominick O'Reilly, a prominent member of the Catholic committee from Kildangan Castle County Kildare, and Earl Conyngham of Slane who wrote: 'I cannot possibly have any just cause for withholding any interest I might have in Meath from you. I only lament for your sake that I have not a greater one, but such as it is, you are welcome to. Long since I wrote to Dean at Slane Castle to use all my interest in favour of you and Somerville. Therefore, cut and carve as you chose'.[44]

Others who offered support were James Farrell of Merrion Square, Lord Fingall of Killeen Castle and Edward Plunkett of Dunsany Castle, who also offered to propose Bective at the hustings. Sir Compton Domville, an MP for Dublin, offered his support, as did William Battersby of Belville.[45] One supporter, P. Barry of Merrion Square (possibly the MP for Cavan) mentioned the bill proposed by Sir Henry Parnell and how it might have troubled the county:

> I am extremely happy that everything is as it should be in our county, and that there is to be no vexatious opposition, although I think my friend, Sir H. Parnell's bill, was a measure as well calculated for that purpose as any could have been devised, and a strong inducement to persons of ever so little pretensions to make themselves troublesome and expensive, not only to individuals but to the counties at large. [46]

The Taylour family held much land in Cavan and would have tenants who not only could vote but also had some standing in the county. Nathaniel Sneyd, who was elected in Cavan, thanked Bective for his support:

> The very noble and generous manner your Lordship condescended to honour me with your support in this county [Cavan] contributed mainly to my obtaining a very triumphant majority on my canvass. The decision of some of the most independent interests in the county rested upon that of your Lordship. The Election Day is fixed for the 18th inst., and for the great favours your Lordship has twice conferred on me, might I be permitted to solicit the still greater honour, that of being proposed by your Lordship at the hustings. Pardon the great liberty I take in making this request.[47]

IV

The early 1820s represent a watershed in terms of the political life for Irish MPs and for Catholic relief. The success of the draft relief bill of 1821 suggested to the Catholic committee that their tactic of presenting petitions to parliament should continue; however, there was dissension in the ranks led by Daniel O'Connell on one side and the old Catholic Ascendancy such as Fingall, Plunkett and Barnwell on the other, together with well-known members of the

Catholic committee such as their spokesman, Richard Lalor Shiel. The accession of King George IV to the throne and his visit to Ireland in 1821 were seen as a good sign, as was the appointment of Marquess Wellesley as lord lieutenant and that of the aforementioned William Conyngham Plunket as attorney general. They were both supporters of Catholic emancipation.[48] By 1823, after a reconciliation with Shiel, O'Connell started up a new Catholic Association with local committees in each parish, which included a rule that allowed the majority of parishioners to become associate members. The subscription for this membership was as low as a penny per month. The association also published a weekly newspaper that had about 6,000 subscribers and published details of the association's activities and plans.[49] The association was suppressed in 1825; however, by that time O'Connell had the ear of Francis Burdett, a radical Whig who proposed the 'Wings' relief bill in May 1825. The Wings represented a compromise agreed by O'Connell where the government would pay the clergy and in compensation raise the property qualification of the electorate in order to dissuade the majority Catholic-peasant vote. This was passed in the House of Commons with a majority of twenty-one, but was defeated in the House of Lords.

Both MPs for Meath, Somerville and Bective, spoke at a county meeting in Navan, chaired by Gormanston, to promote Catholic relief in 1825.[50] Also present at the meeting were Darnley, Thomas Bligh, John Winter, Killeen, Messrs Preston, and Joseph Brown, representing the great and good, Catholic and Protestant of Meath. Both MPs were known to have voted for Catholic relief in 1821 and 1825. Both were also returned unopposed in the 1826 general election. At a meeting of the Catholics of Trim chaired by John Nangle, in 1826, it was resolved that:

> the Earl of Bective and Sir Marcus Somerville do accept our warmest thanks for their uniform steadiness in supporting the cause of our just rights and that they will be pleased to present our petition to the House of Commons, and that Lord Clifton be requested to support its (plea?).[51]

The 1826 election in the Waterford constituency, which returned a member supported by the Catholic Association, was the first indication that the Catholic freeholders could be organised to defy their landlords and vote for a chosen candidate. The Waterford result showed that the interests of the Catholic Association, with

the personal involvement of prominent people such as Daniel
O'Connell and in this case Thomas Wyse, could overcome a very
powerful interest of the major landlord and sitting member. Other
constituencies where pro-emancipation candidates succeeded in
bucking the trend included the nearby Louth, Dublin, Monaghan
and Westmeath. However, in Cavan, even though 800 Catholics
voted against their landlords, the organisation of the registration
and polling of the freeholders allowed the two anti-emancipationist
candidates, Maxwell and Saunderson, to be returned.[52] Retaliation by
the landlords, although effective against individuals, became difficult
against a general revolt, and the Catholic Association, revived by its
victories, began to raise funds again, some of which could be used to
circumvent landlord retaliation.

There was difficulty in forming a government after the 1826
election. The Liverpool administration remained until February 1827
when Liverpool suffered a stroke and was forced to resign. He was
followed by Canning, whose pro-Catholic leanings forced the right-
wing Tories such as Wellington and Peel to resign. Canning died in
office in 1827, and was followed by Viscount Goderich who couldn't
maintain a government, so the anti-emancipationists Wellington and
Peel took over the government with the support of some liberal Whigs.
Wellington had even given a pledge to the king that the government
would not raise the emancipation question and had opposed the
petition of 1828, which was subsequently defeated in the House of
Lords. However, the election in Clare of Daniel O'Connell, who could
not attend parliament because of his religion, forced Wellington into
a U-turn. He realised that the next general election would bring out
more Catholic members and that a change in the law was necessary
to preserve peace. He also reasoned, as set out in his dispatches, after
O'Connell had successfully taken Vesey Fitzgerald's seat:

> The king cannot confer the honour of a peerage upon an Irish
> gentleman, a Member of Parliament for an Irish county [James Daly's
> ennoblement was postponed because of the risk of another such result
> in county Galway] ... His Majesty cannot appoint a Member of an
> Irish county to an office [it was the appointment of Vesey Fitzgerald,
> the defeated candidate in Clare, to the board of trade that had
> caused the by-election in the first place]; and still less can he dissolve
> his Parliament.[53]

The bill proposed by the government went ahead, and in April 1829 parliament finally decided to admit Catholics to its benches and to all offices except the lord lieutenant of Ireland and lord chancellor of England and Ireland and lord keeper and high commissioner of the Church of Scotland.[54] The only security required was that the 40s freehold was raised to £10 on the assumption that this would ensure a Protestant majority in most of the Irish counties.

As on previous occasions, the two sitting MPs for Meath had voted for the relief bills in 1827 and 1828 and finally in 1829. Bective succeeded to his father's peerage in October 1829, and this forced his resignation as MP for Meath. Naper, Killeen and Jack Lawless (of the Catholic Association) offered themselves in election. Arthur Plunkett, Lord Killeen, was proposed by Clifton (John Bligh, MP for Kent) and was returned unopposed. Killeen therefore became the first Irish Catholic to attend the UK Parliament. The honour of being the first Catholic member however went to an Englishman, Lord Surrey, within a month of the passing of the act. Surrey, a friend of the king, took the seat in Horsham when the existing member resigned. Bective's elevation to the peerage did not end his political career; he entered the House of Lords as Irish representative peer and was elevated to the UK peerage a year later. His voting in the House of Lords reflected his liberal views and supported reform, the abolition of tithes, and disestablishment.[55] His son and grandson also entered political life, his son as MP for Westmorland from 1854 to 1870 followed by his grandson who retained the same seat from 1870 to 1892.

Bective's resignation brought about the first electoral controversy since 1812 as elements of the Catholic Association began to focus their attention on the repeal of what they saw was the initial cause of the controversy, the Act of Union. This came to a head when John Lawless, an avowed repealer, put his name forward in the 1830 general election for Meath. With Bective (now Lord Headfort) out of the way, it was Lord Clifton supported by Marcus Somerville and Naper who led the charge against repeal. The Headfort papers show an election address from Clifton to the independent freeholders of Meath stating:

> Gentlemen, the strangely confused state of your county induced me to address you upon the present occasion, and to declare that, although I had it not in contemplation to interfere with the return of your late members, I have come over from England on purpose to oppose the intrusion of a stranger, and that, being now freed from any engagement

in other quarters, I shall be ready on the day of nomination, either in my own person or otherwise, as circumstances may require, to lend my best assistance to uphold the independence of the constituency of Meath.[56]

Further correspondence prior to the election includes resolutions from numerous meetings in Meath, which outline objections to the new candidate (obviously Lawless):

That we feel ourselves called upon to express, in the strongest terms, our abhorrence of the means adopted by some person, chiefly strangers, to agitate and disturb this county, hitherto happily free from party violence and animosities; to stir up strife and ill-will between the higher and lower classes of its inhabitants; to calumniate and excite the popular hatred against the government, laws and institutions of the country: and, above all, to effect that which appears to be the first and immediate object – the making the election of our representatives depend, not on the calm considerate choice of the electors, but on the heated passions of those whose minds may be open to the acts and practices of turbulent and mischievous demagogues. That we call upon all those who value the peace and good order of the country, and the legitimate and salutary influence of rank and property, to unite promptly and firmly in opposing this first attempt to introduce into this county the disorganised principles and practices with which we are threatened; and, as the most probable means of effecting this desirable union at the approaching election, we declare our determination, setting aside all individual views and private parti-alities, to support the re-election of our present respected representatives, Sir Marcus Somerville and Lord Killeen, on this understanding and not otherwise, that they shall both unite fully and frankly with us and with each other in opposing the firmest resistance to the attempts of those who are thus labouring to agitate and divide the county.[57]

The signatories included notable supporters of Bective's campaign, such as Edward Preston, Thomas Barnewall and Charles Dillon. It can also be noted that Bective's replacement as MP, Arthur Plunkett, Lord Killeen, defended the union in parliament in December 1830.[58] Other supporters who publicly opted for the union include John Naper, Dominick O'Reilly and Nathaniel Sneyd.[59] In the end, Killeen was returned unopposed when Clifton, Naper and Lawless declined. However, this in one way was a Pyrrhic victory. Morgan O'Connell replaced Killeen when he resigned his seat in 1832 and Henry Grattan replaced Marcus Somerville when he died in 1831. Both of these repealers were succeeded by Catholic liberals and later by supporters of Home Rule. Thus the 1831 election represented the peak of landlord power in Meath. The electorate from that time on showed an independent spirit and were well prepared to act against their landlords and to make 'a calm considerate choice, for mischievous demagogues', as Clifton stated in his correspondence above.

CONCLUSION

The late-eighteenth century showed a flowering of political thought expressed by the works of Emmanuel Kant, Adam Smith, Thomas Paine and Voltaire. Ideas such as religious tolerance, freedom and liberty were expounded in Ireland by liberal parliamentarians such as Grattan, Hussey and Flood and in England by liberal members of parliament such as Edmund Burke and Charles James Fox, and other members of the Whig party. In France and America these ideals formed the intellectual basis for revolution and similarly in Ireland they formed a major part of the ideals of the United Irishmen. As in France and America, and unlike in Britain, these ideals were to surface in actual rebellion in 1798. However, the excesses of the revolution in France and in particular the 'Terror' and the regicide prompted the suppression of any radical thought or 'Jacobin' sentiment among the British elite, to such an extent that Britain declared war on revolutionary France.

The Irish liberal voice felt that the solution to discontent was to counteract it by concession: 'Catholic emancipation, parliamentary reform, free trade with Britain and measures for improving the conditions of the poor'.[60] In Britain, after the 1798 rebellion, it was felt that the Irish had behaved in a treacherous manner and had allowed the country and its parliament to become a back door into Britain for revolutionary deed and 'Jacobin' sentiment. The British posited, however, that a parliamentary union would, by bringing the full range of liberties enjoyed in Britain, remove the reasons for discontent. In addition, measures to take the religious issues out of Irish politics were proposed as part of this union. In the end the union, as enacted, was diluted by the intransigence of the king, the rise of anti-Popery in Britain, the suppression of liberal sentiment and the need for loyalty in the war against France.

The majority of the 100 Irish MPs on their way to take the seats in the UK Parliament were now left in a bit of a quandary. Their liberal views, as espoused by Grattan and others, which had contributed greatly to the honour of the Irish parliamentarians, were found to be of little consequence in the new assembly and perhaps were seen to be disloyal to the now-United Kingdom, particularly at a time of war against revolutionary France. The Irish MPs were seen to be 'united only in their belief in Catholic emancipation, [and] were equivocal and petty in their approach to the war'.[61] On many occasions they voted in opposition on Catholic relief and as this was deemed to be an unpopular issue, it resulted in a loss of confidence in government and loss of votes for their Whig colleagues. It would seem therefore that Catholic emancipation became the sole expression of the Irish liberal MP. It was also understood among Irish MPs that they were the natural representatives of their community and that a large personal following remained a vital electoral advantage.[62] The fact that the majority of MPs were landowners and that property rights were the only criteria for the franchise meant it was incumbent on those seeking election to ensure that all their freeholders were registered to vote and that their own views represented not only the opinions of the class they came from but also the views of their electorate. In at least three of the four provinces the majority of freeholders could be assumed to be Catholic with a preponderance of pro-emancipation views. Indeed by 1829 it is estimated that 60 per cent of Irish members were pro-Catholic emancipation.[63] In Meath there was an added incentive in that the old Catholic aristocracy still retained land there and were held in high esteem by their neighbours who had acquired their land during the Cromwellian confiscations. Thus the two members for Meath were assiduous in their support for Catholic emancipation and consistently voted for this, whether in government or opposition.

The electoral correspondence with Bective started in 1807 with a letter from John Pratt Winter, who was a prominent Protestant supporter of Catholic relief and a Meath landowner. It would seem that the main reason for this correspondence at that time was the king's refusal to grant a small measure of Catholic relief, forcing the resignation of the Grenville ministry. The support given to the new Portland administration by Thomas Bligh, the sitting MP for Meath, was a concern to the Catholic cause, who mistrusted this new government. They may have felt that if a new election was forthcoming they would need a new supporter on their side and the tone of the letter does suggest that Bective had already made known his support for the Catholic cause. By the time Bligh resigned in 1812, it would seem that Bective had approached a number of his peers with a view of contesting the election. Much of the correspondence promised support, many letters gave advice on whom to approach and also on how to ensure the freeholders were registered. Letters from Gormanston and Fingall, the two Catholic peers, do show that Bective was counted among the supporters of Catholic relief. The extent of the correspondence is quite amazing. There are forty individual replies held in the archive, and among this correspondence another thirty-five names are recommended to Headford as would-be supporters in the event of an election. A number indicated that they had already plumped for the other candidate, Mr Naper, if he were to declare, with the understanding that they would transfer their interest to Bective if Naper declined. Some also promised support only if it would not interfere with the chances of the sitting member, Marcus Somerville. The correspondence with Bective also shows that he had a broad range of correspondents among the prominent members of the Catholic Association. The majority of the seventy-five names mentioned were influential landowners in Meath and probably held 90 per cent of all the land in the county. In the correspondence the number of votes, i.e. freeholders, mentioned ranges between single figures and ninety. The number of 40s freeholders in the early 1800s was estimated to be 1,600, although only 551 people voted in the 1802 election in Meath, which happened to be the only contested election in Meath until 1831. The seventy-five people who were canvassed to support Bective would have had on average twenty freeholders each; however, in the end their votes were not required, as Naper did not declare, and Bective along with Somerville was returned unopposed. In the same way the elections of 1818, 1820, and 1826 were uncontested, which allowed both Bective and Somerville to remain as the duly elected members from Meath. The correspondence in this period reflected this position and generally emphasised the support to be given in the event of the election. More importantly, the correspondence found in the archive seemed to be from close personal supporters, and included letters from important personages such as Gormanston, Conyngham, Fingall and Plunkett.

Both Bective and Somerville continued to support Catholic emancipation until the Act was passed in 1829. When Bective resigned due
to his elevation to the House of Lords, his seat was taken unopposed
by Arthur Plunkett, Lord Killeen, who became the first Irish Catholic
MP in the UK Parliament. In the thirty years after the union the
Catholic cause was served well in Meath by both its MPs, and although
they were not the only Irish MPs to support this cause they were
assiduous in bringing forward petitions and in voting for relief,
on many occasions dividing against the government. The support in
the constituency suggested not only that Bective was trusted by the
Catholic aristocracy, but also that he could be counted among those
Protestants associated with and or indeed members of Catholic relief
organisations.

Meath was also favoured in this respect by having Lord Clifton
of Athboy, a known proponent of Catholic relief, as the MP for
Canterbury in the House of Commons, and also three members,
Darnley, Headfort and Conyngham in the House of Lords. Knowing
the mind of their tenants and voting according to their liberal principles and with the support of like-minded friends and acquaintances
did ensure that the landlord class did hold on to their franchise before
and after the Act of Union. Bective's forced resignation as MP, with
his elevation to the House of Lords; his replacement by Killeen, also
elevated to the House of Lords; and the death of Sir Marcus Somerville
brought about a sea-change in the constituency in 1832. This proved
the end of landlord influence in elections in Meath. Governance,
however, was a different issue – landlords such as Bective maintained
their positions as lord lieutenants of Meath and neighbouring counties,
were prominent in the magistracy and commanders of the militia,
and in this way maintained their control of local government until the
end of the century.

The Darnley Estate
Pre- and Post-Famine

JIM GILLIGAN

BACKGROUND TO DARNLEY FAMILY, ACQUISITION OF LAND AND EXTENT OF ESTATE

In February 1835, while attempting to demonstrate his prowess felling timber on his estate at Cobham Hall, south-east of London, Edward Bligh, Earl of Darnley, aimed his axe at a tree root. The axe, however, glanced off its target and struck the earl's left boot, almost severing his little toe. Within a week he was dead. Tetanus had set in, and, despite the best efforts of his doctors, Bligh's condition deteriorated rapidly. He was only 39 and his son and successor, the new earl, John Bligh, was a mere boy of 8.

The Bligh family originated in Cornwall in England and a John Bligh acquired land in County Meath from Cromwell's government in 1654. In the following century, the Blighs purchased a further 3,000 acres and the estate eventually expanded to 25,000 acres. These lands were situated, in the main, in Athboy, Ballivor, Kildalkey and Rathmore. The Bligh family had also inherited Cobham Hall and almost 10,000 acres in Kent through marriage. John Bligh (1687–1728) became Baron Clifton of Rathmore in 1721, Viscount Darnley in 1723 and finally was created 1st Earl of Darnley in 1725.

The 8-year-old John, who succeeded to the title as the 6th earl after his father's unfortunate demise, would oversee the Irish and English

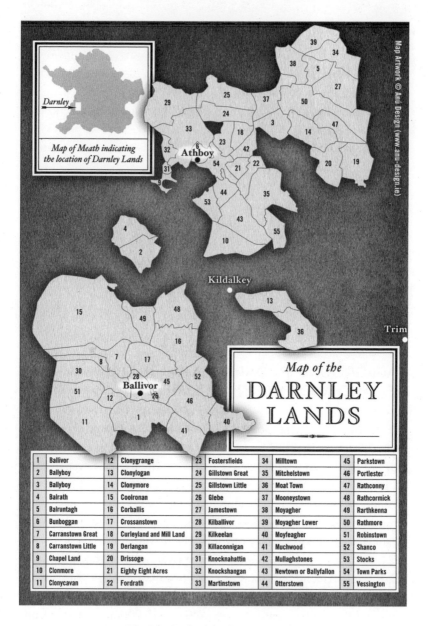

The Darnley lands in County Meath.

1	Ballivor	12	Clonygrange	23	Fostersfields	34	Milltown	45	Parkstown
2	Ballyboy	13	Clonylogan	24	Gillstown Great	35	Mitchelstown	46	Portlester
3	Ballyboy	14	Clonymore	25	Gillstown Little	36	Moat Town	47	Rathconny
4	Balrath	15	Coolronan	26	Glebe	37	Mooneystown	48	Rathcormick
5	Balruntagh	16	Corballis	27	Jamestown	38	Moyagher	49	Rarthkenna
6	Bunboggan	17	Crossanstown	28	Kilballivor	39	Moyagher Lower	50	Rathmore
7	Carranstown Great	18	Curleyland and Mill Land	29	Kilkeelan	40	Moyfeagher	51	Robinstown
8	Carranstown Little	19	Derlangan	30	Killaconnigan	41	Muchwood	52	Shanco
9	Chapel Land	20	Drissoge	31	Knocknahattin	42	Mullaghstones	53	Stocks
10	Clonmore	21	Eighty Eight Acres	32	Knockshangan	43	Newtown or Ballyfallon	54	Town Parks
11	Clonycavan	22	Fordrath	33	Martinstown	44	Otterstown	55	Vessington

estates for almost the whole of the Victorian era. Until he came of age in 1848, three guardians, his mother Emma, 5th Countess of Darnley, the Rt Revd Charles Thomas, Lord Bishop of Ripon – later Archbishop of Canterbury from 1862 until 1868 – and his uncle John Duncan Bligh oversaw the running of the estate. It was an era of huge challenge and change that included the Great Famine, the growth of Irish nationalism and reforms in land legislation that would culminate in the Wyndham Land Act of 1903 and the end of the Darnley estate.

The estate brought in an annual rental close to £20,000 in the post-Famine years. It was the largest estate in Meath, comfortably exceeding the acreage held by any of the other large landowners in the county, such as the Marquesses of Headfort, Conyngham and Lansdowne, the Earl of Fingall, Viscount Gormanston, Lord Athlumney, the Napers of Loughcrew and the Fowlers from Enfield.

STRUCTURE OF THE ESTATE PRIOR TO THE FAMINE

The lands were situated in the barony of Lune on the borders of Westmeath, surrounding the towns of Athboy and Ballivor. However, Darnley also held land further north in the parish of Kilskyre, houses in Trim and Dublin and in Cloontagh in Longford, but some of those were sold in the 1870s. The estate encompassed up to forty townlands of varying extent, and the quality of the land and the size of the farms on the estate varied hugely. The quality and value of land in Ireland can be analysed using the Primary Valuation of Ireland, better known as Griffith's Valuation. Griffith valued land 'according to the nature and depth of the soil, and the quality of the subsoil, all the local circumstances being taken into consideration' and 'at the rate it would reasonably let for by lease to a solvent tenant, on a lease of twenty-one years'.[1] Griffith's valuation of Athboy dates to 1854.[2]

Many of the Darnley-owned townlands attracted a valuation in excess of £1 per acre. A return of valuation completed by 1852 gives an average valuation per acre of 18s 5d for Meath, with most counties well below this. Meath's neighbours, Westmeath and Kildare, were rated at 14s and 13s 10d respectively, while all counties west of the Shannon fell below 10s.[3] Thirteen of the townlands held by Darnley were valued at more than £1 per acre. In Athboy those consisted of Bunboggan, Fordrath, Drisoge, Mitchelstown, Knockshangan and Eighty Eight Acres. Two of the Ballivor townlands were similarly valued, Kilballivor and Glebe, while in Rathmore four townlands had average valuations in excess of £1 per acre, Moyagher, Balruntagh, Ballyboy and Mooneystown. Gillstown Great, Clonimore and Milltown were all close to the £1 mark. In total, those valuable townlands amounted to about 25 per cent of the Darnley lands.

The Darnley estate consisted of a mix of very large, mainly grazing farms, many well in excess of 100 acres, alongside medium to large holdings of from 20 to 100 acres and a substantial number where the rental fell below £10 per annum. Almost half the acreage of the estate was made up of very large farms of 100 acres and above. The large farms on rich pasturelands were dominated by a number of families such as the Hopkins in Gillstown, Mitchelstown and Drissoge and the Pottertons in Rathcormick. They had been Darnley tenants for many years and would remain part of the landscape for most of the century. Other substantial tenants paying in excess of £100 in rent per annum in the 1830s and 1840s included George Cusack in Moyagher and John Dyas and the Battersbys in Boltown. James Campbell held all of Parkstown, while the Lewis family dominated Portlester and Muchwood. Some of those changed over the following decades, but the large farms remained the most significant feature of the landscape.

However, as was common in much of rural Ireland, there were often huge contrasts between townlands in close proximity to each other. The townlands dominated by one or two substantial landholders with very low population density existed side by side with townlands where the pattern was utterly different, with numerous small holdings and large populations dotting the landscape. In Rathmore parish, Jamestown with 535 acres had sixty-six houses in 1841 and Mooneystown, extending to 370 acres, had sixty dwellings. Cheek by jowl with those relatively densely populated stretches of land stood tracts of land almost bereft of human habitation. Milltown, Balruntagh and Moyagher with a combined 1,051 acres held a mere fourteen houses in total. In Kildalkey parish there was a similar pattern. Rathcormick townland with 622 acres accommodated fifteen houses whereas Corballis, only slightly larger at 678 acres, had thirty-five. This probably reflected patterns that long predated the nineteenth century. In general, this pattern mirrored the relative value of the land. The very large farms tended to be in the townlands with the higher values. The townlands with the highest value in Rathmore parish were Moyagher and Balruntagh, both over £1 per acre and both sparsely populated, whereas Jamestown was the lowest valued, at just over 10s. This was partly due to 145 acres of bog, which Darnley himself held. Jamestown, as noted above, was densely populated, with the majority of the farms less than 10 acres. However, Mooneystown bucked this trend, as land here was valued at just over £1 per acre but there was no substantial farm among the thirty-nine holdings listed in Griffith's Valuation.

The largest amounted to 45 acres with the vast majority below 10 acres. Kildalkey parish exhibited a broadly similar pattern: the highest-valued townland, Rathcormick, was dominated by Thomas Potterton with 532 acres, 85 per cent of the townland's area, while the lower-valued Corballis had only one very large farm. Thus, while it is broadly accurate to say that large farms and low populations were generally found on highly valued land, there are some exceptions to this. This can be seen as outlined above with regard to Mooneystown, but it also holds true for other townlands such as Kilballivor.

ESTATE MANAGEMENT AND CONDITIONS ON THE ESTATE PRIOR TO THE FAMINE

Though the Darnleys were absentee landlords and left the running of the estate to their stewards, they were regular visitors to Athboy, staying at Clifton Lodge. John, the 6th earl, paid a visit in 1848 and again in 1850, and throughout his life visited Ireland every second or third year. Indeed, he died in Ireland, at Clifton Lodge, in 1896. The employment of agents or stewards was a common form of estate management in nineteenth-century Ireland. Agents were responsible for collecting rents, usually twice yearly, maintaining accounts, over-seeing improvements and expenditure, carrying out evictions and dealing with petitions from tenants. Darnley paid £600 per annum to his agents in the 1840s, rising to £720 in the 1860s and 1870s.

Throughout the 1840s Lambert Disney was the agent, but soon after the 6th earl took over responsibility for the estate, Disney and his family seem to have emigrated to Stafford in England. Henry Atkinson, who was a JP and resided at Frankville, Athboy, held the position for over twenty years until 1873 when Otway Johnson replaced him. Johnson acted as a land valuer for various landlords in court cases and later worked as agent for Lord Powerscourt in Wicklow. Claude Coghill was the agent in the late-nineteenth and early twentieth century when the tenants purchased most of the Darnley estate under the land acts. All the agents were Protestants, justices of the peace and men of standing in the area.

Most of the large farms were held on leases, usually for three lives or twenty-one years, and many of those dated from the second decade of the nineteenth century. The leases often contained covenants, whereby those leasing the land undertook not to sell or alienate the property, and the penalties for so doing were severe, amounting to a fine to the value of a year's rent or more. There were also clauses preventing tillage on more than a quarter of the land, any corn for grinding was to be brought to one of Darnley's mills and, in some cases, even turf was to be cut in a manner directed by Darnley. Many leases also required the tenant to expend money on drainage, plantations and houses. Even relatively small parcels of land seem to have been subject to a lease, but many of the very small holdings were generally held at will.[4] When the youthful Earl of Darnley took over the running of the estate in the late 1840s, he seems to have exercised similar control.[5] Unlike many absentees, the Darnleys did not allow unchecked subdivision and consequent population explosion on the estate. Thus, in general, there was very little subdivision or subletting, although, as explained earlier, a few townlands with numerous small holdings were juxtaposed with the empty townlands of the large farms. Jamestown and Mooneystown are prime examples of this type of structure, but even here there was minimal subletting. From the evidence of Griffith's Valuation every single holding in Jamestown in the early 1850s, and there were forty-six of them, was held directly from Darnley, and while Mooneystown displays some evidence of subletting it was the exception rather than the rule. Of the forty-two occupiers in Mooneystown, thirty-three held their property directly from Darnley and only nine were subtenants of those who leased from Darnley.[6] In each case there was only one subtenant, often a family member with a house or a house and small garden.

Even before the Famine struck in the 1840s there is evidence that tenants on the estate, including those holding large farms, faced difficulties. A petition addressed to Lady Darnley, probably from the late 1830s, refers to an economic depression, with cattle and corn prices progressing from bad to worse. To add to their woes the petitioners refer to the 'incurable cattle disease which has raged in this country for the last five years, and very fatally in the vicinity of Athboy'. The authors declare that, as a result of their difficulties, they are unable 'to employ as heretofore the labouring poor upon the estate without the prompt assistance which they confidently anticipate from a Landlord whose ancestors have been ever mindful of the comfort and prosperity of their people'. Over eighty people signed their names to the petition and it included all the main landholders such as William Hopkins in Gillstown and his namesake in Mitchelstown, Thomas Potterton in Rathcormick and Tottenham Alley in Fordrath, John Askin of Gillstown and the resident Church of Ireland vicar, Revd Robert Noble. There is no evidence of the response, if any, from Darnley's guardians.[7] At around the same time the Roman Catholic parish priests of Athboy and Kildalkey, Revd James Rickard and Revd John O'Connell respectively, and Revd Robert Noble gave evidence to the Inquiry into the Poor in Ireland. They referred to a combined figure of over 1,600 labourers between both parishes, about one third of whom had regular employment with the rest depending on occasional labour.[8]

For those lucky enough to get employment, wages were in the region of 10*d* daily or 5*s* per week. Workmen's accounts from the Darnley estate in 1838–39 indicate a variety of work such as cutting hedges and timber, levelling ditches, making and repairing gates and fences, cutting poles, drawing stones to the Hill of Ward for repairing ditches, and drawing loads of sand. An indication of the poverty can be gleaned from the fact that for most of the month of December 1839 six or seven men worked daily on the estate cutting timber 'for the use of the poor of Athboy for fuel' and for 'the poor at large of the estate'. The workers were employed on both 24 and 26 December with just a day off for Christmas.[9] The estate also provided another mode of charity for residents in the form of three almshouses built by the 5th Earl of Darnley.[10] These contained accommodation with a garden for twelve poor widows, who had an annual allowance of £5 5*s* and ten kishes of turf.[11] In addition, a number of elderly tenants received weekly allowances. Darnley spent £141 on such allowances in 1847.[12]

Lambert Disney, the Earl of Darnley's agent, was aware of the levels of poverty in the area. Speaking at the first meeting of the Trim Union Agricultural Society in late 1845 he stated that the members were 'too little mindful of the … duties of benefitting the labourers who have been too generally allowed to go on in their misery'. He claimed he had devoted much time on the estate to this object.[13] Even well-off tenants could fall rapidly into poverty. Prudence Walsh, whose husband had once farmed 100 acres in Knocknahattin, petitioned Darnley for assistance in 1834. Her husband lost his farm because of 'unforeseen circumstances and speculations which turned out unfortunate' and died soon afterwards. His widow states that she 'has gone from a state of comfort to comparative indigence' and appeals for assistance to put her house, which is in 'such bad condition and repair as to render it quite unhealthy and uncomfortable … into a tenantable state of repair suiting her condition in life'.[14] Given the number of labourers without regular work and the substantial number of small uneconomic farms, many on the estate were ill-prepared for the onset of famine.

IMPACT OF THE FAMINE

Two different British governments held power during the Famine. Sir Robert Peel's Conservative administration was in office until June 1846 and it responded to the crisis by setting up a scheme of public works, mainly on roads and drainage schemes, and importing a limited amount of maize. The relief works relied heavily on voluntary contributions from the local gentry with grants and loans to supplement the amount collected locally. The Whig government under Lord John Russell that replaced Peel's administration was ideologically committed to a much less interventionist approach, unwilling to interfere with market forces and intent on placing responsibility for the Famine on the property owners in Ireland. Some influential voices in the new government viewed the Famine as an opportunity to realise long-held aims of consolidation of farms and reduction of population. In early 1847 the government announced a major policy change. Soup kitchens would be opened and, in the long term, public works would no longer be used to provide relief. Instead, the Poor Law would be extended, putting more responsibility on localities. This fitted with the prevailing English view that 'Irish property must pay for Irish poverty'.[15]

A partial failure of Meath's potato crop in 1845 was followed by a major crisis in 1846 when the blight struck the crop once again. The north of the county was the worst affected, especially the areas around Kells and Moynalty, but Athboy and surrounding areas were not immune.[16] By late April 1846 Lambert Disney, agent to the Earl of Darnley, was chairing the Athboy Relief Committee, one of many established in the county.[17] The committee catered for townlands that were not part of the Darnley estate in addition to those under the earl's remit. Its aim was to raise funds that would entitle them to additional amounts from the Relief Commission, mainly to purchase meal from food depots. In June 1846 Disney sought a grant of £80 from the Relief Commission and in July requested 100 tickets for admission to public works.[18] In November 1846, John Nolan, secretary to the committee, requested further assistance and enclosed a subscription list for the relief of the destitute in Athboy. The guardians of the Earl of Darnley – who

was now 19 – headed the list of subscribers with a contribution of
£200, about 40 per cent of the £482 donated. Disney himself supplied
£20 while most of the substantial farmers donated £5. Among those
with lands on the Darnley estate contributing were Thomas Potterton,
Tottenham and George Alley, William Hopkins of Mitchelstown, Luke
Rickard of Coolronan, William Moore of Moattown and Samuel Lewis
of Portlester. The parish priests of Athboy, Ballivor and Kildalkey each
donated £5 while the vicar of Athboy, Revd Robert Noble, added £2.
Numerous others contributed amounts from 2s 6d to £3.

The letter to the Relief Commission, dated 6 November 1846, accompanying the subscription list stated that in the barony of Lune there were:

> upwards of three thousand persons in a state of destitution – to support
> this large number, there are at present but a little more than 500
> employed, so that if we did not come forward at this juncture we believe
> that many persons would perish from actual want and that the peace
> of this hitherto quiet district, would be in danger of being disturbed.[19]

In January 1847 Nolan informed the commissioners that they had established a soup kitchen in Athboy 'from which about fifty gallons a day are
distributed' and requested further assistance based on a local contribution of £19 11s 3d. The commissioners recommended a payment of
£19.[20] There were also soup kitchens in Ballivor and Kildalkey.[21]

Meanwhile, Trim Workhouse had witnessed a huge increase in the
numbers applying for admission. A very manageable 200 inmates in
March 1846 had become over 400 in October and by Christmas was
close to 530. The workhouse had been designed to accommodate 500.
In May 1847 the Poor Law Guardians who had responsibility for the
workhouse agreed that a Fever Hospital be erected on the grounds
for forty persons.[22] However, the Poor Law Extension Act passed in
June 1847 aimed to transfer responsibility for relief to Irish taxpayers
and cease government assistance. The new act allowed for limited
forms of outdoor relief, that is relief outside of the workhouse, but it
also signalled the end of the temporary soup kitchens.

In December 1847 Disney called to the Poor Law Commission
offices in Dublin to inform the commissioners that:

> there is very great distress among the labouring population of Athboy
> electoral division, as, notwithstanding the exertions made by the

gentlemen of the district to provide employment, many are without work and actually in a condition tending to starvation.

He persisted in pleading for outdoor relief to be extended to the able-bodied labourers but the commissioners consistently opposed this, and in January 1848 dissolved the Trim Board of Guardians and appointed paid officers to administer relief to the destitute poor of the union.[23]

An analysis of the impact of the Famine on the Darnley estate by comparing population and housing in 1841 and 1851 leads to three broad conclusions. First, many of the townlands dominated by substantial farms that were thinly populated prior to the Famine escaped practically intact and in some cases increased their population. Ballyboy, Clonimore and Gillstown Great in Rathmore parish all increased their population, as did Fordrath in Athboy. Rathkenn Mitchelstown and Muchwood declined but not significantly.[24]

A couple of the townlands with substantial farms did decline, notably Parkstown, which lost five houses out of seven and experienced a drop in population from forty-six to seventeen, a substantial decrease. The townland seems to have changed hands at least twice. In the 1848 rental, Edward Vaughan replaced James Campbell who held the land in 1834 and neither appears in Griffith's Valuation. Instead, William Hone is listed as holding the complete townland in 1854 so Hone or Vaughan may well have cleared a number of tenants from their homes on taking the townland, sometime in the 1840s.

Balruntagh's two houses disappeared over the decade, denuding it of both housing and people as the population declined from twenty in 1841 to zero ten years later. This townland is often combined with Moyfeagher in rentals, as is also the case in the Tithe Applotment Books of 1833. George Cusack Esquire was in possession in 1833 and he still held some of the townland in 1848 as he paid Darnley rent of £572. However, by 1852 Michael Cullen held Balruntagh, Moyfeagher and Moyfeagher Lower so he may also have removed tenants on taking over from Cusack. By 1876, he still held all three townlands and was paying rental of £1,000.[25]

While many townlands suffered loss of population as a result of the Famine, four townlands on the estate bore the brunt of it. These were Jamestown, Mooneystown, Rathconny and Rathmore, all in Rathmore parish. The table below shows the decline in the number of houses in each census from 1841 to 1871.

House Numbers in Four Townlands 1841-71				
	1841	1851	1861	1871
Jamestown	66	45	40	35
Mooneystown	60	38	33	26
Rahconny	42	26	27	26
Rathmore	75	32	31	28
Total	243	141	131	115

Table 16. Source: The Census of Ireland for the Year 1871 Showing the Area
Population and Number of Houses by Townlands and Electoral
Divisions, vol. i, H.C. 1873 [C 662, VIII] 684

Each of the four townlands suffered substantial declines from 1841 to
1851 and the decline continued to 1871 but much less precipitously. In
the Famine decade Jamestown, Mooneystown and Rahonny lost roughly
a third of their houses, while Rathmore lost closer to two thirds, 56.5 per
cent. The 1841 census gives details of the quality of housing on a parish,
but not on a townland basis, categorising dwellings as first, second, third or
fourth class. The table below gives the details for the parish of Rathmore.

Category of Houses in Rathmore Parish, 1841					
	1st Class	2nd Class	3rd Class	4th Class	Total
Rathmore Parish	5	29	215	31	280
	1.7%	10.4%	76.8%	11.1%	100%

Table 17. Source: The Census of Ireland for the Year 1841 Showing the Area
Report of the Commissioners appointed to take the Census
of Ireland for the year 1841, HC, 1843 [504] xxiv, 94

The four townlands being examined accounted for 85 per cent of houses
in the parish, and, as most of the remaining eight townlands featured
substantial farms, the quality of housing there would likely fall into the
first- or second-class category. It can therefore be confidently asserted that
the proportion of third- and fourth-class houses was as high and probably
higher in those four townlands than in the parish as a whole. It was
families living in this category of house that bore the brunt of the Famine.
The four townlands lost 102 houses and over 700 people between 1841
and 1851. It is likely that about eighty of those houses were third class and
twenty were fourth class, the homes of the poorest of the poor. Many of
the tenants in those townlands must have been forced or persuaded to
avail of the assisted-emigration schemes that will be outlined presently.

Finally, the Athboy District Electoral Division also suffered significantly. This area consisted in the main of Athboy town and surrounding townlands, and the overall decline here in the 1841–51 period was 24 per cent. However, the decline varied. The town itself experienced a substantial drop, down from 334 to 210, but a couple of surrounding townlands, not all part of the Darnley estate, had massive rises. The population of Townparks doubled, while that of Eighty Eight Acres went up by 80 per cent. Presumably, this was due to people moving into or near the town from some of the outlying townlands.

EMIGRATION

Evidence suggests that there was only minimal emigration from Meath during the 1830s.[26] Revd James Rickard, the parish priest of Athboy, and his counterpart in Kildalkey, Revd John O'Connell, both agreed when giving evidence to the Poor Law Inquiry in 1836 that only a few labourers had emigrated from the Athboy-Ballivor-Kildalkey area and the main destination was America.[27] By late 1846 emigration from Meath was on the increase. The *Meath Herald* declared in October 1846 that: 'in the memory of the oldest inhabitant in this part of the country the spirit of emigration was never known to have arrived at the height it is at present. Numbers who can muster sufficient funds are wending their way towards the shipping ports for America'.[28]

There is substantial evidence that emigration became a feature of life on the Darnley estate, certainly in the late 1840s. Such assisted-emigration schemes occurred on a number of landed estates in Ireland and took the form of landlord assistance with fares. Some landlords believed it would be cheaper in the long run to compensate or assist a tenant who would leave, rather than have him remain on the estate while unable to pay his rent. It would allow the landlord to get a more solvent tenant or consolidate the abandoned farm into a larger entity. The expenditure on emigration would thereby be recouped over a relatively short time span.

Darnley's accounts for 1848 record an expenditure of over £1,000 assisting tenants to emigrate. The greatest proportion of this was spent paying James Miley, an American packet agent based in Eden Quay in Dublin, the balance due on his account of £929.[29] Usually, shipping agents secured the vessels, negotiated the fare and sourced provisions for the voyage. Miley advertised sailings from Dublin to

New York and Quebec in the local press, claiming to have the fastest ship from Dublin and assuring intending travellers they would get 1lb of bread, flour or oatmeal daily.[30] With fares running from £3 to £3 5s per adult, Darnley's remittance of £929 would cover 300 to 350 persons, assuming some of those travelling were children.

In addition to the cost of fares, Darnley's expenditure on emigration included other forms of assistance. He provided cash for clothing, paid for shoes, sundry travelling expenses, and for dinner for some emigrants prior to their departure. This suggests that those who emigrated were the poorest and had very little in the way of clothing or footwear. The assisted-emigration scheme continued until 1852 at least. In both 1849 and 1850 Darnley paid Miley over £350 in fares, which represented over 100 emigrants each year. Again the accounts show evidence of money being expended on clothes and travel to Dublin for those leaving.[31]

Controversy erupted following the arrival of some of the Darnley tenants in New Brunswick, Canada in 1847. The number of Irish emigrants travelling there trebled in 1847 compared to previous years and the authorities were barely able to cope. The death rate for passengers on board some ships and in quarantine was often stag-gering. The average mortality rate on ships from Cork in 1847 was 18.64 per cent and from Liverpool 15.65 per cent. Ships from Dublin fared slightly better on 8.07 per cent.[32] The Colonial Emigration Office wrote to a number of landlords including Darnley asking for an explanation of their actions. It was alleged that Darnley's tenants were promised money on arrival in Canada but this was not provided and they were left to their own devices. In response, Lambert Disney claimed that Miley was instructed 'that the head of each family should receive a certain specified sum on landing at Quebec; this plan I have adopted in former years, and never heard any complaint of the sum ordered not having been paid'. The failure to do so he ascribed to Miley. Whoever was to blame, the tenants received no extra money.

Darnley has drawn opprobrium for this and other aspects of the voyage, but one of the assertions repeated by historians is incorrect. It was alleged 400 of his tenants travelled on the ship the *Panope* from Dublin in 1847. In fact, as recorded by the Canadian authori-ties, it carried 112 persons, and according to Disney sixty-eight were from the estate. One person died at sea and another, named Catherine Graham aged 60, died in quarantine after arrival. It is not known if she was part of the Darnley party.[33] I was unable to trace the name of the second victim. It appears that more tenants travelled on other ships and evidence from the *Meath Herald* indicates that the emigration scheme continued in the following years. In February 1849 the newspaper reported approvingly that, 'Upward of 200 poor persons have within the last few days, taken their departure for America, from the neighbourhood of Athboy'. The newspaper exhorted other landlords to 'assist the poor, as far as in your power lies, to emigrate', as it had a double advantage: it would remove labour to a market where there was a demand for it, and result in a decrease in taxation at home.[34]

There are very few details on those who availed of emigration. Some are itemised as having rent arrears struck off because they left the area for America. It is unclear if they were part of the assisted scheme and their rents were set at naught as part of it, or if they emigrated using their own resources and left their rent unpaid. Those few names listed in 1848 as having gone to America were generally the holders of very small plots of land from townlands such as Coolronan, Robinstown, Jamestown, Mooneystown, Rahoney Bog and Rathconny. Those townlands were ones where subdivision and small plots were more common and they recorded substantial losses during the Famine.

Tenants often requested assistance towards emigration. A notebook of Tenants' Requests in the Darnley archive, dating from 1851, when the worst years of the Famine were over, records numerous pleas for permission and assistance to emigrate. In February 1851 Pat Caffrey of Chapel Land asked to be sent to America but was informed there was 'No emigration at present', yet the following month it was agreed to fund the emigration of Mrs Kennedy, a widow from Coolronan, and her daughter 'in consideration of her having given up her land'. Not all who emigrated settled abroad as evidenced by the response to a request from B. Corrigan of Rathmore. Darnley advised his agent that 'if he is ever sent, his claim must be way down on the list as he has been to America once and returned again'. There seems to have been minimal emigration to Australia, with the only reference occurring in 1852 when Darnley paid £48 for a passage for a McMullins family. Requests for assistance to emigrate, mainly to America, continued until 1853, but the majority seem to have been refused.[35]

The Irish Folklore Schools' Collection from 1937 has just two references to emigration from the area. Eighteen families were recorded as having left Ballyboy in 1847 while six or seven houses in an area known as The Wood in Kildalkey are recorded as being in ruins due to emigration to America. However, census figures for Ballyboy in Athboy records fourteen houses there in 1841 and fifteen in 1851 while Ballyboy in Rathmore had a mere two in 1841 increasing to three in 1851. Names or details may have been confused in oral transmission, and like all sources this one needs to be treated with caution. It seems likely that most of the emigration originated in townlands such as Jamestown and Rathmore and in the vicinity of the towns of Athboy and Ballivor.

Such schemes have been condemned and viewed as 'shovelling the people out' rather than 'benign assisted emigration' as their supporters preferred to view them. It is doubtful if the tenant had much choice in the matter, as the power relationship of landlord and tenant was tilted strongly in favour of the former. I am not currently aware of any details in the Darnley archives that would provide more information on the rationale and operation of the scheme. Even if there was, it is unlikely that it would shed much light on the emigrants' point of view. In regard to the evidence generally, one can only say that substantial numbers were involved, that the estate provided some funding for food, clothing and transport and it appears some provision was usually made for minimal assistance at the emigrants' destination. Clearly, that assistance wasn't provided for emigrants on the *Panope* in 1847.

The scheme of assisted emigration seems to have been a short-lived one. From 1847 to the early 1850s it is likely that, based on the amount paid to James Miley, 600–700 persons may have been assisted to emigrate. This was a substantial number but it paled into insignificance when compared with the large-scale assisted-emigration schemes on the Palmerston estate in Sligo or the Shirley estate in Monaghan.[36]

RENTALS

Although there are partial rentals for the Darnley estate for the late 1830s, the first of the more comprehensive rentals with records of individual tenants dates to 1848. These give a fairly detailed picture of rents and their payment on the estate. However, accounting dates changed for a couple of years in the late 1840s and some accounts were recorded on a half-yearly rather than a yearly basis. It also appears that Disney was absent, ill, for a time at this period, all of which makes direct comparison of years difficult. The rentals for the mid- to late 1830s averaged over £13,000, rising to over £16,000 just prior to the

Famine. It appears that there was an increase in rent in the region of 20 per cent between July 1841 and July 1842 and the increased rental was maintained up to the Famine. Darnley granted reductions of rent of 20 per cent for the half year to November 1849 and 10 per cent for the following half year, but it appears the abatement did not apply to tenants in arrears. In addition, arrears totalling £1,588 were cancelled in May 1850. Arrears of rents that were relatively high in the 1830s at about 12 per cent of rentals reduced slightly during the 1840s, dropping to just below 10 per cent of rentals on average. However, arrears grew significantly in 1849, with £5,889 outstanding in May and £5,946 due in November. As the worst of the Famine was now over and Disney was replaced as agent, the payment of rents improved and by May of 1850 arrears had been halved to £2,612. In the decade 1850–59 amounts due declined annually, dropping to below £500 by mid-decade and continuing to decline thereafter.

Darnley was for the most part an absentee landlord, but, as noted earlier, visited the estate every two to three years. The bulk of the rental income from the Meath estate was used in the main to fund Darnley's residence and lifestyle in Cobham Hall. Each year between £10,000 and £13,000 was remitted to Coutt's Bank in London for this purpose. The amounts transferred decreased during the Famine years – in 1849 they dropped to £3,300 – but the annual outflow represented a huge drain of funds from the area. Between 1840 and 1880 close to half a million pounds from the Meath estate was deposited with Darnley's bankers. Clearly, the investment of such a substantial fund locally would have made a huge difference to the local economy.

The estate usually spent up to £1,000 annually on improvements to buildings and farms, and amounts averaging about £500 were expended on charities. Among expenses in this category were Protestant organisa-tions such as The Protestant Orphan Society, The Meath Bible Society, The Deaf and Dumb Society and Athboy Sunday School. Darnley also paid a membership fee towards the Sackville Street Club and Trim Agricultural Society. The estate spent money for the provision of turf to schools in Athboy, Ballivor and Moyagher and school books for Coolronan and Ballivor. These were probably religious or quasi-religious publications aimed at promoting the Protestant religion, for the rector Revd Robert Noble was a former Roman Catholic priest turned zealous proselytiser.[37] The charitable and incidental expenses offer revealing insights into aspects of the social and economic life of the estate. In 1849 the estate paid £22 for meals and 18s 6d to Michael Higgins, probably a carpenter, for four coffins, all for the poor of the Rathmore district. Two sick labourers were given allowances for twenty-six and eight weeks respectively, the pensioners in the almshouses were given turf and weekly pensions. The expenditure for Clifton Lodge reveals a very different social milieu with expenditure on wine, candles, groceries, fruit, linen, biscuits, bread, turf and coal.

DARNLEY'S POLITICAL VIEWS

The 6th earl was remarkably reticent when it came to expressing his political views. When he died in 1896 the local newspaper, the *Chatham and Rochester News*, commented that 'the sound of his own voice was to him a cause of terror and dismay ... nothing would ever induce him to utter a word in the House of Lords'. The report also claimed that if he had had more self-confidence and had overcome his shyness and diffidence he could have been a cabinet minister.[38] Evidence of contributions to public discourse in Ireland is also scarce. He was a staunch supporter of the Dublin and Meath Railway, acting as chairman for a time, and clearly the line to Athboy, which opened in 1864, would have been beneficial to the estate. He spoke publicly against the proposed Home Rule Bill of 1893 at a meeting organised by the Marquess of Headfort. Darnley contributed £100 to a fund to fight the bill, describing it as a 'most grievous injustice, not only to the loyal, but to all the inhabitants of this country, and disastrous to the strength and welfare of the British Empire'.[39]

Yet earlier earls, especially his grandfather, the 4th earl, had shown no such reticence in addressing the Lords and took a pro-reform, pro-Catholic line. On two occasions in the 1820s he made strong speeches in favour of an inquiry into the state of Ireland. His first intervention called for a change of approach to Ireland stating that, 'From Henry II to George IV, from Strongbow to Lord Wellesley, I see one unbroken series of English oppression and injustice, and of Irish sufferings and wrongs'. He argued in favour of more rights for Catholics and was critical of the Established Church in Ireland. He identified the potato as the prime cause of much of Ireland's problems as it had led to a 'superabundant population'. He also declared that another cause of poverty was 'the non-residence of a large proportion of the landed proprietors, and the constant drain of money that is thereby occasioned from the country'. As he was mainly an absentee landlord himself he felt compelled to distinguish degrees of absenteeism. Proprietors who got all their income from Ireland and who spent it all in England he described as 'illegitimate absentees'. Others like himself, 'having an equal landed property in this country, and places of residence, which I have not in that [i.e. Ireland]' he deemed legitimate absentees. He noted that there were others, including Lord Lansdowne, in the same situation, who 'will agree with me in considering [it] an indis-pensable duty occasionally to visit his estate in Ireland'.[40] He could have chosen a better role model than Lansdowne, who rarely visited his estates in Kerry and whose agent would be responsible for wide-spread clearances there during the Famine.[41] If, as seems likely, Darnley transferred similar proportions of his rental income to England as the 6th earl did in the 1840s and 1850s, then Darnley must stand accused of hypocrisy on the issue.

Darnley's son, who succeeded to the earldom in 1831, represented Canterbury in parliament from 1818 to 1830 as Lord Clifton and he also supported relief for Catholics. In 1827 he presented a petition from Kildalkey for Catholic relief and even though his constituents narrowly supported an anti-Catholic petition in 1828 he voted in favour of Catholic emancipation the following year. He was not a supporter of Prime Minister Wellington but approved his efforts to have the bill passed 'which I considered paramount to every other question'.[42] It took a degree of political courage to speak in favour of rights for Catholics, particularly as opinion in Kent was at best divided and at worst opposed to concessions to Catholics. A later speech in 1828 proposing the setting up of a select committee to inquire into the distressed state of the poor in Ireland failed to attract a seconder.[43]

CONTINUITY AND CHANGE AFTER THE FAMINE

It is possible to gain some insight into the level of continuity and change on the estate in the decades following the Famine. This can be done by tracing the amendments to occupiers' names in Griffith's original valuation list in the Cancelled Land Books in the Valuation Office and augmenting this with details from Darnley's rentals and information on farm size and rent from the Land Commission Reports of the early 1900s. It was not possible to examine all the Darnley townlands given the amount of information to be analysed spanning almost half a century. Instead, I have focused on a number of townlands, including those dominated by one or two substantial farmers and others with farms of smaller acreages, to arrive at some tentative conclusions. The townlands focused on are Ballyboy, Fordrath, Mitchelstown, Mullaghstones and Otterstown in Athboy parish, Muchwood, Parkstown, Portlester and Robinstown in Ballivor, Rathcormick and Rathkenna in Kildalkey parish and Balruntagh, Clonimore, Gillstown Great and Little, Jamestown and Mooneystown in Rathmore parish. These townlands encompass 7,000 acres, almost a third of the Darnley estate. From those seventeen townlands I have looked at the level of continuity or change among four groups: (i) the substantial farmers owning at least 100 acres and often much more, (ii) farms in the range of 30 to 100 acres, of which there were only eight in the townlands analysed, (iii) small farms from 5 to 15 acres, and (iv) holdings of less than an acre.

In the townlands dominated by the large grazing farms, such as Ballyboy, Fordrath, Muchwood, Parkstown, Portlester, Rathcormick, Rathkenna, Balruntagh, Clonimore, Gillstown Great and Little, there was little or no alteration in the size of the large farms over the five decades to 1900. Even as late as 1905 most of them bore a remarkable resemblance to their extent in 1852. There was some turnover in the occupiers of those farms but many remained in the same family for the duration. The Pottertons remained the dominant presence in Rathcormick and the Rickards held on in Rathkenna until the turn of the century when the Knox Gores took over. The Purdons, who had 324 acres in Clonimore in 1852, held on to them before adding a neighbouring 1900-acre farm in 1887 previously held by the Thompsons. The Cullens in Balruntagh retained their 241-acre holding before departing in the early 1900s, while the Askens' 327-acre farm in Ballyboy changed hands to the Parrs in the 1880s but retained its extent. The whole of Parkstown's almost 350 acres remained as one farm into the 1900s with a change of ownership in 1863, and it wasn't until the turn of the century that a labourer's cottage on a ½ acre was extracted from the estate.

Most of those townlands featured a substantial house belonging to the resident farmer or, instead, a herd's house to minister to the grazing cattle. Griffith's Valuation rated those houses at an annual average of £15 to £20 each with the most grandiose belonging to William Hopkins in Mitchelstown at £45. Those families were always to the fore when addresses were presented to the earl or his agent and they also featured prominently as donors in appeals during the Famine. They were a stable, almost permanent feature of the estate who rarely fell behind in paying rent and seem to have suffered little increase in rents from 1848 to 1876. Rents charged on two Lewis' farms in Portlester did not vary between those years, Potterton in Rathcormick and Alley in Fordrath enjoyed a decrease while others experienced modest increases, especially if there was a change in ownership. Thus, Parkstown went from £315 to £374 and Lewis' farms in Muchwood also saw small increases. Almost all the substantial farmers were Church of Ireland adherents and were clearly the most influential group on the estate.

Only eight farms in the 30- to 100-acre range were identified, and half of those were in Mooneystown. None of the farms altered in size before 1900 and 50 per cent of the owners in 1852 remained in situ at the turn of the century. Four changed hands for some reason, but given the small size of the sample it would be unwise to draw definitive conclusions. A total of forty-four tenancies ranging in size from 5 to 15 acres were identified in the sample townlands above. Families on farms of this size were likely to face a struggle to survive during the post-Famine years. Nevertheless, there was a substantial degree of continuity here also. Very few of the holdings changed in size, and well over 60 per cent of families remained in situ at the end of the nineteenth century. Almost all holdings in this category had houses valued at 15 shillings to £1 5s with a few in excess of this. While some changed ownership in the 1860s, most of the change occurred in the 1880s and 1890s.

Some consolidation took place in those farms but part of it was due to merging farms within families rather than to the landlord taking over the property. Jamestown serves as an example. The Bradys combined two plots, each about 5 acres, the first of which had a house, to make a more substantial 10-acre holding in the late 1880s. Patrick Martin held 7½ acres in 1852, and when he took 2 acres previously held by Clarke he combined both into one farm. Bridget Kerrigan had just 3 acres in 1852 but after Patrick Clarkey departed she got his 6 acres to create a more viable 9-acre plot. Similar practices can be found in Mooneystown. It is not possible to say if Darnley and his agents encouraged such consolidation in the more congested townlands such as Jamestown and Mooneystown, but it is unlikely he opposed it, as it led to more viable farms and probably more certainty regarding the payment of his rent. An unusual feature of some of the farms from the 1-to-15-acre category is that, despite their relatively small size, a number of them had no dwelling, a feature normally associated with large grazing farms. Nine such examples existed in Mullaghstones and most of them changed hands in the 1852–1900 period. It is likely that the occupiers had other farms nearby, or, as Mullaghstones is adjacent to the town of Athboy, had a house in the town.

There were thirty-four holdings in the final category, ranging from a house with no ground to a house with a small garden. Those plots varied from a rood to an acre in size. As explained earlier, tenancies of this size declined greatly between 1841 and 1851 due to death, emigration or eviction. Over the next five decades change continued apace with twenty of the holdings disappearing. Some were consolidated with other small holdings, but most are recorded in the Cancelled Land Books as 'house down' or 'vacant'. The amounts of land involved was so small that it made no appreciable difference when it was absorbed into larger nearby holdings. Only eight remained in the same family name, in contrast to the high degrees of stability experienced in the substantial and medium-sized farms.

ATTITUDES TO THE DARNLEYS

Memories of rack-renting landlords, eviction and forced emigration usually persisted and passed down through the generations in folklore and ballads. Apart from a few fleeting glimpses of antipathy there is no evidence of widespread criticism or vilification of the Darnleys. As this was a family who could trace their presence in Ireland to the Cromwellian era, one would not be surprised if the folk memory harboured burning resentment against them, particularly if the estate had dealt sternly with arrears and distress during the Famine.

Many of the petitions and addresses to the Darnleys followed the well-trodden path of deference and the use of obsequious terminology. The petition from the 1830s, alluded to earlier, describes the landlord as one 'whose ancestors have been ever mindful of the comfort and prosperity of their people' and declares that they 'will ever remember with sentiments of the deepest gratitude' any support he grants. When the young 6th earl visited Athboy in 1850, the town was decorated with welcoming banners and streamers, as was traditional.[44] Darnley had a small number of town tenants in Trim, and they addressed him in the usual flattering terms when he visited the town on attaining

21 years of age and responsibility for the estate passed to him from his guardians. The welcome was a paean of praise to his guardians, father and agent. They assert that the previous earl was 'one of the best and most liberal of kind and indulgent Landlords' and trust that 'his Son will be always found to walk in his footsteps, and that he will come to take up permanent residence among us'. They eulogised Lambert Disney, the estate's agent, for conducting his business in a manner that 'we can safely challenge all Ireland to shew [sic] an Estate in which so much Improvement is visible and such prosperity abounds, and a Tenantry so happy and contented, as that of Your Lordship's Estate; and which is solely attributable to his wise and judicious management'.[45] Incredibly, the Famine and its impact on the district doesn't merit a mention. Addresses such as those were common in nineteenth-century Ireland and were probably authored by the better-off tenants, many of whom were substantial farmers. However, not all agreed with the sentiments they expressed. Two decades later, the then-agent Henry Atkinson received notices threatening him not to carry out Lord Darnley's instructions in the management of his property.[46] It is unclear what those instructions were but evidently they didn't find favour with all on the estate. A year later shots were discharged into Tottenham Alley's residence and the cause was alleged to be Darnley's intention to raise rents. Mr Hopkins, whose family had held the land for generations, declined to pay the increase and Alley took the property. Press reports alleged that Darnley insisted that Alley put three cottier tenants off the farm and received first a threatening notice and then the fusillade of shots, as a result.[47]

Although, Darnley seems not to have attracted the level of odium attached to many landlords there is evidence of animosity. In 1937 the Irish Folklore Commission encouraged children to collect folklore in their districts. Many of the collections featured tales of evil landlords, heroic tenants and priests with supernatural powers. The contributions from the Darnley area include two stories portraying the earls of Darnley in a less-than-favourable light. Contributors from Coolronan and Ballivor National Schools relate similar stories of Lord Darnley and a friend named Mac Suibhne. Darnley said he would lie down on a pathway used by locals going to Mass and pretend to be dead to see what the passing people would do. When a group of people came up the path, Mac Suibhne told them that the landlord was dead, but they answered that it was good enough for him and that they hoped he was in hell. When all the people were out of sight, Mac Suibhne came to tell the landlord he might get up, but Lord Darnley was really dead. The teacher in Coolronan, Bean Nic Conmhidhe, added a note that in some versions of this story it is Mac Suibhne who laid down and died and he was stuck to the ground so that no one could lift the body till the priest came and released him.[48]

Another contributor from Coolronan told a story about one Lord Darnley who was 'very bad and wicked' and whose son had died before he was a full-grown man. The parish priest of Kildalkey, Fr Reynolds, asked Darnley if he would like to see his son and Darnley replied that he would.

The priest went on his knees and prayed a while. Then a noise was heard.

'Do you hear that noise?' said the priest.

'I do,' said Lord Darnley.

'They are opening the chains,' said Fr Reynolds.

He prayed again. The noise was again heard.

'Do you hear that noise?'

'I do.'

'They are opening the gates.'

He prayed again. The noise was heard a third time.

'Do you hear that noise?'

'I do.'

'He is coming up.'

And immediately the ground opened and the son came up, looking as terrible as possible. Then Lord Darnley understood his son was in hell.[49]

Despite those negative views, it seems that the Darnleys ran a well-organised estate. The teacher in Moyagher School in Rathmore parish, Mary Collins, writing in the same collection in the 1930s, stated that 'They were not bad as landlords went, and there were seldom evictions on the estate'.[50] Darnley himself took a personal interest in the running of his fiefdom, and rental policy ensured that subdivision was minimised. In the decades following the Famine there was a huge level of continuity on the estate with most families holding onto their land over the following half-century. The exception was the small uneconomic holdings that amounted to little more than decent-sized gardens.

For the majority of the duration of the Famine, the 6th earl's guardians were responsible for the estate. Even during the worst years most of the tenants seem to have paid their rent, and, apart from the concluding years of the Famine, arrears never grew to unsustainable levels. Yet, a huge proportion of the money collected in rent was transferred to England for the earl's use on his English estate. The estate was never encumbered with debt to the extent that others were, so a much greater percentage of the rentals could have been used to alleviate distress. While the area seems to have avoided the widespread clearances prevalent in other estates, a number of townlands experienced substantial population decline due to death or clearance, as outlined earlier. However, in many such instances the lessee of the land rather than Darnley was responsible for this.

There is very strong evidence that substantial organised emigration took place on the estate. As in all such cases it is difficult to know how many willingly availed of such schemes, and how many were forced to avail of them. Darnley's accounts show that some money was expended on food and clothing for the emigrants, but in many cases this was totally inadequate to meet the rigours of the journey to Canada or the US and enable families to start a new life on a stable footing.

The 6th earl seems to have been a reserved, even a remote character. His grandnephew described him as 'intensely and painfully shy' and the house as one of 'splendour but never relaxed tension' where all had to be done precisely with machine-like punctuality. His very presence 'had the effect of a perpetual inhibition'. In 1850 he married Lady Harriet Pelham, daughter of the Earl of Chichester who is remembered in her old age by the same author as 'stiff as a ramrod and as frigid as a glacier'. She appears to have matched her husband's aloof and cold character.[51]

The centuries-old Darnley domination of the Meath landscape came to a rapid conclusion soon after the death of the 6th earl. Just over sixty years after inheriting the estate, he died in November 1896 and was succeeded by his son Edward.[52] He had a much shorter tenure, dying less than four years later in August 1900. The close proximity of the deaths left the estate liable for substantial death duties while the terms of the Ashbourne Land Act in 1903 made selling the Irish estate an attractive proposition. By the end of the first decade of the twentieth century, most of the lands and the town of Athboy had been sold and the Darnleys' long association with the barony of Lune was at an end.

Can't Pay, Won't Pay: Applications for Rent Abatements on the Gormanston Estate in 1874

DANNY CUSACK

Nora: It's made a great change, Larry. You'd hardly know the old tenants now. You'd think it was a liberty to speak t'them – some of them.

Larry: Of course they all hated us like the divil. Ugh! I've seen them in that office, telling my father what a fine boy I was, and plastering him with compliments, with your honour here and your honour there, when all of the time their fingers were itching to be at his throat.

(from *John Bull's Other Island* by George Bernard Shaw)

The Gormanston estate was owned by the Preston family who first arrived in Ireland from Lancaster in the fourteenth century. After the Battle of Kinsale in 1601 most of the Gaelic Irish lands went to the victors. The Prestons thus acquired lands in counties Dublin and Meath, mostly in the latter.[1] By 1876, they were the fifth largest landowners in Meath, with lands totalling some 9,600 acres.[2] The estate in Meath was based primarily in the east of the county (where Gormanston Castle was built near the village of Gormanston *c.* 1790) with another section (conveniently termed the Nobber estate) in the north of the county. The residence Whitewood House was originally built here as a hunting lodge in the 1790s. In 1868, the Nobber estate consisted of twenty-two townlands and some 227 tenants. It was based around the village of Nobber but included lands to the north and north-east, extending roughly as far as a line drawn between Kingscourt and Drumconrath. The Brittas estate owned by Blighs was located imme-diately to the west, between Nobber and Kilmainhamwood.

The Prestons were a Catholic family with a somewhat chequered career. Along with many of the Anglo-Norman Catholic families, they sided with Charles I against the parliamentary forces in the 1640s and subsequently had their lands forfeited. These were restored after Charles II was reinstated in the 1660s. The Prestons backed the wrong side again when supporting the Catholic James II at the Battle of the Boyne in 1690. Again, their lands were forfeited but largely restored under the terms of the Treaty of Limerick.[3] The Prestons supported Catholic emancipation in the early nineteenth century. By 1874, Edward Preston, the 13th Viscount Gormanston, was 78 years of age. With his death two years later, the estate passed to his eldest son Jenico Preston (born 1837), the 14th Viscount Gormanston, then 39 years of age.

NOBBER ESTATE

Based upon evidence supplied by John Balfe to the Devon Commission in 1844,[4] Peter Connell has described how in the immediate pre-Famine decades the Gormanston-owned land in the parishes of Nobber and Enniskeen was characterised by the large-scale practice of sublet-ting and subdivision.[5] A number of townlands (notably Cortobber and Cloughreagh) had become a refuge for cottiers and labourers. Large-scale evictions of subtenants took place in the early 1840s.[6] The district suffered badly as a consequence, some townlands losing nearly half their population between 1841 and 1851. Post-Famine these much-depopulated townlands came to be dominated by a small number of middle to large tenant farmers. With the worst deprivations of *An Gorta Mór* behind them, conditions for survivors gradually improved during the ensuing decades. Farm prices steadily improved though landlords also increased rents to match those improvements.

The First Gladstone Land Act of 1870 and the Landlord and Tenant Act of 1872 sought to address some of the concerns of tenants and to redress somewhat the imbalance of power between tenants and landlords. While they proved to be inadequate, these measures were the first step in a revolutionary transfer of property ownership in Ireland. They also served indirectly to strengthen the already existing practice of landlords allowing certain tenants abatements on their rents, depending upon the tenant's personal circumstances and on a case-by-case basis.

The Gormanston records confirm that the practice of rent abatements was in place – albeit on a relatively small scale – well before 1874. In 1867–68, the Nobber estate took in some £5,755 in rent, while arrears totalled £510 and abatements only £64 (over half of those granted being to tenants in just two townlands – Muff and Germanagh[7]).

From 1873 until 1879 the world was hit by the 'Long Depression', an economic slump marked by falling prices and declining levels of economic growth. Agricultural prices in Ireland did not begin to decline until the disastrous harvest of 1877–78, however, so the actions by Gormanston's tenants in 1874 described hereunder cannot really be explained by falling farm incomes. Rather they may be said to reflect a 'revolution of rising expectations' amongst farmers who saw their gains during the post-Famine decades threatened by further rent increases. A newfound militancy saw the emergence between 1875 and 1878 of a Meath Tenants' Defence Association in the lead-up to the formation of the Land League in 1879. All of these developments took place in the context of the wider 'Land War' of the 1870s–'90s.

PETITIONERS

In November 1874 a group of tenant farmers on the Nobber estate held a meeting in Kingscourt to consider the issue of rent increases, after which their landlord Lord Gormanston requested Mr Farrelly,[8] the secretary of the meeting, ensured that tenants seeking rent abatements present their cases by way of individual petition. At least eight tenants did so and their letters are retained in the Gormanston Papers in the NLI.[9] Six of these are dated (either 17 or 18 November 1874). The eight petitioners are Thomas McCann (Cortobber), Peter Reilly (Cortobber),

Owen Sullivan (Cloughrea),[10] Laurence Reilly (Muff), Owen Farrelly (Nobber and Spiddal),[11] John Yore (Spiddal), Richard Fagan (Tyrod)[12] and John McEvoy (Muff, Leafin and Rathgillan).[13] Of these, McCann, Sullivan, Laurence Reilly and McEvoy may be regarded as large tenant farmers, Farrelly and Yore as middling tenant farmers and Peter Reilly and Richard Fagan as small tenant farmers. In 1874, their acreage varied from McEvoy's over 200 acres to Richard Fagan's 6 acres.[14]

We shall focus our study upon two petitioners in the townland of Cortobber located a few miles south-east of Kingscourt. In 1835, Cortobber was described as 10 acres bog, 10 acres plantation and 1 acre swamp. Flax, oats and potatoes were produced.[15] The status of Thomas McCann (107 acres) contrasted sharply with that of his neighbour Peter Reilly (14 acres)[16] but the letters composed by these two men stand out as the most substantial and interesting of those submitted.

Thomas McCann set out his claim based upon an ancestral family connection with his farm:

> I farm about 102 acres under your Lordship in Cortobber under seven different agreements. 'The Mill Farm'[17] upon which my ancestors lived from time immemorial, contains about 10a. 3r. at yearly rent of £19/6/- of this there are over 3 acres waste.

He openly acknowledged that much of his land had been acquired progressively over a period of time through the eviction of previous tenants:

> The farm upon which I at present reside belonged to a man named Lynch, who was evicted for non-payment of rent, and to whom I gave £40 for house etc. The remainder of my farm I got from time to time after the previous tenants having been dispossessed for heavy arrears and non-payment. These small farms were advertised for a considerable time for tenants. From their lamentable state of barrenness, and forbidding appearance there could be no person got to take them though viewed by many for that purpose.

In the circumstances he felt he was almost doing Gormanston a favour by taking on the extra land, and that doing so had actually proved an encumbrance:

The late Col. Cruise [Gormanston's agent] persuaded me to take them. I have no hesitation in saying that never since the creation has so much rent been paid out of my holding in the same length of time, as since I took it. Nor would I be able to pay the present rent, but for another farm of forty acres, of good land, I got from my father-in-law on Mr Singleton's property. There are no cattle wintered there, and I bring all the produce of it to my Cortobber farm viz: – about forty tons of hay (there are 10 acres of permanent meadow on it) and from seven to eight acres of corn yearly. With all this manure and a strict adherence to the most approved principles of agriculture I am unable to raise more than six to seven barrels of oats per acre on Cortobber. So that I am obliged principally to pay your Lordship rent off my other farm.

Having set out his circumstances, McCann then came to the point of his letter:

I think, therefore, that I ought to get an abatement from any Catholic landlord. The aggregate rent of the 102 acres I hold from your Lordship is

	£100/5/-
Griffith Valuation	£71/10/-
rent demanded	£137/8/-

which is nearly cent for cent on the valuation.

And, in support of his claim, further elaborates on his circumstances:

Now, my Lord, there are on my farm about fifteen acres of waste land under roads, rivers, glens etc. Which together with cess, rates etc. leaves my arable land at over £1/10/- per acre at present. It is said that land is worth more rent now than it was when I took these lands, that is about twenty-five years ago. This may be true of lands taken for con-acre, or pasture, when the speculator has another means of living, but certainly not otherwise. At least I find in my own particular case, that the additional expense of living, increased dearth of labour, tradesmen etc. have kept pace with, and I might say have passed the increased price of farm produce. And this produce has decreased in quantity owing to unfavourable seasons [?] worm etc.

McCann then states again his inability to pay, before pitching an appeal to Gormanston on the basis of the landlord's supposed good name and the maintenance of harmonious relations between himself and his tenants:

> Hence my Lord I find that it is easier for me to live by tillage when I took these farms than it is now, though the land is in an improved state. I therefore cannot pay anymore than the present rent. But as this estate was always exemplary for the mutual good feeling between landlords and tenants, and relying with unbounded confidence upon your Lordship's proverbial kindness, acute sense of justice, and cordial indulgence to your tenantry, I hope you will take the terror of this threatened increase off the hearts of my poor family; and the scandal of it from the mouths of the people.

Having employed the art of *plamás*-ing along with elements of obsequiousness, the tenant then addresses the man he had pointedly described earlier as a *Catholic* landlord in a somewhat more aggressive and threatening tone. In the course of doing so, McCann outlines the future unpalatable financial scenario he himself faces:

> If this kind of work goes on, very soon the country will be all on fire. Already they say far and near, what a nice example this is for all the Protestant Landlords, the enemies of the people! Would your Lordship even imagine what the Hon. Mr Preston[18] said to me in his office? 'McCann', said he 'I shall make you comfortable for the remainder of your days – you shall get a lease of 21 years – and there shall be yearly rent of £137!' That is, my Lord, I was ordered to pay the sum of £780 in 21 years, above my rent, by way of making me comfortable for the remainder of my life!!

Before sarcastically asking: 'Was there ever such scornful mockery practised on an old tenant?' He concludes on a note of open defiance, sugared with customary felicitations:

> But there is plenty of this sort of thing, and as an old friend of the family I am bound to tell your Lordship that it is setting the tenants mad, and frantic for twenty miles all round. Of this £780 I solemnly declare I shall never pay one shilling. Again, confiding in your Lordship's

consideration, and wishing your Lordship long, happy, and prosperous years, I have the honor of remaining my Lord your Lordship's most obedient and very humble servant ...

Peter Reilly of Cortobber is the most loquacious of the petitioners. He begins by paying the customary respects to Gormanston before setting out succinctly the facts of the matter regarding the financial circumstances of his farm:

> My Lord, Availing myself of your kind condescension to read, and consider each tenant's objections to an increase in rent, who may have such objections, I, Peter Reilly of Cortobber, with confident reliance upon your Lordship's acknowledged kindness of heart, and discerning sense of justice, make the following statement of the principal circumstances and facts relating to my farm.

I hold 14 acres rented at present	£16
Mr Richard Griffith's valuation	£12
Future rent required	£20/14/-

> Hence the present rent is 1/3 higher than the valuation, which is at present too high. But the threatened increase is £8/14 over the valuation, or £1/14/6 per £1 of the valuation.

The recent bad weather along with the inferior quality of the soil and its intricacies had only served to exacerbate his difficulties:

> This ruinous increase I, or any other man, could not pay and live on the farm, as it is naturally very bad land.

> From the peculiarity of the soil there is not perhaps in Ireland another district to which the late seasons have proved so unfavourable. If the seasons come wet, the grass and crops are rendered nearly worthless from scald. If they come dry they are equally injurious as the clay brakes [sic] and hardens in such a way that growth is very much retarded. And these properties make it very hard to till.

Unusually perhaps, Reilly reveals something of the particularities of his family situation:

There are, my Lord, four members in our family namely my mother and two other brothers long grown to man's condition. We are all continually employed on the farm which should therefore show a high rate of cultivation. Moreover, my mother is in receipt of an annuity of $96 = nearly £20 yearly. This she receives from the Govt. of the USA, as a pension for the loss of her second husband, who was killed in the Mexican War. And this annuity she has been expending on the farm for upwards of twenty years in purchasing manure, lime, con-acre and meadows, in draining fencing and reclaiming waste land.

Before setting out the hard facts of his financial situation:

I hope your Lordship will consider, that as we are thus employed upon the farm we should be supported off it. This is set down at the slender
allowance of £20 each	£80
Rent	£16
Buying and repairing farming implements harness etc.	£7
Union rates [?] cess etc.	£1/5/-
Total amount which must come off the farm yearly	£104/5/-

Directly addressing his landlord, Reilly is insistent that, whatever about supposed 'good times', he could never make a reasonable living from his farm and, were it not for mother's annuity, he would be unable to pay the rent:

Now my lord, in my farm there are scarcely twelve acres of land exclusive of waste. Hence it is plain to your Lordship that each acre of these 12 is taxed to produce £8/13/- yearly which I hope your Lordship will admit is enough for an acre of land to do, in this backward locality without taxing it still further.

We don't pay our rent off the farm and I'm inclined to think that we could not pay so much rent for it but for the aforesaid annuity, which will terminate at my mother's death. Notwithstanding the great noise and alarm made by Landlords about good times, and constantly rung in the ears of the poor unfortunate tenants, as a pretext for crushing them with an exorbitant rent, I can verily tell your Lordship, that never since I remember have I derived less money from my farm than I did the present year, by either pasture or tillage.

He begs to be allowed stay in the 'ancestral house' on his 'forefathers' farm, the alternative prospect – emigration – being too much for he and his elderly mother to contemplate:

> My Lord, my forefathers possessed this farm for centuries. And I believe I am paying nearly twice as much for it as my father paid. I have already spent the best of my years upon it, as I am now passed the meridian of life, and my mother is old and infirm. We are not well fit for any other business in life except the drudgery and toil of the farm. In this state together with our love of home and country, and I may add our desire to live under your Lordship and your family; it would be most heart-rending to us to leave our ancestral home, to look for another in some foreign and unfriendly shore.

Having appealed to loyalty to both landlord and country in order to soften the tone of his message, Reilly then insists that it is unjust that all his sweat and labour should be rewarded in this way:

> Nevertheless, your Lordship will drive us even to this alternative, if you don't give us the farm at the present rent which is already very high, being dearer than any other in the townland. It was also worse than any other in the townland, till we improved it. Even if it be worth more I cannot but consider it a grievous wrong, and a great hardship, to be charged rent for the additional value I've given it, at so much labour and expense.

Before finally coming to the point of his letter: 'Therefore I find and your Lordship may see, that I cannot pay one shilling advance on the present rent which is already too much'.

And concluding on a note of humble supplication and expectation:

> I hope that your Lordship will, with your usual indulgence, and paternal consideration and kindness to your tenants, remove this menacing oppression.
>
> Hopefully awaiting your Lordship's reply, and wishing your Lordship many happy and prosperous years over us; with the greatest possible confidence. I have the honor, my Lord, to subscribe myself your Lordship's very humble and most obedient servant.

Having signed off 'Peter Reilly Cortobber Kingscourt', the author adds as a P.S. an apology for the length of his statement [four pages] but states that he could not give 'a satisfactory explanation of his case in fewer words'.

COMMONALITIES

Certain common themes emerge from the letters of McCann and Reilly: Both appeal to their ancestral connection with the land that their forefathers farmed. Both insist that whatever about supposed rising farm prices, increased costs and other encumbrances would make it financially unviable to stay farming in the face of projected rent increases. Both also make reference to the liability of poor unproductive land.

McCann and Reilly each reveal a saving grace that has allowed them to stay in farming despite excessive rents: in the case of the former his use of a nearby productive farm (leased by his father-in-law) on another landlord's estate, and in the case of the latter an annuity paid to his mother. Both appeal in the time-honoured deferential fashion to the supposed good qualities of their landlord, assuring him of their loyalty. Nonetheless, for all their *plamás*-ing and protestations of loyalty, both tenants insist that, when it comes to the demand for increased rent, they can't pay. McCann is much more strident in tone however – not only can he not pay, he will not pay!

McCann also has an extra weapon in his armoury of arguments – the employment of a form of moral blackmail against his Catholic landlord, with the threat of the scandal Gormanston would create should he destroy his tenants with ruinous tents. Reilly, on the other hand, employs his own brand of guilt-inducing moral blackmail by painting the alternative scenario of himself and his aged mother being forced from farming into some other occupation – even into emigration. A largely rhetorical device to be sure, but nonetheless effective.

The one theme common to all petitioners was the appeal to ancestral claims. Richard Fagan recalled his 'forefathers who always punctually paid their rents';[19] Owen Sullivan his 'Father and Grandfather [who] lived under you for the last 100 years'; John Yore his 'ancestors' who had enjoyed their land for 'centuries'; Laurence Reilly the role of his uncle, father and grandfather. Like middle-aged Peter Reilly with his aged mother, several petitioners naturally enough mentioned personal family circumstances in the course of explaining their case: Fagan had 'a young helpless family to support'; Sullivan was 'an old man now' with 'a large family'; Yore likewise had 'a large family to support'.

Several petitioners thought it worth their while to put Gormanston in the picture regarding the recent (and not so recent) history of their farms. Sullivan recalled how five families had lived on his land previously and 'left it wild, fit to give nothing', and some with between five and seven years in arrears with rent. Laurence Reilly described how four of his uncles had worked so industriously to reclaim bad land – 'made an immense dale of drains, made ditches, scoured gripes and raised stones' – that they had all died prematurely from the severity of their labours. Owen Farrelly recalled that his grandfather Philip Farrelly had been born at Whitewood in 1713. A granddaughter of Philip's (and cousin of Owen's) who had inherited the farm from her brother had married out thus denying Owen's brother Philip his rightful inheritance. His cousin had taken her new husband into the house; the farm had subsequently gone to rack and ruin, acquiring heavy arrears in the process. In 1870 John Gearty had described how his father had purchased – and permanently improved – 1 acre of land from one of eight labourers at Whitewood, each of whom had been granted 7 acres of land by Gormanston's ancestors. On the strength of this, Gearty was now seeking to acquire the other 6 acres of this allotment, currently leased by a farmer residing on a neighbouring estate.

Petitioners liked to emphasise the improvements they had effected on their leases. As noted previously, Laurence Reilly wrote of the massive amount of work carried out by his uncles on land reclamation. Likewise, John Gearty made reference to the lasting improvements undertaken by his father since 're-built and improved' further by himself.[20] They were also at pains to explain the complexities and peculiarities of their own tenancies, comparing and contrasting different plots of land, distinguishing not only between different townlands but between locations within the one townland. Laurence Reilly, for example, observed that his dwelling house at Muff was situated in the northern and coldest part of that townland. Similarly, Owen Farrelly noted that his farm occupied the worst part of the townland of Muff, being situated on the northern side which was colder than the south (or sunny) side.[21] He acknowledged that he could afford a high rent for his good land in the neighbouring townland of Spiddal, but not so for Muff.

The petitioners have this in common: they all insist they cannot afford the rent increase demanded by Gormanston. Furthermore, they contend that the current rent they are paying is excessive when measured against Griffith's Valuation, especially when much of the land could be regarded as poor land in the first place. All conclude nonetheless by paying customary respects to their landlord.

SURVIVORS

Unfortunately, we do not know the outcome of these appeals since Gormanston's replies are not recorded. It seems likely however that most if not all were granted abatements. In the cases of McCann and Reilly, we know that both survived whatever financial difficulties confronted them in 1874. McCanns are recorded in the 1901 and 1911 censuses as occupying a substantial farmhouse at Cortobber. Indeed, Edward McCann, a bachelor, was still farming here as recently as the late 1930s.[22] Reillys likewise are recorded at Cortobber in both 1901 and 1911; they too occupied their small farm as recently as the late 1930s.[23] Of the other petitioners, Sullivans, Reillys (Laurence) and Fagans were still recorded at their townland addresses in 1911.[24] Farrellys, Yores and McEvoys had gone by 1901.[25] So, altogether, of the eight petitioners in 1874, five appear to have survived on their farms until 1901. Of the other three, it is difficult to conclude whether or not their leaving resulted from financial problems.

In the case of the Farrellys and the Yores there is little or no evidence to go on. For the McEvoys (easily the most substantial landholders included in our case studies), it is unlikely that financial difficulties alone dictated the outcome. In 1867 rent had been paid in full and 'no arrears' recorded for the McEvoy tenancies.[26] When John McEvoy of Muff, who had appealed for an abatement in 1874, died in 1881, his land had been divided between his sons Philip and Dr James McEvoy.[27] In that same year Gladstone's Second Land Act had established, along with a Land Commission, judicial rent courts which allowed tenants apply for a binding legal ruling as to the amount of rent to be paid. In the first year of its application (1882) this procedure resulted in tenant applicants having their rents reduced by an average of 20 per cent. The land courts had the power to fix rents for fifteen years and effectively removed the landlords' rights to fix the rent payable.

In 1888 the McEvoy brothers had each applied to the judicial rents court for an abatement. This suggests that, whatever about the success or otherwise of their father's application fourteen years earlier – and other applications in the interregnum – the brothers were unhappy with Gormanston's latest response. Dr McEvoy was successful in his appeal to the court – obtaining a substantial abatement – but Philip McEvoy was not.[28] Whatever about the circumstances, both brothers nonetheless surrendered their tenancies within the next decade or so. By 1901 there were no McEvoys whatsoever at Muff. Dr McEvoy is recorded in Nobber village (of which Gormanston was also the landlord) practising as a medical doctor. There is, however, no record of his brother Philip or any other siblings in the locality.[29]

Interestingly, a third brother, Laurence McEvoy, had emigrated to Mexico some years previously. A letter dated 1894 from Laurence to his sister Kate back home in Ireland survives.[30] This suggests that McEvoys were still living in Muff up until then at least. As well as revealing the author's nationalistic opinions with regard to Ireland and British politics, the letter provides an interesting insight into one Irishman's perceptions – somewhat jaundiced as they are – of the people and culture of his adopted land.[31] The existence of a doctor in the family and the fact that another brother was established in business overseas suggests that it may have profited the McEvoys to surrender their long-standing tenancies at Muff and adjoining townlands when careers in the professions or commerce seemed more attractive than farming.

In at least one case, and quite possibly as many as three, the direct descendants of the eight petitioners mentioned at the outset are still resident in 2015 at their 1874 townland addresses. We can state conclusively that the Sullivans of Cloughreagh have farmed their land continuously from at least the mid-1800s.[32] And it seems likely that the Reillys of Rathgillan and the Fagans of Nobber (the Cregg Road) are descendants of petitioners. In the eventuality only a limited number of evictions for rent arrears were enforced on the Nobber estate during the severe economic recession/mini-Famine of 1879–80. Seven actual evictions (five at Cloughrea) are recorded with another eight tenants recorded as 'to be evicted'. With the exception of one tenant who surrendered his property prior to eviction, the arrears involved substantial sums of money. None of the 1874 petitioners were amongst those evicted or listed for eviction in 1879–80.[33]

Both the Gormanston Nobber estate and the neighbouring Bligh estate at Brittas – one with a Catholic and the other with a Protestant landlord – would seem to have been characterised by a relative degree of stability during this period; that is to say, there were very few evictions and there was a recognisable continuity of tenantry. The Brittas estate did show a marked increase in arrears with the agricultural recession beginning in 1874: £51 in 1874, £91 in 1875,

£204 in 1876, £528 in 1879.[34] There were nevertheless very few evictions, even fewer it would seem than on the Gormanston estate. Indeed, the rental rolls for the Brittas estate reveal a remarkable degree of stability of tenantry for the century from 1822 until 1931.[35]

One only has to look north to the neighbouring Shirley estate in County Monaghan for evidence of the effect of the agricultural recession on tenant farmers. A tenant right meeting was held at Carrickmacross on 4 June 1874, a Farney Tenants' Defence Association having been founded the previous month.[36] Although no such counterpart organisation existed in Meath until at least 1875, the elements of commonality in the letters of tenant farmers to Gormanston remarked upon earlier do suggest at the very least a degree of collusion and informal association. Farmers from north Meath and south Monaghan would have been meeting and socialising at fairs in Kingscourt and Carrickmacross. They recognised their common interests and banded together in an expression of collective solidarity. What is noticeable in the case of our eight petitioners is the apparent transcendence of class difference within the ranks of tenant farmers. Large, middling and small tenant farmers acted in concert.

CONCLUSION

This study has illustrated the value of using one historical source (the evidence of John Balfe to the Devon Commission in 1844) to complement another (the Gormanston estate papers) and thus provide a wider context for the subject under discussion. It is clear from Balfe's evidence that parts of the Nobber estate had a 'history of trouble'. Balfe himself had blamed the system of tenure that had developed in the 1820s for the problems of the 1840s, and compared it unfavourably with the system prevailing in the neighbouring estates of Bligh (Brittas) and the Revd Taylor.[37] It is not too much to suggest that the events of the 1870s might be explained, at least in part, as a legacy of the 1840s and by ongoing systemic failures on at least one of Lord Gormanston's estates.

Two of the petitioners in our study, Thomas McCann and Peter Reilly, compared their current rents in 1874 and how much they were now being asked to pay, with the rental value set down in Griffith's Valuation some twenty years previously. This was a tactic commonly used by tenant farmers during the Land War. McCann was paying £100 5s rent per annum, an increase of 40 per cent on Griffith's Valuation, and was now being asked to pay £137 8s, an overall increase of 92 per cent. Reilly fared nearly as badly. In 1874 his annual rent of £16 represented a 33-per-cent increase over Griffith's Valuation, and his landlord was now seeking £20 4s, an overall increase of 72 per cent.[38]

It is true that, compared to landlords, tenant farmers had benefited disproportionately from the economic prosperity of the decades immediately following the Great Famine. Increases in agricultural income averaged 40 per cent between the early 1850s and the late 1870s and exceeded increases in rent that averaged only between 20 and 30 per cent.[39] As we have seen, however, the rent increases being sought by Gormanston in the cases of McCann and Reilly well exceeded the approximately 40-per-cent increase on Griffith's Valuation that would have been needed to match increases in agricultural income. We do not know exactly by how much McCann's and Reilly's personal incomes increased during this period. Nonetheless, the figures presented in these cases – when set against national averages – would suggest that their current rents were about right and that the higher rents being demanded were well above those justified by any rise in prices. It would be true to say that Gormanston was effectively punishing his tenants for having improved their farms between 1850 and 1874.

The letters of petition have given us an insight into the economic situation of the tenant farmers on the Nobber estate in 1874. We have also been given some insight into their self-perceptions as to their relationship both to the land itself and to their landlord. More than that, we have been afforded some insight into the social and economic conditions prevailing in Ireland at the outset of the 'Long Depression' in the lead-up to the formation of the Land League in 1879 and the mini-Famine of 1879–80, all within the wider context of the ongoing 'Land War'.

The letters reveal something of the individuality of the authors while at the same time highlighting common concerns and attitudes. Ancestral connection to the land was most apparent. Moreover, this study of a small number of tenant farmers in a small number of townlands on the Nobber estate has served as a microcosm of the situation throughout north Meath and the county as a whole in the mid-1870s.

More than mere lists and statistics, the letters have given us an insight into the human side of the story of landlord/agent/tenant relations. They have given the tenant farmers a voice, and allowed us to hear that voice. At the same time, it must also be recognised that this is an exclusively male voice. And, while it is indeed a voice from below, it is not a voice from the bottom. It was after all the voice of those who were literate and those who had land in the first place. Other groups and classes in society – notably the landless agricultural labourer (not to mention his wife) – remain voiceless. For all that, it should be clear that estate records – properly utilised – can serve as an invaluable tool in researching the economic and social history of a given locality and, indeed, by extension, of the county and country as a whole.

John Sweetman and the Irish Land Question, 1879–81

BRIAN CASEY

INTRODUCTION

> It is ... indisputable that the last quarter of the nineteenth century was
> a period of agricultural crisis ... more numerous bankruptcies, lower
> rents and untenanted farms.[1]

> It is proposed to diffuse useful information on the Irish land question
> by public meetings, instructive pamphlets, and the establishment of
> numerous farmers clubs throughout the country.[2]

The Great Famine of 1845–1850 acted as a Darwinian agent in
removing weak links in the class system in Ireland. While horrendous
numbers of dead and departed are obvious consequences of it, another
important change was how the entire system of landholding and
ownership had changed. There was a change in the landscape with the
disappearance of the despised middleman, the cottier class had essential
been wiped out and the rundale system of farming was no more. There
was extensive subdivision of holdings and landlords faced responsibilities to meet Poor Law rates for tenants with valuations under £4.
This saw the landlord class' numbers depleted as they could not sustain
their estates or support impoverished tenants that could not pay their

rents because of the havoc of their destitution. Clearances and assisted-emigration programmes took place on numerous estates, which helped secure the idea of 'bastard landlordism' remaining resolute in the Irish psyche. Those who went bankrupt generally saw their estates enter the Encumbered Estates Courts, bought by neighbours seeking to expand what they had or by investors that made their money from trade, keen to find a new way to expand their fortune and join the ranks of respectability that land brought.

Post-Famine Ireland saw an unprecedented period of prosperity for the country as many now had a better life and the vicissitudes of modernisation meant that monetary income had become more important to maintain and sustain a certain standard of living. At the eve of the Land War, 1879–82, small farmers had become dependent upon a level of purchasing power beyond their means and, with sources of credit diminishing, they needed to borrow more. This presented problems for shopkeepers and other members of the middle classes who were now reliant upon the farming classes for survival, and resulted in them being forced to begin calling in credit because their own resources were diminishing in this vicious circle as the urban/rural alliance became more obviously desperate.[3]

The birth of the Irish National Land League in October 1879 followed a lengthy period of economic and social crises that began with the Long Depression of 1874. This economic malaise had its origins in North America and reached a crescendo in Ireland in 1877 following a series of poor harvests and the utter collapse of the potato crop from a yield of over 4 tons an acre in 1876 to 1.6 tons an acre in 1879.[4] The Land League was an all-embracing and evocative movement that soon demanded fair rent, fixity of tenure and freedom of sale (three Fs) from the British government. The mass mobilisation of tenants had been discussed for a number of years prior to this as a plethora of tenant defence associations and farmers clubs were established as a response to the 1870 Land Act, which is discussed in further detail below. As the Land League grew into this supra-national organisation, these clubs and associations disappeared or merged with the league, which became Europe's largest mass peasant movement in the nineteenth century. It was generally a disciplined and highly effective organisation, with all the farming classes and urban tenants such as shopkeepers, tradesmen, publicans, teachers and journalists becoming involved as part of the 'challenging collectivity'.[5] Its success could be measured by the extra-legal prosecutorial courts and power of the crowd in asserting control over tenants in areas where it was particularly strong. Its erudite local leaders politicised the countryside by using the land question as the conduit to involve as many as possible and also to include people not previously active in prior mass political movements. While it was key to the League's success, its very nature meant that the differing views on the land question would struggle to find a middle ground because of the varied interpretations that leaders in each province had. In the west, the system of landholding saw a real social malaise reaching crisis proportions. Western Fenians were aware that armed insurrection would not succeed and they now focused their attention to the material conditions of the poorest farmers. 'The manner in which the tenant movement translated for the first time in Irish history, an economic crisis for the peasantry of the west into a political problem for the government, marks a major milestone on the road to modernisation.'[6]

Generally, the post-Famine period was one of economic prosperity with a myriad of agricultural statistics reflecting this. However, as Virginia Crossman has recently shown, this did not trickle down with utter destitution being only one bad harvest away for many.[7] While there was a very positive state of affairs by 1876, there was a noticeably poor harvest in 1877, followed by a partial recovery in 1878 but a total failure in 1879 that ran the risk of a repeat of the Great Famine of 1845–50. Heavy rain in March and April 1877 saw record low yields and the insipid response of landlords often saw tenant frustrations spill over into violence against landlords, land agents, bailiffs, process servers and grabbers, which resulted in stern response from the government.[8] It also saw the revival of the mass meeting as ambiguous rhetoric, with violent metaphors, was used to great effect.[9] Despite the disasters presented by the Famine because of the over-dependence upon the potato, along with the Poor Law and Devon Commission all remarking on this and the challenges presented by rudimentary farming methods, nothing was done to diversify farming either by landlords or government, as tenants were content with subsistence and the ambiguous protection that they could claim was problematic. Furthermore, tenants were genuinely unable to make improvements due to a lack of significant spare capital that was necessary to invest, ignorance of the necessity of investment and lack of security of tenure. Jonathan Bell and Mervyn Watson also argued that these farming techniques were adequate for farmers as they were only interested in subsistence, fearing the penalties that would be imposed if they improved.[10]

There had been discussions on land reform since at least the 1830s with James Fintan Lalor and William Conner being two of the best-known writers on it and the pre-Famine Devon Commission calling for comprehensive reform, but nothing happened as the blight arrived just as the commission delivered its report. The land question had moved onto another plane by the 1870s as the provincial press offered a new public space for those ideas to be aired and refined and expressed to a much wider audience than previously. While there was a genuine appreciation of the complications surrounding land reform, it was distilled into the ambiguous, simple and evocative rallying call, 'the land for the people' as efforts were made to find some sort of resolution with politicians, political theorists, economists and grassroots social radicals all actively engaged in efforts to find a satisfactory solution to an inherently compli-cated and vexing question. However, who 'the people' actually were remained deliberately vague. It eventually seemed to mean the middling sort of farmer to the detriment of small farmers and labourers who were not part of the imagined community of sturdy peasants that eventually made up the Irish nation.[11] The subject of this article, John Sweetman, was a moderate voice in the call for land reform, which was tempered by his Catholicism and the fact that he was also a progressive landlord. This article also shows the utility of using biography to explore contem-porary issues and how individuals formulated their ideas in various fora.

JOHN SWEETMAN AND THE IRISH LAND QUESTION

John Sweetman was born in 1844 and has been described as a 'religious man with considerable energy' who enjoyed reading leading Catholic journals, possibly to compensate for his lack of a university education. His autodidactic nature also saw him develop an interest in agricul-tural matters and he was elected a member of the Royal Agricultural Society in November 1877. He was an astute and progressive landlord, having received generous praise from tenants because of his effective estate management. One tenant, Thomas Tadham, had written a salutary letter to the *Freeman's Journal* to state that his landlord granted 35-per-cent abatements on all holdings, gave tenants perpetual leases on their farms and oversaw the construction of good-quality houses for labourers on the estate. Other progressive landlords such as the 3rd Earl of Clancarty and Henry Villiers Stuart also did this. Good-quality housing was seen to be an important element of the moral rehabilitation of the 'deserving poor' that dominated debate in the Victorian and Edwardian period. Having such quality housing would allow a placid and amenable tenantry to remain.[12] Tadham expressed the gratitude of tenants to Sweetman for his foresight, and said that if other landlords adopted similar plans then the ongoing crisis could have been abated. He was concerned with landlord zeal in transforming arable land into grassland in order to make a quick profit to the detriment of farmers.[13] He took over the management of the Drumbaragh estate from his mother in the 1870s and began proposing the notion of federation of farmers clubs being established across Ireland. 'Long before Davitt's Land League was conceived, Sweetman wrote that the land would never be properly cultivated until the farmers had security'.[14]

The Victorian period saw a general move towards grazing in Britain and Ireland as heavily indebted landlords had to deal with numerous charges to manage their estates and they struggled to sustain them.[15] Their failure to increase rents generally during the post-Famine period saw them struggle to sustain their extravagant lifestyles. Grazing offered a way of easing debt because it was highly profitable with minimal investment required. Sweetman was part of an inchoate group of individuals that emerged in the 1870s and demanded reforms of the land-tenure system in Ireland; their requests for land reform were ignored prior to the emergence of the Land League in 1879. While there had been sustained discussion on the need for land reform throughout the nineteenth century, this reached a crescendo in the 1870s as more attention was now being paid to the issues of land tenure and reform of the land laws. There were diverging opinions on how this was to be achieved: western neo-Fenians demanded wholesale reform and the breaking up of large farms with land redistributed accordingly in order to alleviate poverty in the west, while eastern farmers were more conservative in how they wanted to achieve reform. Both the Devon Commission and the Famine showed that 'Irish rural poverty and low agricultural productivity were primarily the result of an oppressive land system'.[16] However, for the purposes of this article, attention will be limited to Sweetman's ideas.

Sweetman attended a tenant-right meeting that was held in the Rotunda in Dublin in April 1873. Those in attendance were keen for some form of remedial legislation to be brought in, because they felt landlords were working against the spirit of the 1870 Land Act by exploiting its loopholes and forcing tenants into new agreements.[17] This meeting also saw a secret agreement reached between Fenians and MPs to support Butt's movement for three years and was the birth of the 'New Departure'.[18] The Act failed to attain the objectives its framers hoped it would accomplish. However, despite its limitations, it was the first effort of the British government to interfere with private property, which left the purists aghast. Terence Dooley has recently shown how the 1870 Land Act caused great consternation amongst the propertied classes. It was anathema to traditionalists as it forced tenants to accept more restrictive leases and forgo claims for compensation. The most notorious example was that of the Leinster Lease, on the Duke of Leinster's estate.[19] It was an important precursor to much more comprehensive legislation that helped to expedite the decline of landlordism in Ireland through a series of Land Acts in 1881, 1885, 1890, 1903 and 1909. Traditionalist landlords saw it as an affront to the concept of private property. 'Although landlords had already suffered a series of electoral and psychological setbacks in the 1870s, they were still powerful, wealthy and prepared to fight.'[20] Following this meeting, Sweetman became an articulate but much-ignored figure regarding the land question during the 1870s and 1880s.

Negative contemporary portrayals of landlords as being bumbling incompetents who were more interested in drinking and shooting than in working abounded. For every landlord who fitted this stereotype, there was one who went against it, with Sweetman being one of the latter. A shrewd, serious and responsible landlord, he happily embraced the sense of duty of such landlords who prevented large numbers of tenants slipping into utter destitution, though efforts to raise them out of poverty were limited. John Bright had earlier suggested that peasant proprietorship was the best system for survival, and that the new landowners who emerged because of the Encumbered Estates Courts embittered the agrarian struggle because they failed to invest and improve standards and did not have the same sentimental attachment to land this irked farmers.[21] Those who bought estates under the Encumbered Estates Court frequently cleared and consolidated uneconomic holdings and created large grazing tracts: this left people aggrieved, especially in the west as they believed that the very best land was being taken up for grazing, which was much more profitable and less labour-intensive.

The economist, MP and philosopher John Stuart Mill wrote extensively on Irish land and was an obvious influence in Sweetman's train of thought. His writings were influential for numerous writers on the Irish land question in the 1870s. Mill was one of the great intellectual radicals of the mid-Victorian period and sincerely believed his political ideas could have a direct impact on political affairs.[22] These writings certainly provided a coherency for the ideas of grassroots social radicals looking for land reform in the 1870s, and his thoughts influenced their speeches and writings.

Despite being a landlord himself, Sweetman was critical of Irish landlords, arguing that many were feudal in their outlook to the neglect of their tenantry. Their arrogant assertiveness caused tenants to air their grievances at public meetings under the banner of tenant defence associations, farmers clubs and, later, the Land League. Sweetman was amenable to public opinion taking this forum, as, coupled with a sympathetic provincial press, it formed a profoundly powerful public sphere in late-Victorian provincial Ireland. In a circular addressed to the Irish National Land League from 21 October 1879, Sweetman suggested that: 'Tenant Defence Associations must be organised in every county and assistance be rendered to farmers who may be called upon to defend themselves against an unjust or capricious exercise of landlord power'.[23] His later political career made it evident that Sweetman was aware of the power afforded by popular liberalism and the march of democracy as the landlord/aristocratic nexus began to lose influence.

Despite the sincerity of his ideas and writings, Sweetman was generally treated with a degree of condescension by politicians as he failed to have his ideas, such as the Land Purchase Company, taken seriously. Furthermore, his efforts at establishing a Catholic colony in Minnesota did not take off because of a lack of political support. There seems to be a certain political naiveté in his thought process and the evidence suggests that he did not appreciate the magnitude of the burgeoning movement, partially because he was dislocated from the Home Rule Party and he tried to change its direction in order to temper its radicalism, as he believed that peasant proprietorship was too much to be demanding from a landlord parliament.

The land question was a vexed one that remained incongruous to political leaders in the four nations of Great Britain and Ireland. David Howell, Paul Readman, Jeremy Burchardt, Keith Snell and Ewen Cameron have all explored how utterly challenging and divisive the land question was in England, Scotland and Wales. W.E.Vaughan, Philip Bull, Terence Dooley, Barbara Solow and this author have examined the Irish dimension from a variety of perspectives. Security of tenure, according to Sweetman, was crucial to the prosperity of Ireland and solid legislation without causing 'pecuniary loss to landlords as the land will never be properly cultivated until farmers have security of tenure, and the people will never be contented until they have some stake in the country'.[24] Sweetman believed that 'it is absurd to expect farmers to cultivate the land as it should be or to have a manly feeling of independence unless they are free from the fear both of arbitrary eviction and of having their rents raised'. Because land tenure was such a complex issue, Sweetman wanted to dedicate himself 'to the task of endeavouring to obtain a change in the present system of landlordism'. Landlords needed to be re-educated in how to behave regarding their responsibilities, and it was important to remove the power of arbitrary eviction, which could be carried out by calling in the hanging gale, a common form of estate control useful in effectively suppressing dissent.

The trauma of the Famine left Ireland with a rather weak political class. No one had been groomed to succeed Daniel O'Connell and there was a vacuum following his death. The Independent Irish Party that emerged in the 1850s was an ineffectual body and it was not until the emergence of the Home Government Association and Isaac Butt that something resembling a coherent political force formed in post-Famine Ireland. Some members of the Catholic clergy were circumspect about supporting the Home Government Association because of the sizeable Protestant presence in it.[25] The Meath by-election of 1871 showed how cooperation between Catholics and Protestants could become a vital cog in the campaign for legislative autonomy if it was correctly utilised. John Martin, a Presbyterian and former Young Irelander, was returned, and this buoyed the Home Rule movement, but the calling of an election in 1874 caught them off guard.[26] His faction in the House of Commons primarily focused their attention upon Home Rule. Despite this, there was a tacit awareness that land would dominate future hustings, so they began drawing up a land bill to fix the defects of Gladstone's solo effort – the 1870 Land Act. The fragmented and incoherent motley of MPs and the emergence of the precarious Parnell/O'Connor Power nexus meant that this bill, while unlikely to ever be passed, could barely pass muster within the Irish Parliamentary Party. Both O'Connor

Power and Parnell wanted to take Irish representation in a different direction and remove the carpetbaggers that jumped on the Home Rule bandwagon. Butt's credibility as leader was further challenged when he failed to get any reasonable support from members of the Central Tenant Defence Association. This association proposed various changes to Butt's thoughtful land bill and this reflected either their inability or their refusal to respect his excellent legal skills. The defeat of this amendment damaged Butt's credibility and ability to lead the Irish faction in the House of Commons.[27] Butt was a man for the large questions and his background as a northern Tory limited his ability to bring the party any further. While the land question was now seen to be the engine to drive Home Rule, the question remained as to who would be the driver. The answer was soon apparent as Parnell became the supreme figure in the movement, though he had 'hesitated about peasant proprietorship because he feared that Westminster might feel less disposed to grant Home Rule to a people who had emasculated the political power of the aristocracy'.[28] Following the election of William Gladstone as prime minister and the success of the Irish Parliamentary Party, Parnell's position was greatly strengthened. A land conference was held that April, the Land League was spreading and economic decline was intensifying, and all this led to a more formidable phase of the agitation. The land conference advocated a more radical programme for the Land League to adopt, calling for the suspension of evictions for two years for anyone who held a farm worth £10 or less.[29]

Prior to Parnell's assent as leader of the Irish Parliamentary Party, Sweetman penned a letter to the *Freeman's Journal* in which he expressed concerns that the private disputes between Butt and O'Connor Power were detrimental to the well-being of farmers. The perilous state of the agricultural economy and the infighting within the Irish Parliamentary Party were an unnecessary distraction for political gains, and he was concerned that this *imbroglio* meant that the importance of the land question was lost on its members. The attention of Irish MPs was on Home Rule as the major issue, but the reality was much different in provincial Ireland, and Sweetman was keenly aware of this. The emergence of tenant defence associations and his correspondence with various members was indicative of this new political milieu emerging. He correctly asserted that there would be a new land act within the next five years, and that there was a need for farmers 'to make a strenuous effort to obtain their rights' by using their vote to return members who would campaign in the House of Commons for land reform. David Thornley argued that Butt struggled to enforce his personal authority upon the party. He lacked moral courage or the necessary ruthlessness that Parnell certainly had.[30] Sweetman exchanged ideas with Thomas Robertson, a grazier, member of the Central Tenant Defence Association and divisive commentator on the land question, from Athy, on various aspects of the land question through the pages of the *Freeman's Journal*. In this exchange, both came to the consensus that the land question was of secondary importance to Home Rule for MPs. Sweetman also saw organisation as key in effecting beneficial change for tenant farmers, and he advocated the formation of a central tenant right club in Dublin where all other organisations could come together because 'the trade unions in England show us the strength of union and the present state of the Irish party shows the weakness caused by the want of it'.[31]

The inherent flaw in the land system that retarded prosperity, according to Sweetman, was the presence of a small-farmer class that could not sustain themselves adequately on their holdings. This flew in the face of arguments put forward by western radicals, who were of the opinion that the nefarious graziers and their lust for land and respectability were limiting the development and prosperity of the country. This highlighted the entrenched complexities of the various issues that went beyond the evocative rallying call, 'the land for the people' that succeeded in giving a coherency to an otherwise haphazard farming polity. The emergence of tenant defence associations and farmers clubs in the 1870s reflected the obvious dissatisfaction with the 1870 Land Act. In February 1878, Sweetman made an effort to get these unaffiliated groups to unite in order to present a more coherent front in efforts to achieve legislative reform.[32] He failed to appreciate the disparate voices that existed within the land movement and were becoming more pronounced. While the vast majority of them were of the one opinion in presenting a united voice in arguing for improved conditions, the radical, left-leaning Ballinasloe Tenant Defence Association rallied strongly against unity of action, fearing the consequences for small farmers. Despite this obvious dichotomy owing to the issue of class, Matt Harris sent the rules of the Ballinasloe association to Sweetman in September 1878 as Sweetman attempted to get them all to work together as allies were scarce for tenant righters in parliament.[33] He was encouraged by the establishment of the Meath Tenant Defence Association that sought to revive the spirit of previous gatherings and 'to foster a sound public opinion in favour of the tenant classes throughout the county, and in the cases of individual hardship from landlord injustice and oppression to bring public opinion to bear on the oppressors' and to confront the evils of insecurity of tenure while building a great farmers' union for all of Ireland.[34] At the same time that Davitt addressed the crowds in Irishtown at the first meeting of the Land League in April 1879, Sweetman called for an Irish farmers' union. This was welcomed by the *Weekly Northern Whig*, which said: 'every well-wisher of the Irish farmer should at this moment, encourage the adoption of a scheme fitted to promote union and enthusiasm'.[35] Elections were now seen to be an important element of the farmers' armory and their ability to use it needed to be overseen if they wanted to ensure success and achieve justice. However, the only way they were going to get success was by working for it 'and All Ireland [is] uttering a unanimous voice in the hope' that legislation would be enacted.[36]

To counteract the rising influence of the grazier as a competitor for land, western radical Matt Harris suggested limiting tenant right to smaller farmers, arguing that universal tenant right would only benefit the stronger farmers. To him graziers were 'a class of men who are more exacting and avaricious than the landlords themselves and who, in the course of time, would become more cruel and tyrannical than the landlords are or ever have been'.[37] They saw themselves as part of a new elite that was emerging in the countryside and they did not have the same sentimental attachment to the land as other landlords may have had, and as David Seth-Jones argued, they treated land and cattle in the same vein, in that the only purpose both served was to make money. Harris' utter contempt for the graziers and his desire to exclude them from land-reform legislation saw him being accused of begrudging farmer prosperity. Kerry also had to deal with the vexed issue of graziers with Thomas O'Rourke, secretary of the Kerry Tenant Defence Association, informing John Sweetman that they were like vampires sucking 'on the life blood of the nation and whose sole ambition is to turn this old and fertile land into a huge bullock walk' and they only engaged in the poltical process out of self-interest.[38]

Such restrictive proposals were a clear threat to graziers who saw: 'fixity of tenure is an absolute quantity, and we can see no possible reason for attempting to make it the exclusive prerogative of a section of the agricultural community'.[39] Such a disagreement reflected the chasm between the radical and moderate wings of the nascent land movement, and how its western members dominated its early ideology. Thomas Robertson, a grazier from Athy, County Kildare and member of the Central Tenant Defence Association, blamed landlords for the shift towards grazing and 'the proof that he is unable is to be had in almost every large holding throughout the country'.[40] He correctly asserted that the eleven-month grazing system left larger farmers as vulnerable as their smaller counterparts, and he exchanged letters with Sweetman on this over the pages of the *Freeman's Journal*.[41]

The establishment of an association to help tenant farmers to negotiate with landlords on more equal terms in the law courts had failed previously, therefore the necessity of a farmers' union was becoming more prevalent with the deteriorating economic circum-stances. The responses of landlords during this crisis and their general aloofness from their tenants did not help their case and attracted a great deal of hostility. Many still thought in pre-Famine terms, in that poverty meant absolutely nothing: tenants had an obligation to pay their rents (which many had no issue with) and they should sell possessions to meet their obligations. This attitude grated most profoundly with the strong farmers who believed that if they were expected to reduce certain aspects of their lifestyle to meet rent, then rents could be reduced as well.[42] The *Weekly Northern Whig* reflected some of the opinions held by Sweetman, saying that farmers should not be afraid of uniting because no landlord would dream of evicting a farmer for joining a union, 'for the indignation of public opinion would be such that the power of the landlord would not last much longer'.[43] However, what played out during the Land War certainly challenged this belief.

The geographical spread of tenant defence associations and farmers clubs is indicative of the level of interest there was in land prior to the Land War, with branches existing in each province and thirty-one recorded in the Sweetman papers, held in the NLI. While the 1870 Land Act was part of Gladstone's mission at pacifying Ireland, it didn't go nearly close enough and the Land War forced their hand. However, the virulence of the agitation caught everyone by surprise.

Sweetman joined the Irish Liberal Club in 1878 and identified himself an advanced Irish liberal who was in favour of religious equality and denominational education. In preparation for the next general election, he contended that only those who were sincere in their quest to achieve land reform should be elected. It is during this period that we see more vocal criticisms of MPs taking place, as they were held up to public scrutiny in a much more obvious way.[44] Sweetman could be misguided in his writings and hope to influence the direction of the land movement. One critical example was his failed efforts at progressing the Tenant's Central Association, which was established to counter the Land League. He was eager for it to take a central role in the movement by 1880 despite the resolute control that the Land League now had. Along with Maurice Butterly and A.J. Kettle, he had hoped it could play a role in selecting candidates for the 1880 general election. However, there was confusion regarding the circular sent out by Sweetman as Butterly and Kettle were both of the opinion that it had been issued as Butterly remarked to Sweetman in a previous letter on 20 March 1880, that he believed it had merged with the Land League. Previous meetings saw poor turnouts and the circular drafted by Kettle was problematic for Butterly, who was in disagreement with Kettle on several aspects. While he believed that the association had merged with the Land League, he was not certain as he was not present at the previous meeting. Although it was suggested a subsequent meeting be held to ascertain what happened, this was never called and the association disappeared without a whimper afterwards.

CONCLUSION

Irish historiography has rehabilitated the lot of landlords since the 1970s as vast swathes of empirical evidence debunks contemporary assertions that they were heartless, capricious evictors. However, as L.P. Curtis has recently argued on several occasions, it fails to appreciate the fact that the threat of eviction was something that landlords could and did use to assert control over a potentially wayward tenantry.[45] Furthermore, Ann Andrews has recently illustrated how the Repeal press, particularly *The Nation*, played a role in stirring anti-landlord animus in the early 1840s. Those that survived the Famine and participated in the Land War were survivors and remembered this vitriol that was used to great effect during the Land War.[46] The Land League became Europe's largest peasant movement in the nineteenth century and its success was down to its numerous grassroots leaders who politicised poverty and appealed to an increasingly educated and politically aware farming class. This also gave a powerful coherency to their disaffection. However, it was tempered by the rising confidence of the Catholic middle classes that exploited the poverty of the smaller farmers in order to further their own aims. While the Land League initially represented the interests and challenges presented to small farmers in the west of Ireland, their interests were soon superseded by strong farmers in Leinster and Munster and this became the dominant narrative of the Land League in terms of both its direction and later historiography. The demands of larger farmers won out in the end, partially because they were so forceful in their demands for unity of action.[47] Sweetman believed that the historicist nature of some of the speeches was overstated. 'I grant that something must be allowed for national antipathies, owing to past grievances, wrongs, but this cause has, I think, been vastly exaggerated.' Some of the Catholic middle-class leaders cited notions of confiscation in previous milieus in order to justify the egregious nature of the country in 1879 and their actions.[48]

Sweetman was a moderate and was not keen on any reform that could be construed to be radical or socialistic. Proper infrastructural investment was seen to be key for improvement while also securing tenure. This was the panacea for Ireland because 'everyone that knows Ireland is aware that for the most part the land is wretchedly cultivated'. Tenants were depending upon the goodwill of the landlord and this was risky because the landlord had ultimate control over the tenant, and this inflamed animosity which in turn saw an intense hatred of England emerging.[49]

Sweetman was very suspicious of the Land League. He thought the radical elements within it were going to spread disorder across the countryside. The Land League had succeeded in undermining elite culture and this dissension from what was the acceptable order that had existed heretofore was seen to be a real threat to the stability of the countryside. However, what the Land League offered was an alternative sphere of political discourse as it highlighted the various social and economic problems present in the countryside. Their sense of community remained firmly rooted in the local and rural, excluding towns, and they had an alternative form of jurisprudence. This gradually changed as they became increasingly aware of class divisions in the countryside and the failure of the post-Famine prosperity to permeate all classes.[50] Former farmers clubs that merged into the Land League were determined that their woes not be neglected and, along with the government and landlords, they were taken aback at the virulence of the campaign in the west. A Fenian-artisan-small-farmer nexus was emerging, and this was something that alarmed the more moderate elements that were aligned with the Home Rule movement rather than with the Fenians and associated themselves with Parnell more than with Davitt. Despite these divisions, nationalist politicians soon gained unprecedented power over the rural population.[51] Its sophisticated radicalism, which was in part influenced by agricultural trade unionism in Britain and by popular liberalism, meant that it did not fit into the liberal paradigm that he advocated frequently in the letters page of the *Freeman's Journal*. While he feared it, the divisions within the movement limited its effectiveness and as Samuel Clark argued, 'we frequently hear that peasants have difficulty getting organised because they are too individualistic, are tied to local community groups ... and have little means of communicating with one another'.[52]

John Sweetman was a self-proclaimed liberal who did not necessarily want to interfere in private property but rather facilitate the ability of tenants to transfer through an overhaul of the Bright Clauses of the 1870 Land Act or making tenant right more robust through perpetual leases for tenants. While extolling his qualities as a liberal, he stated: 'People often differ as to the meaning of the word liberal. By a liberal I mean one who is in favour of liberty as opposed to a despotism of progress which aims to improve the laws as opposed to conservatism which considers them already perfect'.[53] He was Gladstonian in his sympathies but certainly not sympathetic to the radical wing. He frequently extolled his opinions on the pages of the *Freeman's Journal*, which resulted in him attracting some odium, ridicule and support. Sweetman was quite conservative in his politics, respecting the authority of the Catholic clergy in these matters and being unashamed in his hostility to the western radicalism that threatened a moderate tenant-right platform that could embrace all as he had hoped. He was keen to work with other like-minded moderates to effect some beneficial change to legislation as a result of the inadequacies of the 1870 Land Act. His not-atypical commentary saw him assert that investment in agricultural improvement was poor because of a lack of security of tenure. He was hostile to violence or even the threat of it and his conservatism was akin to that of many Irish Catholic liberals and had some resemblance with that of James Daly in Mayo. Like Daly, he was also a harsh critic of the system of landlordism, seeing it as a pernicious and inept institution that had delayed the development of the country. This was a common theme amongst liberals at the time and reflected the growth of popular liberalism in the age of the Grand Old Man.

His efforts at establishing an Irish Farmers' Union coincided with the rise of the Land League that dominated the domestic political landscape in the provinces. The Irish Farmers' Union was to be open to all farmers in Ireland and would be allowed to vote for a delegate to a central council.[54] In a letter, Thomas Dowling informed Sweetman of the importance of a central body to represent the interests of tenant farmers, otherwise the disjointed structure that had heretofore existed would indeed be ineffectual.[55]

The Meath Aristocracy and the First World War, 1914–18

KEVIN LYNCH

INTRODUCTION

It could be argued that the sight of 'Big Houses' in County Meath is commonplace; all a testament to the success of the county and the landed gent in political, industrial and agricultural arenas since the time of the Ascendancy. These Big Houses all vary in size but the grander examples were affiliated with the aristocracy of Meath, such as Headfort, Summerhill or Killeen Castle. However, by the end of the First World War in 1918, the prominence and celebrity associated with these families and their properties had disappeared. This watershed event happened during the period 1912–18 when some of the most significant moments in Irish history occurred, such as the third Home Rule Bill, social reforms, the First World War, the 1916 Rebellion and the 1917 Irish Convention. The reaction of the Meath aristocracy to these immensely significant events was a feature at this time. This article focuses on the following families: the Everards, the Conynghams, the Gormanstons, the Headforts and the Plunketts, both the Dunsany and the Fingall branches, all of whom were residents in Meath. While the sources available on each family vary, there is enough evidence to illustrate their reaction to these said events.

The first significant threat to the continuance of the aristocracy in Meath came with the Land Acts beginning in 1881, which were a response to the Land War of 1879–81. These acts affected the lifestyle and political strength of the landed aristocrat in Meath. The 1903 Wyndham Land Act brought about a level of stability for the Meath peer because it slowly eradicated land agitation by encouraging land-owners to sell whilst also aiding tenants to buy.[1] Meath peers then attempted to restore their permanence in the county, but another threat loomed.[2] The next problem for the aristocracy of Meath came in 1912 from the political arena; as the third Home Rule Bill threatened to cut the aristocracy from the political, social and financial security that the union with mainland Britain provided.

The Liberal Party held the office in London from 1905 to 1916 and the influence of the landed aristocracy of Britain and Ireland was further eroded through a series of measures that were brought in. It was during this time that the 'People's Budget' was introduced to help finance old-age pensions and the National Insurance Act. To finance these social benefits, the Chancellor of the Exchequer Lloyd George proposed to tax unearned increments of land sales and land values, higher death duties and impose a super tax on incomes above £3,000, which ultimately threatened all large landowners. The House of Lords attempted to stop this budget but failed because the power of the upper house had been severely curtailed by the Parliament Act of 1911. Lloyd George then initiated the 'land campaign': he sought to reform land taxation and introduced a 'single tax', which frightened the landed classes because it threatened the foundations of their existence.[3] Their existence was further menaced because they were liable for the costs incurred by these political and social changes initiated by London. These changes also threatened the aristocracy of Ireland; however, the prospect of Home Rule was also a threat. The Liberal government in London had become reliant on the Irish Parliamentary Party to stay in power, and in return for nationalist support, the Liberal Party had to introduce a third Home Rule Bill, which the upper house was unable to prevent due to the Parliament Act of 1911.

In Meath, hostility over land issues was diminishing; the United Irish League and the 'Back to Land' Movement were unable to maintain a presence in the county, and it was stated in the *Meath Chronicle* that 'they never had any genuine agitation in the district to get back the land'.[4] However, the introduction of the third Home Bill in 1912 endangered the permanence of the Meath peer while also widening the gap between nationalist and unionist camps. Following its instruction, a very stringent Anti-Home Rule movement was initiated by Edward Carson: this led to the creation of the Ulster Solemn League and Covenant in 1913 (Ulster Letter), which recorded the signatures of unionists who swore to resist Home Rule at any cost. It was an overwhelmingly northern movement but southern unionists still subscribed to it. Thirteen residents from Kells subscribed to the Ulster Letter. While they were the only people from Meath to do so, it suggests that inflexible unionist sentiment towards the Home Rule Bill was not confined to the northern counties.[5] No peers from Meath subscribed to the Ulster Letter but the Marquess of Headfort subscribed to the Anti-Home Rule campaign of the Irish Unionist Alliance (IUA) and donated £25.[6] Lords Langford and Dunboyne were also quick to subscribe to the Anti-Home Rule campaign.[7] Viscount Gormanston's position on the subject was more complex because he was a Catholic who was opposed to Home Rule. His brother stated, 'I know you won't join Redmond or Dillon but the anti-Catholic campaign disgust[s] me ...'[8] His sister Ismay Crichton-Stuart was also concerned about the treatment of Catholics in the northern counties by Anti-Home Rulers.[9] Gormanston would later sign a national declaration against the scheme of Home Rule alongside other Catholic unionists.[10]

Although neither the Marquess of Headfort nor the Marquess of Conyngham subscribed to the Ulster Letter, both men attended a unionist meeting in Kells and their contribution to it would suggest that their unionist sentiment was more stringent than that of other Meath peers. Speakers at the meeting declared:

> We protest at the Home Rule Bill at present before Parliament upon the following grounds ... it is a measure for the creation of a separate Irish Parliament which will produce most dangerous confusion, involving a disastrous conflict of interests and classes, and a serious risk of civil war ... this measure will endanger commercial relation between Ireland and Great Britain, and will submit Ireland to a double form of taxation, both by the Imperial and Irish Parliament ... this measure will imperil personal liberty, and freedom of opinion, and the spirit of tolerance in Ireland ... this measure cannot be final, and, instead of effecting a settlement, it will pave the way for further efforts towards the complete separation of Ireland from Great Britain.[11]

Representatives from the Ulster Unionist Party Samuel and Quinn also attended the meeting. When Samuel spoke at the meeting he referred to his audience as Irishmen, not unionists, as he believed that all 'Irish men and women, whatever their politics or creeds, or classes may be, were … going to be swindled' by Home Rule because he believed that Irishmen would no longer have access to imperial money.[12] Quinn was labelled as the 'bearer of a message from Ulster'; he declared, 'Ulster Unionist will never submit to this Home Rule Bill'.[13] This inflexible Ulster unionist response is notable because it received much applause from the Kells audience. Furthermore, the Marquess of Headfort voiced his support and thanks to Mr Quinn after his speech, to which the Marquess of Conyngham seconded him.[14]

On the eve of the First World War, the future position and role of the aristocracy in Meath was unclear. Land agitation was non-existent; Home Rule threatened their livelihoods, their lifestyles, their connection with London and the security that it provided. It was only a matter of time before the Home Rule Bill would be ratified by the House of Lords because they were unable to veto the bill. The Meath peers who opposed Home Rule also knew that it was inevitable, so they were cautious as to how they would voice their opposition to the bill. Therefore, it can be suggested that Meath peers did not sign the Ulster Letter because they did not want to be associated with the very stringent Ulster opposition to a bill that would be eventually ratified. A 'New Moderate Party' was briefly formed by southern unionists so that they could voice their opposition the Home Rule Bill without being associated with Ulster unionists. Viscount Gormanston, Lord Fingall and Sir Everard aligned themselves with this new party.[15] The new party declared, 'in the interests of the United Kingdom and the Empire, no less than those of Ireland, the settlement of Irish Government should be lifted above the sphere of party politics'.[16] The New Moderate Party clearly wanted nationalist and Ulster unionist members to be removed from the decision-making process because the Irish Parliamentary Party was getting stronger and the divide between Ulster and southern unionists was also growing. The New Moderate Party declared: 'we desire, moreover, to disassociate ourselves from the fears expressed in Ulster and elsewhere, that under any system of Irish government Protestants would be exposed to religious and civil disabilities. We unhesitatingly record our convictions that whatever results the settlement of this question has in store for us, religious intolerance or civil oppression need not be feared'.[17] By supporting the New Moderate Party, Meath peers were able to voice their opposition to Home Rule without being stained by the more severe drives for union.

The outbreak of war across Europe in 1914 was received with great apprehension. Nevertheless, peers all across the British Isles felt a duty to join the army and go to war. Lord Dunsany made no secret of the fact that he detested war but he still felt obliged to rejoin the army in 1914 because he was from a noble society that, at this time, was still perceived as a military class.[18] The aristocracy of the British Isles was traditionally described as the warrior class; therefore, many peers viewed the war as an opportunity to justify their existence.[19] Similarly in Ireland, peers strove to justify their existence but they had to contend with the ever-growing sentiment of Home Rule within the populace; they believed that war in Europe would help unite Ireland and maintain the union with mainland Britain.[20] Meath peers also believed that if they fought alongside Irishmen, their political and social status would be maintained within a new Ireland. Lady Dunsany perceived the war as an opportunity: when discussing her son's involvement, she stated, 'Randal and his generation will be muffs if they can't make something of it'.[21] Sir Horace Plunkett also believed that it would unify unionist and nationalist camps against a common enemy and in doing so would relieve the growing tension on the home front.[22]

Upon hearing news of the war, the peers of Meath quickly set about making preparations. Lord Gormanston considered the possibility of forming a 'Louth/Meath battalion': as he already had 450 men at his disposal, all he needed was cars.[23] The first public efforts made by the peers of Meath came after John Redmond declared that the Irish Volunteers would serve as a home guard in Ireland so as to free up British troops stationed in Ireland.[24] Redmond's proclamation encouraged many peers to join the ranks of the Irish Volunteers, illustrating the importance of the war to the nobility of County Meath. Sir Horace Plunkett wrote to Redmond stating, 'your speech last night relieved much anxiety here and I think you will find it will give the Irish Volunteers exactly the help they want. I was able to induce a kinsman of my own to join them today'.[25] This clearly indicates how keen Sir Horace Plunkett was to include Redmond and the Irish Volunteers in the war effort. The Marquess of Headfort stated in *The*

Irish Times, 'I gladly welcome Mr. Redmond's declaration in the House of Commons ... I propose forthwith to join the local corps of the National Volunteers, and thus contribute my part to the defence of a united Ireland against a common enemy'.[26] Many peers joined the Irish Volunteers and the *Meath Chronicle* stated, 'every day brings more evidence of the marvellous change wrought since the historic utterance of the Irish Leader (Redmond) was heard in the House of Commons ... in the face of the national emergency that has arisen class barriers have broken down, and the common impulse is to draw together and present a united front'.[27] This statement clearly articulates how nationalists perceived the current state of affairs: they recognised that opposing forces were being united, but also that this 'marvellous change' was dissolving any prominence that the peers may have had.[28]

The Irish Volunteers would never fight on the front and this was primarily due to Kitchener and the War Office in London not allowing them to be kept in their same divisions under Irish officers. Lady Fingall noted that 'the Irish were distrusted' at this time and that this is why Kitchener would not allow them to join.[29] Before the collapse of negotiations between the Irish Volunteers and the War Office, many Irish peers had already run out of patience. Lord Fingall resigned his post in the Irish Volunteers due to their inactivity, stating that 'his duties had never been defined' and that his position was more like 'a fifth wheel on a coach'.[30] Before this resignation, Lord Fingall's frustration had become apparent at an assembly of 2,000 Irish Volunteers. They had gathered at Slane Castle to be inspected with Lords Fingall and Dunsany the primary officials, both of whom installed much cheer in the men, but the mood changed when Mr White, MP of North Meath, spoke:

> Mr White got up and told these luckless men (all longing to do the right thing if allowed) that they should accept the War Office instruction but must remain under their own leaders. It was sickening. He must know that no sane man in power would accept a force under these conditions, he must know that they would be useless, that in case of invasion they would be mere armed civilians, liable to be hung and their villages burnt – it can't be that these wretched politicians are going to ruin the only chance there has been of making a loyal and contented Ireland. And these poor sheep will follow from habit – it is contemptible that they can believe them.[31]

Lord Dunsany clearly expresses the frustration felt by his fellow peers who had joined the Volunteers; he also highlights the division amongst nationalists regarding the war. Lord Fingall stated that even supporters of the war were 'sharply divided both upon enlistment for service abroad and upon the necessary steps to enable the Volunteers to render efficient service at home'.[32] Colonel Moore of the Irish Volunteers strongly condemned Lord Fingall's public resignation and suggested that he should join Kitchener's army if he wanted to defend the Empire.[33] Lord Gormanston continued to manage and inspect the Volunteers of County Meath with the help of the County Surveyor of Meath, James Quigley. Over two days Lord Gormanston inspected the 400 men of the Kells Corps, 440 men of the Navan Corps, 200 men in Slane, 400 men in Ardcath and 200 in Athboy.[34] Eventually he too would resign his post, albeit on better terms than Lord Fingall. Afterwards, Colonel Moore wrote to him thanking him for the work done, 'you are obliged to leave us but I hope one day you will join us again'.[35] This brief collaboration between the nobility of County Meath and the Irish Volunteers proved to be unconstructive and led to resentment between the two parties. Therefore, the drive to unify nationalists and unionists to combat a common enemy had backfired.

Recruitment and conscription would remain significant issues throughout the war and Lord Fingall became the primary figure for the recruitment drive in County Meath as Lord Gormanston had been appointed to the position of railway transportation officer at Kingsbridge Station in 1915.[36] Many peers in Ireland had become disillusioned by the unwillingness of the Irish populace to enlist.[37] Gormanston, who had been patron of the Voluntary Recruitment League, withdrew his patronage as he had become a 'firm believer in the need for universal service at the present time'.[38] Lord Fingall continued the recruitment drive in counties Longford, Meath, Westmeath, Kings, Queens and Louth. On one occasion, whilst accompanied by Captain Murray Wight at an Oldcastle rural district meeting, he called for the formation of a recruitment committee in the district and suggested that it would be better to join the British Empire than any German enterprise in Ireland as Ireland has already contributed significantly to the British Empire and should stand to gain from it.[39] Fingall was heckled, members of the Oldcastle rural district shouted 'Let him go with them, he will not be much of a loss', and as they left the building Councillor Ryan shouted 'bye bye' to them both.[40] This encounter illustrates the resentment that had grown towards the issue of enlistment and Lord Fingall. Upon leaving the meeting, Fingall declared, 'it only remains for me to thank you for receiving us, and although you don't see your way to forming a committee, I presume that the majority are in accordance with the views we hold, that all young men should join the army'.[41] This statement exemplifies one peer's inability to read the writing on the wall, the deteriorating position of aristocrats in County Meath and the growing resentment towards them; consequently, enlistment into the British army suffered.

At a recruitment meeting in Navan, in February 1916, it was argued how best to maintain the strength of the battalions of the Leinster regiments. While many sentiments of appreciation were voiced for the efforts made by Lord Fingall and Sir Nugent Everard, there were revelations concerning a method to maintain the numbers in the Leinster regiments.[42] Even with separation allowances and other remittances promised, the recruitment drive in Ireland never reached the same fervour as it did on mainland Britain. Nevertheless, Sir Nugent Everard continued to promote and organised many recruitment meetings in Navan. On one occasion, he even campaigned from the pulpit, for which he was severely criticised because it was in a Catholic church.[43] Lord Fingall also continued to encourage enlistment – at a function in Athlone that was commemorating eight local men who had been killed on the front, he stated:

> there was not one of the wives or mothers or daughters of the men that they had come there to honour who would not sooner that their beloved young men had been to the front and had done their duty than have them to remain at home as slackers … he appealed to the mothers, wives and daughters of the men they honoured to do their utmost to send out other men to avenge their losses.[44]

Lord Fingall was clearly playing on the emotions of the recently bereaved and this method can be perceived as insensitive. These harsh methods proved to be unpopular and destructive to the already politically sensitive issue of enlistment, which in turn led to low enlistment figures in Meath.[45]

The aristocracy of Meath also contributed to the war effort through other avenues. After the failure of negotiations between the Irish

Volunteers and the War Office, Sir Horace Plunkett continued giving his contribution by developing industry. Whilst presiding over an Irish Agricultural Organisation meeting, he stated:

> every man capable of patriotic sentiment, and who was not called upon to risk his life at the front, felt in honour bound to work for those who did, and to serve his country in some other way ... the appeal to the organised farmers on behalf of a Belgian and general relief fund, to recognise their obligations not only to those who were fighting their battles at the moment, but to their country.[46]

Similarly, Sir Nugent Everard believed that industry and agriculture within Meath could aid the war effort. As a member of the Meath County Committee of Agriculture and the County Meath Joint Technical Instruction Committee, Everard set about reorganising industry and the agricultural economy in Meath. He recommended that a 'number of committees, local and central, should be formed to represent different branches of industry' to the international market.[47] Everard would later become a colonel in the 5th Battalion Prince of Wales Leinster Regiment (formally the County Meath Militia) and serve on the Belgian front.[48] His efforts with the agricultural industry in County Meath showed farmers in the county that it was possible to aid the war effort whilst improving industry and profits. In Everard's absence, Lady Everard continued his work. She voiced her husband's views at meetings as well as initiating her own movements.[49] During the war, there was a shortage of potatoes and she then became involved in the debate to stop the export of potatoes from Meath.[50] She encouraged the development of tillage orders by the Irish Horticultural Society and Vegetable Product Committee; these tillage orders were carried out in 1916 and, one year later, the amount of land being tilled for potatoes rose from 8,000 to 12,000.[51]

The contribution of the aristocratic women of County Meath to the war effort was substantial and, like the efforts of the men, it attempted to unify the home front by assisting the Leinster regiments. Lady Headfort sold St Patrick's Day flags at a prominent London hotel to raise funds for wounded soldiers.[52] In Meath, Lady Everard was the president of the Women's Committee; the Marchioness of Conyngham was the vice-president and Lady Fingall was a member. The main purpose of this committee was to collect clothing, comforts and funds for the Leinster regiments.[53] On one occasion, Lady Everard presided over a meeting of ladies from County Meath and she proposed that these ladies, who were 'citizens of a great Empire could render service to their country in her hour of need', by organising Red Cross classes to teach first aid, nursing and sewing so to make garments to send to wounded men.[54] Lady Headfort expanded on this suggestion by proposing that these Red Cross classes should teach women to 'meet the present need, either in respect of work in our own districts, or … for filling any gaps which may occur in the ranks of those already engaged in ambulance work'.[55] Her suggestion received great praise, as did Lady Plunkett who had already initiated similar classes in Ratoath. These steps taken by the ladies of County Meath illustrate how they also felt compelled to support the war effort.

Due to the active role peers took in the recruitment drive in Meath, they received much criticism from political bodies. John Sweetman was a notable figure in public life at this time due to his activity within the Meath County Council and his involvement with the *Sinn Féin* publication. He publicly opposed any Irish involvement in the war and at a meeting of the Drumbaragh Irish Volunteers, which had just been inspected by Lord Gormanston and James Quigley, he declared:

> our aim is simple … to secure and maintain the rights and liberties common to all the people of Ireland … we in Ireland must drill and arm in order that we may be in a position to take advantage of the future. West Britons are trying … to induce the Irish Volunteers to put themselves under the English Government … England always wants Ireland to do the hard fighting for her but it is time for Ireland to think of herself.[56]

The Drumbaragh Volunteers quickly aligned themselves with Sweetman.[57] The following articles from *Sinn Féin* damning the war effort can be credited to Sweetman due to references to nobles from County Meath:

> a jingo speech delivered by Lord Ashbourne from a non-political Gaelic League platform in Tyrone. His Lordships incitements to Tyrone peasants to aid England were based on a professed pro-French fervour of his own … We counsel the boys and girls who listen to Lord Ashbourne's harangue, from a platform of which he violated the neutrality, to watch whether his lordship will join the French foreign legion. If he does not, they will recognise humbug when they meet him again.[58]

England wants men ... Lord Dunsany, Lord Fingall ... and a
hundred pillars of the unionist alliance appear decked in nationalist
feathers to urge the volunteers to "go under the war office. For calm
impudence we prefer Dunsany, whose last public appearance in Dublin
was on the platform of the we-will-not-have-home rule meeting ...
Lord Dunsany is an ex-British officer under 40 years of age, why does
not he go out and fight?[59]

Sweetman clearly targets the nobility as he perceives them as the main
enforcer of the war effort in Meath, and his rhetoric is identical to
that of the Provisional Committee (Irish Volunteers). These analogous
efforts would later make them indistinguishable to the public and
both thwarted the recruitment drive and amplified any resentment
towards the nobility of County Meath.

During the First World War, one of the most defining events in
Irish history occurred: the Easter Rising of 1916, in which many of
the Meath aristocracy were intrinsically involved. Upon hearing of
the rebellion, the peers of the county sought to combat the revolt.
Lord Gormanston successfully defended Kingsbridge Station from
rebel attack, Sir Everard used his vantage point in the Sackville Street
Men's Club to record the movements of rebels in the GPO, Lord Fingal
escaped an ambush at Dunboyne Castle and went on to fight the
rebels in Dublin, and Sir Horace Plunkett, with the help of Lady Fingal,
ferried foodstuffs to British troops fighting in Dublin. Lord Dunsany
was the only Meath peer to be wounded in the rebellion; he was shot
in the face when driving into Dublin to combat it. Although the revolt
greatly affected the peers of Meath, it was the aftermath that was to
have the most significant effect. Even though the rebellion initially
had little support, it reinvigorated nationalist sentiment in the local
populace, to which the nobility were unable to respond.

One of the first repercussions of the rebellion was a complete stand-
still in the recruitment drive in Meath.[60] When it resumed, the county
peers were not present. It was noted that their involvement in the
drive only helped to strengthen nationalist sentiment in the county
and 'gave the "extreme patriots" a further pretext for opposing' the
recruitment effort.[61] Peers may also have simply feared for their safety,
but their absence is noted during a week-long recruitment march by
the 2nd and 5th Battalions of the Leinster Regiment, which marched
through all the major towns in the county: Trim, Athboy and Navan.[62]

The rebellion also further weakened the position of the southern unionists because Ulster unionists and their sympathisers were now able to justify their campaign for partition. Initially, southern unionists had not taken the concept of partition seriously because they believed it was impracticable, so they did not perceive it as a threat.[63] As the possibility of partition gained momentum, southern unionists began to contest it.[64] Mr George F. Stewart, the chairman of the IUA, sent a letter to Lloyd George, stating:

> as a direct result of the rebellion and in consequence of it proposals appear to have been formulated with the object of excluding certain counties in Ulster and for handing over the government of the rest of Ireland to the Nationalists during a period of war … we are convinced that the proposal to so hand over the Government of the South and West of Ireland to the Nationalist at this stage will not assist the Empire in the prosecution of the war. On the contrary we think it will bring about the gravest dangers to England from the standpoint and we believe that it may weaken the position of the country at the conclusion of the war'.[65]

Regardless, the IUA was unable to combat the growing threat of Home Rule and partition, the writing was on the wall and with the approaching Irish Convention of 1917, the idea of partition gathered strength.

Partition was perceived as a way to protect loyal British subjects in the northern counties, and this concept was initiated in 1912 when the Home Rule Bill was first introduced.[66] By 1914 it was further promoted in the House of Lords, when it was insisted upon in the amended bill that the nine counties of Ulster should be excluded from the scheme.[67] On the eve of the Irish Convention in 1917, partition had become the key issue in Irish politics and Lloyd George had hoped that the Irish would 'endeavour to find a settlement for themselves'.[68] Sir Horace Plunkett stated, 'I confidently believe we shall ultimately come to a settlement'; however, there were challenges for the convention.[69] It consisted of 101 members, supposedly from all political initiatives in Ireland. However, Sinn Féin chose to ignore the convention, so not all political positions were present.[70] Sir Horace Plunkett presided over it, as he was believed to have no political connections.[71] Plunkett continuously communicated with Redmond throughout the convention and on one occasion he wrote, 'I think I can report that things are going well so far here ... the procedure that you explained so perfectly to them but which many of them have, I fear, already forgotten'.[72] On another occasion he sent him confidential material, '... if Carson gets it there may be trouble' and when speaking of the unofficial Sinn Féin members at the convention, he said, '... whose speakers, I notice give a much fuller account of our proceedings than we do', for which they gained more support.[73] Although Plunkett believed he had no political connotations, he clearly aligned himself with the Irish Parliamentary Party, which, he believed, needed him and other southern unionists to maintain control in parliament.[74] In return, Plunkett and southern unionists expected safe-guards for themselves as they had now come to accept that some form of self-government would occur. However, the Irish Parliamentary Party had now lost all the prominence that it once had.[75] Sein Féin was now the dominant nationalist party in Ireland because the Irish Parliamentary Party was in decline.[76] Moreover, the concept of partition grew stronger, further weakening the status and continual existence of the aristocracy in Meath.

The First World War, during which the aristocracy of Meath fought on the continent and on the home front, ended in 1918. The war with Germany would have direct consequences for many of the aris-tocratic families in Meath; Marquess Conyngham was the only peer from County Meath to lose his life as a consequence of the war.[77] Lord Dunsany lost his cousin Sir Richard Levinge in October 1914.[78] The Marquess of Headfort lost his grandson, Capt. George Taylour, at Menin – he was killed while cutting barbed wire on the front.[79] Lord Langford lost his daughter in the early months of 1916 after she became ill while nursing wounded soldiers.[80] Lord Langford also lost his son George Cecil Rowley of the King's Royal Rifles.[81] His death would prove disastrous for the family because Lord Langford's remaining son lacked the psychological ability to retain the title.[82] Lady Gormanston's brother, Col Patrick Butler, whilst serving on the western front, described how he had lost close friends and how he prayed 'that I may not show fear ...'[83] His statement shows the great strain that the war placed on the peers of the British Isles, regard-less of the financial and social strains that many were facing at home. The aristocracy of Great Britain suffered greatly as a consequence of the war, but in Meath, aristocrats also suffered the serious change that the First World War brought, weakening them to a point from which they would never recover, leaving the peers utterly demoralised.[84]

The narrative of the Big Houses in Meath is reliant on the persistence of the peers who maintained them. Political and economic success ensured the continuance of the lifestyle of the landed peer in Meath; however, through social reforms, this security became null and void. This irreversible threat was in the making since the 1880s, but it was during the period of 1912–18 when the celebrity, prominence and security of the aristocrat in Meath truly came to an end. In 1912 the Home Rule Bill kickstarted a rivalry between two political and militant forces, unionism and nationalism. The coming of the First World War gave the nobility of Meath respite from these political issues, and during this period they attempted to secure their own objectives. They would ultimately fail to arrest the growing threat of Home Rule because they were unable to manage the complexities of the home front with the demands that the war in Europe imposed. The shock of the Easter Rebellion illustrated their inability to recognise the growing menace around them, but their actions during it demonstrated their devote loyalty to Britain as well as the perplexity of their position in Ireland. During the 1917 Irish Convention, Lloyd George had hoped that the Irish might 'find a settlement for themselves', as did the aristocracy of Meath, but the convention only helped to secure the position of the Sinn Féin party and the concept of partition.[85] After the First World War, the aristocracy struggled to recover – it was suggested that the First World War generation was not 'decimated but decapitated … our born leaders are dead'.[86] Although only one Meath aristocrat lost his life as a result of the war, by 1918, the aristocracy that remained was unable to maintain its prominence; the political role, the land, the way of life and their traditional role was now gone.

The Loughcrew Fires

MALACHY HAND

Loughcrew House was built in 1823 by James Lenox Naper and designed by Charles Robert Cockerell. Cockerell was a famous architect who designed Gilson School in Oldcastle and many famous buildings in England. Loughcrew House was a large mansion of neo-classical design with a fine Athenian Ionic portico, was surrounded by a 1,000-acre demesne and was the centre of a large estate of thousands of acres. This house replaced a 'long house', the outline of which can be detected in what are now the historic gardens near the old Plunket church and also close to an Anglo-Norman motte.

In 1778, Fr Thomas Allen was evicted from a house at Millbrook where priests from Oldcastle and Moylagh resided. Folklore suggests that it was because of this eviction that a curse was put on Loughcrew House, which states:

> Three times will Loughcrew be consumed by fire! Crows will fly in and out of the windows. Grass will grow on its doorstep.

And so it was: three times it was 'consumed by fire'. The first fire occurred on 28 April 1888 at 2 p.m. Water was carried in barrels from nearby streams, but in spite of this much of the house was gutted. One wing was saved by people who built a wall of cut sods to keep the flames from spreading from the main structure. Most of the furniture and valuables, including most of the books from the library, were saved due to the bravery of the staff. The events surrounding this

Loughcrew House in 1935. (Berry Collection, Meath County Library)

Three men and a trap on the Naper estate (note the name Captain Naper on
the ironwork on the shaft) (Berry Collection, Meath County Library)

fire were recorded as part of the Irish Schools' Folklore Collection
in 1938. The manuscript, reproduced below, was written by Eileen
Jenkins, a local schoolteacher, and was based on information gleaned
from Mrs Dixon of Loughcrew Farm, stewardess to Capt. W.L. Naper.

The second fire was in September 1959, on the Sunday of the
All-Ireland Football final. Nigel Naper and his family, who had a few
years previously come from England to farm the estate, had to deal
with this disaster. Noel Mahon, a local lad at the time, related that,
before realising that there was a fire, he had smelled the lovely burning

scent of the pitch pine timber that was used in the construction of the house. He had then made his way to the mansion where a small trailed fire engine had arrived from Oldcastle. The fire lasted a couple of days and was a great spectacle when news got out of the inferno. The *Meath Chronicle* reported that:

> Oldcastle fire brigade was quickly on the scene. The Kells, Navan and Trim were also summoned, since water had to be taken from the lake more than a mile from the mansion. Seventy five lengths of hose were to be employed for the purpose.[1]

The final burning was in April 1964. The house was still being restored from the previous fire and it was unoccupied as the Naper family were in temporary lodgings in the Kennel yard. Four Meath fire brigades from Navan, Trim, Kells and Oldcastle fought the disastrous fire. There was not much furniture as it was still in storage from the previous conflagration but a lot of books, paintings and sporting equipment were lost. About £2,000 worth of tools and machinery belonging to the contractors were destroyed.

The house was subsequently demolished and all that remains now are the four pillars of the portico, a reminder to the passer-by of the great edifice that once graced this beautiful landscape.[2]

Photographs taken in April 1964 on the occasion of the third burning of Loughcrew House. (Meath County Library, courtesy of Denis McCarthy)

Notes

INTRODUCTION

1 William J. Smyth, *Map-making, Landscapes and Memory: A Geography of Colonial and Early Modern Ireland, c. 1530–1750* (Cork, 2006), p. xix.

2 Ibid., pp xix–xx.

3 Colm Lennon, *Sixteenth-century Ireland: The Incomplete Conquest* (Dublin, 1994), pp 209–212, 230–4.

4 Peter Connell, *The Land and People in County Meath, 1750–1850* (Dublin, 2004), p. 11.

5 For more, see Raymond Gillespie, *Seventeenth-century Ireland: Making Ireland Modern* (Dublin, 2006).

6 Smyth, *Map-making, Landscapes and Memory*, p. xx.

7 Terence Dooley, *The Big Houses and Landed Estates of Ireland: A Research Guide* (Dublin, 2007), p. 13.

8 Author of *Divine Right? The Parnell Split in Meath* (2007).

9 One contributor, Kevin McKenna, had recently completed a PhD on the Clonbrock Estate in Galway and another, Joe Mooney, a Masters' thesis on the Headfort estate at Kells. Brian Casey was engaged in the arranging and cataloguing of the Headfort Papers under a research studentship in the National Library.

CHAPTER 1

1 Mark Clinton, 'Settlement Dynamics in County Meath: The Kingdom of Lóegaire' in *Peritia* (2000), xiv, pp 377, 379, 383; Michael Moore, *Archaeological Inventory of County Meath* (Dublin, 1997), p. 60; Goddard H. Orpen, 'Subterranean Chambers at Clady, County Meath', *JRSAI* Second quarter (1890), pp 150–4.

2 Roger Stalley, *The Cistercian Monasteries of Ireland* (London, 1987), p. 13; Aubrey Gwynn and R. Neville Hadcock, *Medieval Religious Houses: Ireland* (London, 1970), pp 115–6, 128; F.H.A. Aalen, *Man and Landscape in Ireland* (London, 1978), p. 123.

3 Stalley, *The Cistercian Monasteries of Ireland*, p. 40; Flannan Hogan, 'The Last Monks and Abbots of Bective' in *Ríocht na Mídhe*, vol. VI, no. 2 (1976),

p. 12; Anthony Cogan, *The Diocese of Meath Ancient and Modern* (Dublin, 1862), i, p. 116.

4   Stalley, *The Cistercian Monasteries of Ireland*, p. 205; Cogan, *The Diocese of Meath Ancient and Modern*, i, p. 117; M.T. Flanagan, 'Lacy, Hugh de (*d.* 1186)', *Oxford Dictionary of National Biography* (Oxford University Press, 2004) [www.oxforddnb.com/view/article/15852, accessed 8 February 2009].

5   Stalley, *The Cistercian Monasteries of Ireland*, pp 45, 107, 158–60, 193–4; Harold G. Leask, *Irish Churches and Monastic Buildings*, vol. III (Dundalk, 1996), pp 27–8, 145–7; Gwynn and Hadcock, *Medieval Religious Houses: Ireland*, p. 128.

6   Aalen, *Man and Landscape in Ireland*, p. 123; B.J. Graham, *Anglo-Norman Settlement in Ireland* (Athlone, 1985), pp 25–6; Gwynn and Hadcock, *Medieval Religious Houses: Ireland*, p. 119; Cogan, *The Diocese of Meath Ancient and Modern* (Dublin, 1862), i, pp 118–9; Will of Frances Georgina Bolton, dated 4 April 1879, D7/10/8, 1&2, RCB Library.

7   Stalley, *The Cistercian Monasteries of Ireland*, p. 160.

8   Mervyn Archdall, *Monasticum Hibernicum*, vol. iii (London, 1786), p. 517.

9   Hogan, 'The Last Monks and Abbots of Bective', p. 3.

10   Ibid., pp 6–8.

11   Ibid., p. 8.

12   Newport B. White (ed.), *Extents of Irish Monastic Possessions 1540–41* (Dublin, 1943), pp 267–70; Archdall, *Monasticum Hibernicum*, iii, pp 517–8; Cogan, *The Diocese of Meath Ancient and Modern*, i, p. 120; Hogan, 'The Last Monks and Abbots of Bective', pp 8–9; Gwynn and Hadcock, *Medieval Religious Houses Ireland*, p. 128.

13   C.E. Challis, 'The Debasement of the Coinage, 1542–1551' in *The Economic History Review*, New Series, vol. 20, no. 3 (Dec., 1967), pp 441–66; Brendan Scott, *Religion and Reformation in the Tudor Diocese of Meath* (Dublin, 2006), p. 97–8; Stalley, *The Cistercian Monasteries of Ireland*, pp 228–32.

14   Scott, *Religion and Reformation in the Tudor Diocese of Meath*, p. 97.

15   James Morrin (ed.), *Calendar of Patent and Close Rolls of Chancery in Ireland, Henry VIII–Elizabeth* (1861), i, pp 280, 281; Cogan, *The Diocese of Meath Ancient and Modern*, i, pp 118–9.

16   *Calendar of Patent and Close Rolls of Chancery in Ireland, Henry VIII–Elizabeth*, i, p. 293; Cogan, *The Diocese of Meath Ancient and Modern*, i, p. 119; Harold G. Leask, 'Bective abbey, County Meath' in *JRSAI* series VI, vol. VI (1916), p. 48.

17   Leask, 'Bective Abbey, County Meath', p. 48.

18   Cogan, *The Diocese of Meath Ancient and Modern*, i, p. 119.

19   A rent roll of Bective [County Meath] under the Tenants Names set by Barthol. Dillon, sold at Bloomsbury Auctions Sale 614, 24th May 2007; Leask, 'Bective Abbey, County Meath', p. 49; Cogan, *The Diocese of Meath Ancient and Modern*, i, pp 119–20.

20   R.C. Simington (ed.), *The Civil Survey, A.D. 1654–56*, vol. v (Dublin, 1940), pp 239–41.

21   Leask, 'Bective Abbey, County Meath', p. 46; *The Civil Survey, A.D. 1654–56*, p. 136; Beryl F.E. Moore, *Bective Abbey Notes*,

Meath County Library; Moore, *Archaeological Inventory of County Meath*, p. 178; John Healy, *History of the Diocese of Meath* (Dublin, 1908), i, p. 289.

22 Edward McKeever, *History of Kilmessan and its Environs* (Bective, 1972), p. 14; Fairs and Markets Commission Ireland HC, 1852–53, p. 100.

23 Art Kavanagh, *The Landed Gentry and Aristocracy Meath* (Dublin, 2005), p. 45; *Ordnance Survey Field Name Books, County Meath, 1835–6, Balsoon Parish* (typescript, MCL, Navan); G.E. Cokayne with Vicary Gibbs, H.A. Doubleday, Geoffrey H. White, Duncan Warrand and Lord Howard de Walden (eds), *The Complete Peerage of England, Scotland, Ireland, Great Britain and the United Kingdom, Extant, Extinct or Dormant, new ed.*, 13 volumes in 14 (Gloucester, 1910–1959), i, p. 283.

24 Bernard Burke, *Genealogical and Heraldic Dictionary of the Landed Gentry of Great Britain and Ireland* (London, 1868), p. 109.

25 *Freeman's Journal*, 28 September 1811.

26 Kavanagh, *The Landed Gentry and Aristocracy Meath*, p. 48. Weston St John Joyce, *The Neighbourhood of Dublin* (Dublin, 1913), pp 316–7.

27 *Newry Commercial Telegraph*, 7 March 1828; Virginia Crossman, *Local Government in Nineteenth-century Ireland* (Belfast, 1994), pp 7–9.

28 W.E. Vaughan, *Landlords and Tenants in Mid-Victorian Ireland* (Oxford, 1994), p. 6.

29 *Freeman's Journal*, 20 February 1840; Crossman, *Local Government in Nineteenth-century Ireland*, p. 2.

30 Cogan, *The Diocese of Meath Ancient and Modern*, iii, p. 323; Dan Daly, *Robinstown Education 1800–1995* (Robinstown, 1995), p. 3.

31 L.J. Proudfoot, 'Spatial Transformation and Social Agency: Property, Society and Improvement, *c.* 1700 to *c.* 1900' in B.J. Graham and L.J. Proudfoot (eds), *An Historical Geography of Ireland* (London, 1993), pp 227–8; Terence Dooley, *The Decline of the Big House in Ireland* (Dublin, 2001), pp 30–1; Terence Dooley, *Sources for the History of Landed Estates in Ireland* (Dublin, 2000), pp 3–4, 8.

32 Bective parish registers, burials; Bective D7/10/8 1&2 RCB library, *Landowners in Ireland, Return of Owners of Land of One Acre and Upwards* (Dublin, 1876) p. 65; John Bateman, *The Great Landowners of Great Britain and Ireland* (London, 1883), p 46; U.H. Hussey de Burgh, *The Landowners of Ireland* (Dublin, 1878), p 43.

33 *Ordnance Survey Field Name Books, County Meath, 1835–6, Bective Parish* (typescript, MCL, Navan); Dooley, *Sources for the History of Landed Estates in Ireland*, p. 5.

34 Valuation of Ireland 1854, Parish of Bective.

35 *Ordnance Survey Field Name Books, County Meath, 1836, Bective Parish* (typescript, MCL, Navan); Samuel Lewis, *A Topographical Dictionary of Ireland* (London, 1837); Christine Casey and Alistair Rowan, *The Buildings of Ireland: North Leinster* (London, 1993), p. 162; Mark Bence-Jones, *A Guide to Irish Country Houses* (London, 1988), p. 35; Terence Dooley, *The Decline of the Big House in Ireland* (Dublin, 2001), p. 40.

36 Terence Dooley, *The Decline of the Big House in Ireland* (Dublin, 2001), pp 39–40.

37   *Ordnance Survey Name Books, County Meath, 1836, Bective Parish* (typescript, MCL, Navan).

38   *The Parliamentary Gazetteer of Ireland* (Dublin, 1846); www.excavations.ie Meath 2000:0746 Bective (viewed 30 March 2009).

39   William Wilde, *The Beauties of the Boyne and its Tributary, the Blackwater* (Dublin, 1849), p. 109.

40   Valuation of Ireland, Parish of Bective.

41   L.M. Cullen, 'Man, Landscape and Roads: The Changing Eighteenth Century' in William Nolan (ed.), *The Shaping of Ireland: The Geographical Perspective* (Cork, 1986), p. 127.

42   James Fairbairn, *Fairbairn's Crest of the Families of Great Britain and Ireland* (Clearfield, 1905), p. 61.

43   George Briscoe, *The Best of Times: Memoirs of a Countryman* (Bective, 2005), p. 90.

44   Helen M. Roe, *Medieval Fonts of Meath* (Longford, 1968), p. 25.

45   *Meath Chronicle*, 25 December 1926.

46   UCD Dept of Folklore MS 190. Schools Collection, Robinstown.

47   Terence Dooley, *Sources for the History of Landed Estates in Ireland* (Dublin, 2000), p. 1.

48   *Anglo-Celt*, 12 September 1850; Bective D7/10/8 1&2 RCB library; Irish architectural archive www.dia.ie (viewed 30 March 2009); Bective D7/19/2.10 RCB library; *Biographical Succession List for the Diocese of Meath* Canon Leslie, RCB Library; *The Irish Times*, 5 May 1859; Healy, *History of the Diocese of Meath*, ii, p. 236; Samuel Lewis, *Topographical Dictionary of Ireland* (London, 1837); Roe, *Medieval Fonts of Meath*, p. 25.

49   T. Jones Hughes, 'Landholding and Settlement in the Counties of Meath and Cavan in the Nineteenth Century', p. 114; John O'Meara, 'The Meath Road' in *Journal of the Irish Railway Record Society* (spring, 1957) p. 234; Stephen Johnson, *Lost Railways of Dundalk and the North East* (Catrin, 2006), pp 7–9.

50   Elizabeth, Countess Fingall, *Seventy Years Young* (London, 1937), p. 135.

51   *Hansard* HC Debate 23 July 1889, vol. 338, c. 1100, HC Debate 8 August 1889, vol. 339, cc 852–70.

52   Irish Land Commission. The Land Law (Ireland) Act, 1881 Judicial rents as notified to the Irish Land Commission during the months of September, October, and November 1890, HC 1890–91, (c.6263), p. 515.

53   Leask, 'Bective abbey, County Meath', p. 49.

54   *Biographical Succession List for the Diocese of Meath* Canon Leslie, RCB Library; *Irish Times*, 5 May 1859.

55   UCD Dept of Folklore MSS. 190. Schools Collection, Robinstown.

56   Return of untenanted lands in rural districts HC (1906) (205) p. 345.

57   Fingall, *Seventy Years Young*, pp 198–201; Lord Dunsany, *My Ireland* (London, 1937), pp 123–8; Kavanagh, *The Landed Gentry and Aristocracy Meath*, pp 213–20; *Meath Chronicle*, 1 November 1902, 17 February 1906, 19 May 1906, 14 April 1979; Bective D7/19/2.10 RCB library; *Irish Independent*, 14 November 1908; *The Irish Times*, 22 December 1908; Slater's national commercial directory of Ireland (Manchester, 1894).

58 Dooley, *The Decline of the Big House*, p. 160.

59 *Census Returns, 1911*. Unpublished census returns, NAI.

60 Dooley, *The Decline of the Big House*, p. 161.

61 Kim O'Rourke, 'Descendancy? Meath's Protestant Gentry' in David Fitzpatrick (ed), *Revolution? Ireland 1917–1923* (Dublin, 1990) p. 100.

62 Irish architectural archive www.dia.ie (viewed 30 March 2009).

63 George Briscoe, *The Best of Times: Memoirs of a Countryman* (Bective, 2005), pp 77–8; *Meath Chronicle*, 12 March 1923.

64 *The Irish Times*, 20 Apr. 2006; *Meath Chronicle*, 30 January 1926; Irish Tourist Association, Topographical and General Survey, 1942; Local studies section, County Library, Navan; Briscoe, *The Best of Times: Memoirs of a Countryman*, p. 135.

65 Briscoe, *The Best of Times: Memoirs of a Countryman*, pp 79, 84, 119.

66 Bence-Jones, *A Guide to Irish Country Houses*, p. 35; Briscoe, *The Best of Times: Memoirs of a Countryman*, p. 120.

67 Briscoe, *The Best of Times: Memoirs of a Countryman*, p. 121.

68 T. Jones Hughes, 'Landholding and Settlement in the Counties of Meath and Cavan in the Nineteenth Century' in Patrick O'Flanagan, Paul Ferguson and Kevin Whelan (eds), *Rural Ireland 1600–1900: Modernisation and Change* (Cork, 1987), pp 111–2.

CHAPTER 2

1 J.C. Beckett, *The Making of Modern Ireland 1603–1923* (London, 1966), p. 60.

2 J.P. Prendergast, *The Cromwellian Settlement of Ireland* (London, 1865), pp 90–1.

3 Beckett, *Modern Ireland*, p. 60.

4 J.G. Simms, 'The Establishment of Protestant Ascendancy, 1691–1714' in T.W. Moody and W.E. Vaughan (eds), *A New History of Ireland, Volume IV: Eighteenth Century Ireland 1691–1800* (Oxford, 1986), p. 12.

5 R.C. Simington (ed.), *The Civil Survey, A.D. 1654–56, v: County of Meath* (Dublin, 1940). Note: this reference applies to any reference to the Civil Survey hereafter.

6 Parish maps with terriers, showing forfeited lands in County Meath, commonly known as the 'Down Survey', executed under the direction of Sir William Petty, 1657, and copied by Daniel O'Brien, 1786 (NLI, MS 715). Note: this reference applies to any reference to the Down Survey hereafter.

7 'Books of Survey and Distribution' for counties Louth and Meath, compiled *c.* 1703, listing proprietors of land in 1641, and grantees and lands granted in 1688, with acreages (NLI, MS 974).

8 Available at: www.1641.tcd.ie/.

9 B. Nugent, *A Guide to the 18th Century Land Records in the Irish Registry of Deeds* (Meath, 2012).

10 P. O'Connell, 'The Parish and District of Kilbride' in *Ríocht na Midhe*, ii (1962), pp 5–16.

11 B. Graham, 'Medieval Settlements in County Meath' in *Ríocht na Midhe*, v (1974), pp 40–59.

12 Graham, *Medieval Settlements*.

13 Listed as part of Oldcastle parish in Books of Survey and Distribution but was later in the parish of Kilbride, now a part of the modern Mountnugent parish.

14 B. Graham, 'The Mottes of the Norman Liberty of Meath' in H. Murtagh (ed), *Irish Midland Studies* (Athlone, 1980) [as cited in E. Sheridan, *The Parish of Clonmellon/Killalon* (Meath, 2001), p. 21].

15 Sheridan, *Clonmellon/Killalon*, p. 21.

16 As cited in Sheridan, *Clonmellon/Killalon*, p. 21.

17 M.R. Carty, *History of Killeen Castle* (Meath, 1991), pp 3–4.

18 T. Harris, 'Fairs and Markets in the Environment of County Meath' in *Ríocht na Midhe*, ix (1998), pp 149–169.

19 J. Brady, 'Anglo-Norman Meath' in *Ríocht na Midhe*, ii (1961), pp 38–45.

20 Source: Naper family records.

21 J.G. Simms, 'Meath Landowners in the Jacobite War' in *Ríocht na Midhe*, ii (1962), pp 55–58.

22 Examination of Patrick Lord Baron of Dunsany. 1641 Depositions (MS 840, fols 016r–017v), accessed at www.1641.tcd.ie

23 K.V. Mulligan, *Buildings of Meath* (Meath, 2001), p. 34.

24 W.J. Smyth, 'Exploring the Social and Cultural Topographies of Sixteenth and Seventeenth Century County Dublin' in F.H.A. Aalen and Kevin Whelan (eds), *Dublin, City and County: from Prehistory to Present (Studies in Honour of J.H. Andrews)* (Dublin, 1992), p. 140.

25 Rentals and estate accounts of the Plunketts, Earls of Fingall in Counties Cavan and Meath and in Dublin City, *c.* 1668 to 1793 (NLI, MS 8024) (henceforth cited as Fingall Papers MS 8,024).

26 A survey of the estate of William Naper, in the baronies of Half Fore and Kells, County Meath. By Sherrard and Brownrigg. 1778 (NLI MS 2,754) (henceforth cited as 'Naper Survey 1778').

27 Simington, *Civil Survey*, p. 264.

28 This section relies heavily on details provided in C.C. Ellison, 'Bishop Dopping's Visitation Book 1682–1685' in *Ríocht na Midhe*, v (1975), pp 3–13. The original document was also viewed at the RCB Library (RCBL MS D7/18.4).

29 Simms, *Meath Landowners*, p. 55.

30 Fingall Papers MS 8,024.

31 Source: Ussher Visitation 1622 (RCBL MS D7/18/1).

32 Ellison, Dopping's Visitation, p. 9.

33 Ibid.

34 Naper Survey 1778.

35 Ellison, Dopping's Visitation, p. 8.

36 P. Cassidy, 'Non-conformist Religions Denominations in County Cavan in the Seventeenth and Eighteenth Centuries' in J. Cherry and B. Scott (eds), *Cavan History and Society* (Dublin, 2014), pp 204–205.

37 Ellison, Dopping's Visitation, p. 8.

CHAPTER 3

1   For the organisation of feudalism in Ireland, see J. Otway-Ruthven 'Knight service in Ireland' in *Journal Royal Society of Antiquaries of Ireland*, lxxxix, pp 1–15.

2   Mark Hetzloff (ed.), *John Norden's The Surveyors Dialogue (1618): A Critical Edition* (Surrey, 2010), p. 34.

3   Antiquissime roll (http://chancery.tcd.ie/document/Other/antiquissime-roll/61) (23 April 2013).

4   For more on Roger Mortimer, see Ian Mortimer, *The Greatest Traitor: the Life of Sir Roger Mortimer, 1st Earl of March, Ruler of England 1327–1330* (London, 2003).

5   Bernard Burke, *Burke's Peerage and Baronetage* (London 105th edition, 4th impression of 1st impression 1969/70), pp 725–7; A.J. Otway Ruthven, *A History of Medieval Ireland* (London 2nd edition, 1980), p. 243.

6   The battle of Crécy, 1346, in northern France was one of the most important battles in the Hundred Years' War.

7   Burke, *Burke's Irish Family Records*, p. 323.

8   Books of Survey and Distribution, County Eastmeath (NLI, Ms 974, p. 72).

9   Interview with Anthony Tisdall, 14 September 2012.

10   (NLI, MS 974); R.C. Simington (ed.), *The Civil Survey, A.D. 1654–1656 County of Meath with Returns for the Meath Baronies* (Dublin, 1940), v.

11   John Ainsworth (ed.), *Report on Private Collections, the Tisdall Papers (from 1630) Tisdall x*, (NLI, report no. 290), p. 2276.

12   See Marion Rogan, *Charles Tisdall of County Meath, 1740–51: From Spendthrift Youth to Improving Landlord* (Dublin, 2014).

13   Burke, *Burke's Irish Family Records*, pp 1104–9.

14   Interview with Anthony Tisdall, Ascot, September 2013.

15   Charles Tisdall's account book, 16 October 1749, hereinafter Tisdall account book.

16   C.C. Ellison (ed.), 'Bishop Dopping's Visitation Book 1682–1685' in *Ríocht na Midhe*, v (1972), p. 11.

17   Simington (ed.), *The Civil Survey A.D. 1654–1656 County Meath*, p. 229.

18   William Sheppard, *The Court Keepers Guide: Or a Plaine and Familiar Treatise, Needful and Usefull for the Helpe of Many that are Imployed in the Keeping of Law Days, or Courts Baron* (London, 1650), p. 70.

19   Book containing records of courts leet and courts baron held in the manor of Martry, County Meath, 1789–92, hereinafter 'court book' (NLI, n. 4704, p. 4692).

20   Court book, NLI, n. 4704, p. 4692.

21   Edmund Curtis (ed.), 'The Court Book of Esker and Crumlin, 1552–1600' in *Journal of the Royal Society of Antiquaries of Ireland*, xix (1929), pp 45–64, 128–48, xx (1930), pp 38–51, 137–49; Herbert Wood (ed.), *The Court Book of the Liberty of St. Sepulchre* (Dublin, 1930).

22   Rent roll and list of securities of Michael Tisdall, relating to property in Kells Upper and Navan Lower baronies, c. 1792 (NLI, n. 4704, p. 4692).

23   William Scroggs, *The Practice of Courts Leet and Courts Baron* (3rd edition Dublin, 1714).

24   Court book, not dated.

25   *Report from the Select Committee on Manor Courts, Ireland; Together with the Minutes of Evidence, Appendix and Index*, HC 1837 (494), xv.

26   Raymond Gillespie, 'A Manor Court in Seventeenth Century Ireland' in *Irish Economic and Social History*, xxv, pp 81–7.

27   Scroggs, *The Practice of Courts Leet and Courts Baron*, p. 94.

28   Court book, not dated.

29   Ibid.

30   John Ainsworth, 'Survey of Documents in Private Keeping' in *Analecta Hibernica*, xxv (1967), pp 159–60.

31   NLI n. 4704, p. 4692; Tisdall account book, 1740–51.

32   *Report from the Select Committee on Manor Courts* HC 1837 (648), xv.1, 123–4.

33   Tisdall account book, 12 April 1748.

34   *Report from the Select Committee on Manor Courts* HC 1837 (648), xv.1, 12, 45, 68–9.

35   *Report from the Select Committee on Manor Courts* HC 1837 (494), xv.1, 13, 298–9.

36   Compensation sought by James Clarkan from Thomas Lee at a court held in Martry on Monday 15 June 1789.

37   Court book, not dated.

38   Court book, not dated.

39   NLI, n. 4704, p. 4692.

40   A map of Mount Tisdall alias Bloomsberry in the County Meath, the estate of Herr Brooke Esq. surveyed by B. & County 1802, Longfield collection (NLI, MS 21 F 14/46).

41   Court book, not dated.

42   Distraint was the remedy by which landlords sought to secure the payment of arrears by seizing the goods of the debtor, selling them and retaining what was owed.

43   NLI, n. 4704, p. 4692.

44   Court book, not dated.

45   *Report from the Select Committee on Manor Courts* HC 1837 (494), xv.1, 13, 298, 299.

46   Tisdall account book, 20 June 1744; 16 December 1746; 16 October 1749.

47   NLI, n. 4704, p. 4692.

48   Court book, 1 March 1790.

49   NLI, n. 4704, p. 4692.

50   Court book, 1 November 1792.

51   Court book, p. 25.

52   Court book, rules governing trespass.

53   Court book, not dated.

54   Walter J. King, 'Untapped Resources for Social Historians: Court Leet records' in *Journal of Social History*, xv (1982), p. 704.

55   Court book, not dated.

CHAPTER 4

1 John Smith, *The Oldcastle Centenary Book, a History of Oldcastle Commemorating St Brigid's Church 1904–2004* (2004), pp 182–3.

2 Rental of the estate of James Lenox Naper (1733–1814), NLI, MS 3031.

3 L.M. Cullen, *An Economic History of Ireland Since 1660* (London, 1972), p. 78.

4 Kevin Whelan, *The Tree of Liberty* (Cork, 1996), pp 5, 25.

5 J.L.W. Naper, *Observations on the Elective Franchise and Fixity of Tenure as Connected with Agricultural Improvement Addressed to the Landlords, Landholders and Tenants of Ireland* (Dublin, 1843), pp 3, 27.

6 Cormac Ó Gráda, *Ireland: A New Economic History 1780–1939* (Oxford, 2001) p. 100.

7 Peter Connell, *The Land and the People of County Meath 1750–1850* (Dublin, 2004), p. 56.

8 Rent of the estate of James Lennox William Naper of Loughcrew (November 1791–December 1811), NLI, MS 3,094.

9 Tithe Applotment Books, County Meath, Oldcastle and Moylagh parishes, (microfilm, NAI).

10 The ratio for conversion used is 1 Irish acre to 1.62 statute or 8 statute to 5 Irish acres.

11 J.L.W. Naper, *An Address to the Land Holders of the County of Meath in Particular and those of Ireland in General on the New Poor Law Bill* (Dublin, 1837), pp 7–8.

12 Rent roll of J.L.W. Naper minor (year ending November 1810), NLI, MS 3,094. Rent Roll of J.L.W. Naper (year ending November 1824), NLI, MS 5,773.

13 NLI, MS 3,094.

14 Rental of the estate of J.L.W. Naper, MS 3868 (1855), NLI.

15 J.L.W. Naper, *Practical Hints for the Relief and Employment of the Poor of Ireland in Continuation of a 'Plan of Labour Rate'* (Dublin, 1831).

16 *Freeman's Journal*, 5 August 1831.

17 Peter Connell, *The Land and People of County Meath 1750–1850* (Dublin, 2004), p. 44.

18 *Abstract of Population Returns for Ireland, 1831* HC 1833 (634) xxxix 72.

19 Naper, *Plan of Labour Rate*, pamphlet (1831), pp 5–6.

20 NLI, MS 5,773.

21 Smith, *Oldcastle Centenary Book*, p. 184.

22 *Freeman's Journal*, 22 January 1829.

23 *First Report of His Majesty's Commissioners for Inquiring into the Conditions of the Poorer Classes in Ireland* County Meath, Barony of Demifore, HC 1835 (369) xxxii Pt. 1.1, xxxii Pt. 11.1.

24 J.L.W. Naper, *An Address to the Landholders of County Meath in Particular and those of Ireland in General on the New Poor Law Bill* (Liverpool, 1837), pp 3–18.

25 John O'Donovan, *Ordnance Survey Field Name Books, Oldcastle and Moylagh Parishes* (1836), p. 1,126, MCL.

26 *The Census of Ireland for the Year 1851. Part 1 County of Meath*, HC 1852–53 [1494] xlvi. 561.

27 *Report from Her Majesty's Commissioners of Inquiry into the State of the Law and Practise in Respect to the Occupation of the Land in Ireland*, HC 1845 [605] [606] xix 186.

28 Naper estate, rent roll 1847–53, MCL.

29 *The Census of Ireland for the Year 1851. Part 1 County of Meath*, HC 1852–53 [1494] xlvi. 561.

30 *Fourth report from the Select Committee of the House of Lords Appointed to Inquire into the Operation of the Irish Poor Law and the Expediency of Making any Amendment in its Enactments; and to Report Thereon to the House Together with the Minutes of Evidence.* H.L. 1849 (365) xvi 831–5.

31 Richard Griffith, *Valuation of the Several Tenements Comprised in the Union of Oldcastle situated in the County of Meath* (Dublin, 1854), pp 26–8.

32 Naper estate accounts 1847–9 MCL.

CHAPTER 5

1 'Thomas Cherburgh Bligh' (www.historyofparliamentonline.org/research/members/members-1790–1820) (date accessed 16 April 2014)

2 Headfort Papers (NLI, MSS. 25,300–453; 26,679–739).

3 Election Correspondence 15 October 1807 (NLI, Headfort Papers, MS 48,884 F/9 /1).

4 R.B. McDowell, 'Revolution and the Union, 1794–1800' in W.E.Vaughan, T.W. Moody (eds), *A New History of Ireland, iv, Eighteenth-century Ireland, 1691–1800* (Oxford, 1986), p.367.

5 Gearoid O'Tuathaigh, *Ireland before the Famine 1798–1848* (Dublin, 1990), p.47.

6 Asa Briggs, *The Age of Improvement* (London 1979) p. 179.

7 Election Correspondence 18 October 1811 (NLI, Headfort Papers, MS 48,884 F/9 /2).

8 Ibid., F/9 /4, 28 September 1812.

9 Ibid., F/9 /5, 1 October 1812.

10 Ibid., F/9 /5, 16 August 1812.

11 Ibid., F/9 /5, 3 October 1812.

12 Ibid., F/9 /7 3, October 1812.

13 Ibid., F/9 /7 4, October 1812.

14 Ibid., F/9 /8 4, October 1812.

15 Ibid., F/9 /9 5 October 1812.

16 James Kelly, 'O'Beirne Thomas Lewis (1749–1823)', in H.C.G. Matthew and Brian Harrison (eds), *Oxford Dictionary of National Biography* (Oxford, 2004); online edition, Lawrence Goldman (ed.), October 2009, (www.oxforddnb.com/view/article/20438) (accessed May 19, 2014).

17 *The Eclectic Review*, vol. 1, pt 1 London 1805, p. 459.

18 NLI Headfort Papers MS 48,884 F/9 /10 6 October 1812.

19 C.J. Woods, 'Pollock, John', in James McGuire and James Quinn (eds), *Dictionary of Irish Biography* (Cambridge, 2009).

20   Election Correspondence 8 October 1812 (NLI, Headfort Papers, MS 48,884 F/9 /14).

21   Ibid., F/9 /11, 7 October 1812.

22   Ibid., F/9 /11, 7 October 1812.

23   Ibid., F/9 /15, 8 October 1812.

24   Ibid., F/9 /16, 8 October 1812.

25   Ibid., F/9 /18-22, 9–12 October 1812.

26   Ibid., F/9 /22, 12 October 1812.

27   Ibid., F/9 /21, 12 October 1812.

28   Ibid., F/9 /24, 14 October 1812.

29   Ibid., F/9 /24, 14 October 1812.

30   Ibid., F/9 /27–30, 19–21 October 1812.

31   Ibid., F/9 /31, 21 October 1812.

32   Ibid., F/9 /32, 21 October 1812.

33   Ibid., F/9 /33, 22 October 1812.

34   Election Correspondence, 24 October–13 November 1812 (NLI, Headfort Papers, MS 48,884/2 F/9 /35–36).

35   Ibid, F/9 /45, 28 October 1812.

36   Briggs, *The Age of Improvement*, p. 198.

37   (www.historyofparliamentonline.org/research/parliaments/ parliaments-1790-1820) (22/7/2014).

38   C.J. Woods, 'Plunkett, Arthur James 8th earl of Fingall Viscount Killeen', in *Dictionary of Irish Biography*.

39   S.J. Connolly, 'Union Government 1812–23' in W.E. Vaughan (ed.), *A New History of Ireland, v, Ireland under the Union, I 1801–1870* (Oxford, 1989), p.49.

40   Connolly, 'Union Government 1812–23' in *A New History of Ireland, v*, p. 67.

41   *Freeman's Journal*, 16 June 1818.

42   Election Correspondence, 19 April–22 April 1817 (NLI, Headfort Papers, MS 48,884/2 F/9 /42-43).

43   Ibid., F/9 /46, 29 June 1818.

44   Ibid., F/9 /47, 48, February 1820.

45   Ibid., F/9 /50–56, March 1820.

46   Ibid., F/9 /51, 16 March 1820.

47   Ibid., 16 March 1820.

48   Connolly, 'Union Government 1812–23' in *A New History of Ireland, v*, p. 69.

49   Connolly, 'Mass Politics and Sectarian Conflict', in *A New History of Ireland, v*, p. 86.

50   *Freeman's Journal*, 2 September 1825.

51   Ibid, 24 October 1826.

52   Connolly, 'Mass Politics and Sectarian Conflict', in *A New History of Ireland, v*, p. 99.

53   (www.historyofparliamentoN.L.I.ne.org/research/surveys/surveys-1820-1832) (4/08/2014).

54   Briggs, *The Age of Improvement*, p. 232.

55   'Headfort', (http://hansard.millbanksysteMScom), (6/08/2014).

56   Election Correspondence, 1830, (NLI, Headfort Papers, MS 48,885 F/10 /1).

57   Ibid, F/10 /3, 22 July 1830.

58   'Arthur Plunkett' (www.historyofparliamentoN.L.I.ne.org/research/members/members-1790-1820) (09/08/2014).

59   *Belfast Newsletter*, 2 November 1830.

60   McDowell, 'Revolution and the Union, 1794–1800', in *A New History of Ireland*, iv, p. 351.

61   Briggs, *The Age of Improvement*, p. 157.

62   S.J. Connolly, 'Aftermath and Adjustment' in *A New History of Ireland*, v, p. 49.

63   (www.historyofparliamentonline.org/research/surveys/surveys-1820-1832) (Date accessed 4 August 2014)

CHAPTER 6

1   *Report from the Select Committee Appointed to Inquire whether the Present Townland Valuation of Ireland made by the Committee of Valuation under the Act 16 Vict. C. 52, can be made Available for the Imposition of Poor Rate and Other Local Rates in that Country*, pp iii–iv (513), HC 1844, vii, 463–4.

2   *General Valuation of Rateable Property in Ireland, Union of Trim, Valuation of the Several Tenements*, (Dublin, 1854), Athboy, pp 99–116, Kildalkey pp 116–126, Killaconnigan, 126–134, Rathmore, 134–139. See also Union of Trim, p. 109 and Union of Kells, p. 109.

3   *Return of the Several Counties, Counties of Cities, and Counties of Towns in Ireland, of which the Valuation Under the Act 9 and 10 Vict . c. 110, has been Completed*, p. 11, (553), H.C. 1852, xlvii, 547.

4   Medway, City Ark, Darnley Papers, U565/E115. A copy is also in NLI, Microfilm P4572.

5   Medway, City Ark, Darnley Papers, Notebook of tenants' requests, U565/E851.

6   *General Valuation, Union of Trim*, pp 135–36.

7   Medway, City Ark, Darnley Papers, U565/E903.

8   *First Report from His Majesty's Commissioners for Inquiring into the Condition of the Poorer Classes in Ireland; Appendix D: Containing Baronial Examinations Relative to Earnings of Labourers, Cottier Tenants, Employment of Women and Children, Expenditure and Supplement Containing Answers to Questions 1 to 12, Circulated by the Commissioners*, 1836 [36] xxxi, p. 107.

9   NLI, MS 5,200, Workmen's accounts in respect of the estate of the Earl of Darnley in County Meath, 1839–40.

10 Samuel Lewis, *A Topographical Dictionary of Ireland*, 2 vols (London, 1837), Athboy, vol. I, pp 81–2.

11 A kish is a large square wicker basket used to carry turf.

12 Medway, City Ark, Darnley Papers, U565/32.

13 *Drogheda Argus and Leinster Journal*, 25 October 1845.

14 Medway, City Ark, Darnley Papers, U565, E902.

15 For an outline of relief measures during the Famine see Christine Kinealy, 'The Operation of the Poor Law During the Famine' in John Crowley, William J. Smith and Mike Murphy, *Atlas of the Great Irish Famine* (Cork University Press, 2012), pp 87–95.

16 For an overview of the Famine in Meath see Peter Connell, 'County Meath during the Famine', in Crowley, Smith, Murphy, *Atlas of the Great Irish Famine, 1845–52*, pp 334–340.

17 NAI, RLFC 3/1/1714.

18 NAI, RLFC 3/1/2809 and RLFC 3/1/4338.

19 NAI, RLFC 3/1/2943 and RLFC 3/2/22/31.

20 NAI, *RLFC* 3/2/22/28.

21 Danny Cusack, *The Great Famine in County Meath* (Meath County Council, 1996), p. 35 and Bríd Hiney and M.J. McGearty, *Killaconnigan alias Ballivor, A History of Ballivor Parish* (Ballivor 2014), p. 158.

22 MCL, Trim Poor Law Guardian Minute Books, BG 155 A4, 28 May 1847.

23 *Papers Relating to the Proceedings for the Relief of Distress, and State of Unions and Workhouses in Ireland 1848*, pp 123–136, HC 1847-48 [956] xxix, 447–460.

24 All calculations based on census of population figures for 1841 and 1851. See *The Census of Ireland for the Year 1851 Showing the Area Population and Number of Houses by Townlands and Electoral Divisions, vol. I, County of Meath,* pp 207–08, [1494], HC 1852, xlvi, 215–6.

25 Medway, City Ark, Darnley Papers, U565/E852 for 1834 and U565/E33 for 1848. A copy of the latter is also in NLI, Microfilm P4571. MCL, Darnley Rental 1876 and Valuation Office, Revised valuation books for the individual townlands.

26 Connell, *Land and People of County Meath*, p. 229.

27 *First Report … into the Condition of the Poorer Classes in Ireland; Appendix F,* H.C. 1836 [38], xxxiii, p. 107.

28 *Meath Herald*, 3 October 1846.

29 Medway, City Ark, Darnley Papers, U565/E33.

30 *Anglo-Celt*, 9 June 1848, p. 2.

31 Medway, City Ark, Darnley Rentals, U565/E33.

32 Charbonneau, André, and Drolet-Dubé, Doris, *A Register of Deceased Persons at Sea and on Grosse Île in 1847* (Ottawa, 1997), p. 9.

33 *Papers Relative to Emigration to the British Provinces in North America and to the Australian Colonies, part I, British provinces in North America,* HC 1847–48, (50) xlvii, pp 46–47 and Charbonneau et al, *A Register of Deceased Persons*, p. 30. For commentary on this episode see, Donald McKay, *Flight from Famine* (Toronto, 1990), p. 192, Moran, Gerard, *Sending Out Ireland's Poor: Assisted Emigration to North America in the Nineteenth Century* (Dublin, 2004) and Hiney et al, Killaconnigan, p. 161. The first two refer incorrectly to Darnley as a Kilkenny landlord while McKay wrongly asserts that 400 Darnley tenants were on the *Panope*, an error repeated in Hiney.

34 *Meath Herald*, 24 February 1849.

35 Medway, City Ark, Darnley Papers, Notebook of Tenants' requests, U565/E850.

36 Desmond Norton, *Landlords, Tenants, Famine: The Business of an Irish Land Agency in the 1840s* (Dublin 2006), pp 49–56, Patrick J. Duffy, 'Assisted emigration from the Shirley Estates 1843–54, in *Clogher Record* XIV: 2 (1992), pp 7–62

37 James Martin (Thady M'Blab), a native of Millbrook, near Oldcastle excoriated Noble in verse describing him as 'the sleek vicar, Noble Bob'. See Thady M'Blab, *Reformation the Third or the Apostate N-l-n, and the Perverts of Athboy: A Poem in Four Cantos with Notes* (Dublin, 1838), pp 5–120. I am grateful to Marion Rogan for drawing my attention to this source.

38 *Chatham and Rochester News,* 19 December 1896.

39 *The Irish Times,* 9 March 1893.

40 Speech of the Earl of Darnley in the House of Lords on Thursday 8 April 1824, on moving for an Inquiry into the State of Ireland (London, 1824).

41 See Gerard J. Lyne, *The Lansdowne Estate in Kerry under W.S. Trench 1849–72* (Dublin 2001), pp 25–57.

42 *See* www.historyofparliamentonline.org/volume/1820-1832/member/bligh-edward-1795-1835. Accessed 28 February 2015.

43 Speech of the Rt Hon. Earl of Darnley on the State of the Poor of Ireland delivered in the House of Lords on Thursday 1 May 1828, on his Lordship's motion for a Select Committee to inquire into the distressed state of the people of that country (London, 1829).

44 Medway, City Ark, Darnley Papers, Sketch of the town of Athboy, County Meath *c*.1850, U565/P023. (A copy is also in NLI, Microfilm, p. 4573.)

45 Medway, City Ark, Darnley Papers, U565/E905. Copy also in PRONI, 'An address of welcome from the tenants of the town of Trim to the Earl of Darnley on his arrival to visit his estate', 1848, T2852/22.

46 *Freeman's Journal,* 7 January 1862.

47 *Cavan Observer,* 10 January 1863 quoted in http://archiver.rootsweb. ancestry.com/th/read/IRL-CAVAN/2005-11/1133229802 accessed 16 February 2015.

48 MCL, Irish Folklore Commission, Schools' Collection MSS. 189 on microfilm.

49 Ibid.

50 Ibid.

51 Wingfield-Stratford, Esmé, *The Lords of Cobham Hall* (London, 1959), pp 423–5.

52 *The Irish Times,* 16 December 1896 and *Chatham and Rochester News,* 19 December 1896.

CHAPTER 7

1 Information for this section is based largely upon the Introduction to the Index to the Gormanston Papers in the NLI written by Sonja Tiernan in 2008.

2   Out of a total of approx. 11,000 acres in Meath and Dublin combined.

3   My thanks to Peter Connell for drawing my attention to the significance of these facts.

4   *Evidence Taken before the Commissioners Appointed to Enquire into the Occupation of Land in Ireland* [Devon Commission] (British Parliamentary Papers 1845), pp 260–68. John Donnellan Balfe (1816–80) was born at Sallybrook House, Drumconrath, County Meath, conveniently located to places such as Cloughrea and Cortobber on the Gormanston estate. Young Irelander, informer, journalist and politician, he emigrated to Tasmania in 1850 where he had as colourful and controversial a career as he had in Ireland. Cf. Stefan Petrow, 'Idealism Betrayed: John Donnellan Balfe, Supergrass of 1848' in Richard Davis and Stefan Petrow (eds), *Ireland and Tasmania 1848: sesquicentenary papers* (Crossing Press, Sydney, 1998), pp 70–137.

5   Peter Connell, *The Land and People of County Meath, 1750–1850* (Four Courts Press, Dublin, 2004), p. 241. He suggests Cloughreagh (the townland occupied by petitioner Owen Sullivan mentioned later) as an excellent case study.

6   Employing his local knowledge to full effect, Balfe was able to describe insightfully how a system of subtenants acquiring land without formal leases had developed since the mid-1820s. Gormanston's land agent Richard Cruise would appoint a head tenant whose responsibility it was to collect rents from the subtenants on the agent's behalf. In at least one instance (at Cortobber) the appointed tenant had neglected to pass on all of the collected rent. In 1840 Richard Cruise died and his son Alexander took over as Gormanston's agent on the Nobber estate. By then a large number of subtenants had fallen into arrears with their rents through no fault of their own. Some were able to negotiate agreements to stay on but Gormanston ordered the eviction of many others, notably at Cloughreagh [Report of Devon Commission, *op.cit.*, pp 260–64].

7   NLI MS 44,389/1. According to Griffith's Valuation these were two of the poorest townlands in Nobber parish.

8   Presumably Owen Farrelly of Nobber, one of the petitioners referred to below.

9   NLI MS 44,393/8. There is also a letter from John Gearty (Whitewood) dated four years earlier (8 December 1870) on a separate matter. Gearty was petitioning Gormanston to have 6 acres of an adjoining farm occupied by James Flood transferred to himself.

10 The townlands of Cortobber and Cloughreagh are located between Kingscourt and the village of Drumconrath.

11 Spiddal is located just south of Nobber village.

12 It has not been possible to locate Tyrod. It is not a townland; it appears to have been a place name which has since gone out of popular usage. It is likely that it was located near the village of Nobber and in the townland of that name.

13 As per Griffith's Valuation. The townlands of Muff, Leafin and Rathgillan are located just north of Nobber village. No address is given in McEvoy's letter of 1874 though his residence was probably at Muff. McEvoys appear to have been at this location for at least 125 years. On 1 May 1749 Thomas McEvoy of [Moyle?] signed an indenture with Jenico Preston granting him a thirty-one-year lease for 'land and

parks adjoining the great road and north side of the parish of Nobber'. This would equate roughly with the townlands of Muff and Leafin. 'Moyle' may be another name for Muff. Another indenture dated 9 November 1750 grants McEvoy and two of his brothers a thirty-one-year lease of 129 acres in the neighbouring townland of Lower Germanagh [NLI Ms 44, 359/2].

14   Based on information contained in the letters in NLI. Most but not all of the petitioners revealed their approximate acreage in 1874. McEvoy did not, but in 1881 the McEvoys held at least 228 acres at Muff (see footnote (26) below). At the time of Griffith's Valuation (c. 1851), the acreage of the petitioners varied from McEvoy with 264 acres to Peter Reilly with 22 acres. McCann held 129 acres. Despite reference in Fagan's letter of 1874 to his land having been 'held and enjoyed by [my] forefathers', he is recorded in neither Griffith's Valuation nor the Tithe Applotments.

15   Ordnance Survey Field Name books (1835–36). The townland had a population of 100, of whom half were Protestant.

16   The second largest and second smallest respectively of the petitioning farmers.

17   The Griffith's Valuation map shows a corn–mill and kiln here.

18   This presumably is a reference to Jenico Preston (1837–1907), 14th Viscount Gormanston, the son of Edward Preston (1796–1876), 13th Viscount Gormanston and the 'Lordship' to whom the letter was addressed. Since Edward was 78 years of age at the time and his son Jenico only 37, it was presumably the latter who was handling the day-to-day affairs of the estate. Jenico Preston is also recorded in December 1874 as one of three men overseeing the Kingscourt Petty Sessions. He later served as Governor of Tasmania 1893–1900. Significantly, in 1895 the visiting Michael Davitt warned Gormanston's fellow Catholics in the colony that he was a bad Irishman and one of the worst landlords [Richard Davis, Gormanston 14th Viscount (1837–1907) in *Australian Dictionary of Biography*, vol. 9 (Melbourne University Press, 1983)].

19   Though, as noted previously, he is recorded in neither Griffith's Valuation nor the Tithe Applotments. It may be that his father married into the farm and that he is recorded under a different surname.

20   It is not known whether Gearty's request was granted. Geartys lived at Whitewood Cross on the Nobber-Kingscourt road in the residence that until the early 1980s served as a public house. Geartys married into the McDermotts who are still resident and farming at this location.

21   Land facing north was noted for being less profitable than that which faced south and received more sunlight. In neighbouring County Monaghan poet Patrick Kavanagh had one of his characters famously warn his daughter never to marry a man from a townland ending in *duff*. This signified north-facing land and was sure to dictate a life of toil and drudgery for any woman marrying into such a farm. Kavanagh's own Shancoduff provides a classic example.

22   Land Valuations Office records, Dublin. Information also from J.J. O'Reilly (Cortobber) 22 May 2013. O'Reilly grew up in the old McCann farmhouse, his mother Katie Clarke and uncle John Clarke having purchased the farm from Edward McCann.

23 Ibid. James Reilly, a bachelor (?) sold up in 1938.

24 That is, assuming that the Fagans recorded at Nobber were the same as those recorded at Tyrod in 1874. It seems likely that they lived out the Cregg Road, about ½ mile from the village, where there have been Fagans until quite recently.

25 Census of Ireland 1901. Though see endnote 29 below regarding McEvoys.

26 NLI MS 44,389/1 [Gormanston Papers].

27 Letter from James Plunkett and Son Solicitors (Dublin) to Philip McEvoy (Muff), 28 Apr. 1881 [NAI].

28 *British Parliamentary Papers on Ireland, Return of judicial rents fixed by sub-commissioners and Civil Bill Courts, notified to Irish Land Commissioners,* May–June 1888, p. 254. Dr James McEvoy was granted an abatement of £17 that reduced the annual rent for his 113 acres at Muff from £104 to £87 (bringing it roughly in line with the Poor Law Valuation of £83). Philip McEvoy received no abatement on the annual rent for his 115 acres at Muff of £102 (being, as it already was, roughly in line with the Poor Law Valuation of £98).

29 Census of Ireland 1901. James McEvoy (52), medical officer, is listed along with his wife, two daughters, one granddaughter and a servant.

30 Letter from Laurence McEvoy (Pichualco, Ciapas, Mexico) to his sister Kate (Muff) 25 April 1894. Copy retained in the Kilmainhamwood History Committee Archives, residence of Joe Gogarty, Eden, Kilmainhamwood, County Meath.

31 Chiapas, where McEvoy was resident, is the southernmost state of Mexico, noted in recent decades as the base of the Zapatista National Liberation Movement and the location of a popular uprising in 1994.

32 Indeed, the name Owen (the same as the 1874 petitioner) is recorded on the 2013 electoral roll.

33 One possible exception is Mrs Fagan (Nobber) who is listed amongst those for eviction in 1880. She may have been the widow of Richard Fagan (Tyrod) who applied for an abatement in 1874.

34 Vol. 3 (1857–76) and Vol. 4 (1877–92) of the rental records of the Brittas estate retained in the Meath County Library, Navan.

35 Vols 1–6 of the rental records of the Brittas estate.

36 Index to the Shirley Papers (D3531) retained at PRONI.

37 Devon Commission, *op cit.*, p. 263.

38 NLI MS 44,393/8. See extracts of letters quoted earlier in this essay.

39 Terence A.M. Dooley, 'Estate Ownership and Management in nineteenth century and early twentieth century Ireland' in *Sources for the History of Landed Estates in Ireland* (Irish Academic Press, Dublin, 2000), pp 3–16. See also W.E. Vaughan, *Landlords and Tenants in mid-Victorian Ireland* (Clarendon Press, Oxford, 1994), p. 21 and p. 48, for a comparison of rents and agricultural output 1851–80. I am indebted to Peter Connell for drawing my attention to these sources, which help us to judge the justice or otherwise of the proposed rent increases.

CHAPTER 8

1   Cited in Alun Howkins, *Poor Labouring Men: Rural Radicalism in Norfolk, 1870–1923* (London, 1985), p. 1.

2   *Weekly Northern Whig*, 5 April 1879.

3   Samuel Clark, *Social Origins of the Irish Land War* (Princeton, 1979), pp 231–2.

4   Gerard Moran, '"Near Famine": The Roman Catholic Church and the subsistence crisis of 1879-82' in *Studia Hibernica*, no. 32 (2002), p. 156.

5   See Clark, *Social Origins*, chapter 8.

6   J.J. Lee, *The Modernisation of Irish Society* (Dublin, 1971), pp 66–7.

7   Virginia Crossman, *Poverty and the Poor Law in Ireland, 1850–1914* (Liverpool, 2013).

8   Samuel Clark, *Social Origins of the Irish Land War* (Princeton, 1879), pp 3, 225.

9   See Stephen Ball, 'Crowd Activity During the Irish Land War, 1880–90' in P.J. Jupp and Eoin Magennis (eds), *Crowds in Ireland, c. 1720–1920* (London, 2000), pp 212–48.

10 Jonathan Bell and Mervyn Watson, *A History of Irish Farming, 1750–1950* (Dublin, 2008), chapter 18; idem, *Irish Farming: Implements and Techniques* (Edinburgh, 1986), pp 3–10.

11 Brian Casey, 'Matt Harris and the Irish Land Question, 1876–82' in *Rural History*, 25:2 (2014), pp 183-201.

12 See Brian Casey, 'Land, Politics and Religion on the Clancarty Estate, East Galway, 1851–1914' (PhD thesis, Maynooth University, 2011), chapter 1.

13 *Freeman's Journal*, 11 January 1878; 5 November 1879.

14 *Meath Chronicle*, 20 January 1961.

15 See L.P. Curtis, 'Incumbered wealth: Landed indebtedness in post-Famine Ireland' in *American Historical Review*, vol. 85, no. 2 (1980), pp 332–67.

16 S.J. Connolly (ed.), *The Oxford Companion to Irish History* (Oxford, 2004), p. 153.

17 *Freeman's Journal*, 18 April 1873.

18 T.W. Moody, *Davitt and the Irish Revolution, 1846–82* (Oxford, 1984) pp 120–4.

19 Terence Dooley, *The Decline and Fall of the Dukes of Leinster, 18872–1948: Love, War, Debt and Madness* (Dublin, 2014), pp 39–40.

20 K.T. Hoppen, *Ireland Since 1800: Conflict and Conformity* (London, 1999), p. 101.

21 J.C. Beckett, *The Making of Modern Ireland, 1603–1923* (London, 1966), pp 352–3.

22 Paul Adelman, *Victorian Radicalism: The Middle Class Experience, 1830–1914* (Essex, 1984), p. 48.

23 Irish National Land League Circular in John Sweetman papers, NLI, MS 47,574/3.

24 Letter from Royal Agricultural Society to John Sweetman, 7 November 1877 in John Sweetman papers, MS 47,573/1.

25 R.V. Comerford, *The Fenians in Context: Irish Politics and Society, 1848–82* (Dublin, 1998), p. 188.

26 Gerard Moran, *A Radical Priest in Mayo: Fr Patrick Lavelle, the Rise and Fall of an Irish Nationalist, 1825–86* (Dublin, 1994), pp 132, 136.

27 David Thornley, *Isaac Butt and the Home Rule Party* (Dublin, 1964),

28 Lee, *Modernisation*, p. 77.

29 James S. Donnelly, *The Land and the People of Nineteenth Century Cork* (London, 1975), p. 263.

30 David Thornley, *Isaac Butt and Home Rule* (Dublin, 1964), pp 218–19.

31 John Sweetman papers, NLI, MS 47,573/2.

32 Ibid.

33 Letter from Thomas O'Rourke to Sweetman, 9 October 1878 in John Sweetman papers, MS 47,573/4.

34 John Sweetman papers, MS 47,573/5.

35 *Weekly Northern Whig*, 5 April 1879.

36 Ibid.

37 *Freeman's Journal*, 6 April 1878; 13 April 1878; 20 April 1878.

38 Donnacha Seán Lucey, *Land, Popular Politics and Agrarian Violence in Ireland, 1872–86: The Case of County Kerry* (Dublin, 2011), p. 15.

39 *Connaught Telegraph*, 6 April 1878.

40 Ibid., 6 April 1878; 20 April 1878.

41 See also Brian Casey, 'Land, Politics and Religion on the Clancarty Estate, East Galway, 1851–1914' (PhD thesis, Maynooth University, 2012), chapter 4.

42 Clark, *Social Origins*, pp 233–5.

43 *Weekly Northern Whig*, 5 April 1879.

44 See Casey, 'Clancarty', chapter 4; Donnacha Seán Lucey, *Land, Popular Politics and Agrarian Violence in Ireland, 1876–82: The Case of County Kerry* (Dublin, 2011).

45 See L.P. Curtis, *The Depiction of Eviction in Ireland, 1845–1910* (Dublin, 2011); idem 'Demonising the Irish landlord since the Famine' in Brian Casey (ed.), *Defying the Law of the Land: Agrarian Radicals in Irish History* (Dublin, 2013).

46 Ann Andrews, *Newspapers and Newsmakers: The Dublin Nationalist Press in the Mid-Nineteenth Century* (Liverpool, 2014), chapter 1.

47 Donnelly, 'The Land Question in Nationalist Politics', in Thomas Hachey and Lawrence J. McCaffrey (eds), *Perspectives on Irish Nationalism* (Lexington, 1989), pp 90–1.

48 John Sweetman papers, MS 47,574/7.

49 Ibid.

50 See Eric Hobsbawm, *Nations and Nationalism since 1780, Programme, Myth and Reality* (Cambridge, 1990), p. 101.

51 Clark, *Social Origins*, p. 280.

52 Samuel Clark, 'The Importance of Agrarian Classes: Agrarian Class Structure and Collective Action in Nineteenth Century Ireland', in P.J. Drudy, *Ireland, Land, Politics and People* (Cambridge, 1982), p. 11.

53 John Sweetman papers, MS 47,573/2.

54 Ibid., MS 47,573/9.

55 Thomas Dowling to John Sweetman, 2 April 1879, MS 47,573/9.

CHAPTER 9

1 Fergus Campbell, *Land and Revolution: Nationalist Politics in the West of Ireland 1891–1921* (Oxford, 2008), p. 83.

2 Terence A.M. Dooley , '"A World Turned Upside Down": A Study of the Changing Social World of the Landed Nobility of County Meath 1875–1945', in *Ríocht Na Midhe*, Vol. XII (2001), p. 207.

3 David Cannadine, *The Decline and Fall of the British Aristocracy* (London, 1992).

4 *Meath Chronicle*, 29 January 1916.

5 Ulster Covenant, available at www.proni.gov.uk/index/search_the_archives/ulster_covenant.htm [10 November 2011].

6 Papers of the IUA, Statement of receipt to anti home rule, 1912, D989/A/9/2.

7 Papers of the IUA, Statement of receipt to anti home rule, 1912, D989/A/9/2.

8 Brick to Lord Gormanston, 3 October 1912, (NLI, Gormanston papers, Ms 44,426/4).

9 Ismay Crichton-Stuart to Lord Gormanston (his sister), 12 December 1912 (NLI, Gormanston papers, Ms 44,426/80).

10 Viscount Hythe to Lord Gormanston, 25 July 1912 (NLI, Gormanston papers Ms 44,452/8).

11 *The Irish Times*, 1 August 1912.

12 Ibid.

13 Ibid.

14 Ibid.

15 Ibid., 26 October 1912.

16 Ibid.

17 Ibid.

18 Mark Amory, *Biography of Lord Dunsany* (London, 1972), p. 26.

19 Cannadine (1992), p. 73.

20 Patrick Buckland, *Irish Unionism: One, the Anglo and New Ireland 1885–1922* (Dublin, 1972), p. 32.

21 Amory (1972), p.153.

22 Sir H. Plunkett to John Redmond, 4 August 1914 (NLI, Redmond Papers, Ms 15,221). Peter Martin, 'Dulce et Decorum: Irish Nobles and the Great War, 1914–19', in Adrian Gregory and Senia Paseta (eds), *Ireland and the Great War, 'A War to Unite Us All'?* (Manchester, 2006), p. 32.

23 Peter Clinton to Lord Gormanston, 19 August 1914 (NLI, Gormanston papers, Ms 44,425/1).

24 Martin (2006), p. 31.

25 Sir H. Plunkett to John Redmond, 4 Aug 1914 (NLI, Redmond Papers, Ms 15,221).

26 *The Irish Times*, 7 August 1914.

27 *Meath Chronicle*, 8 August 1914.

28 Ibid.

29 Elizabeth Mary Margaret Burk Plunkett Fingall, Countess Fingall, *Seventy Years Young: Memories of Elizabeth, Countess of Fingall, told to Pamela Hinkson* (London, 1991), p. 348.

30 *The Irish Times*, 1 September 1914.

31 Amory (1972), p.115.

32 Ibid.

33 *Meath Chronicle*, 5 September 1914.

34 Meath County Police Report (MCPR, October 1914 (NUIM library).

35 Maurice Moore to Lord Gormanston 21 September 1914 (NLI, Gormanston papers, Ms 44,453/4).

36 Colleague to Lord Gormanston, 17 August 1915 (NLI, Gormanston papers, Ms 44,462/3).

37 Martin (2006), p. 34.

38 *The Irish Times*, 31 August 1915.

39 *Meath Chronicle*, 22 January 1916.

40 Ibid.

41 Ibid.

42 *The Irish Times*, 1 March 1916.

43 *Meath Chronicle*, 18 March 1916.

44 *The Irish Times*, 1 January 1916.

45 Meath County Police Report (MCPR), February 1916.

46 *The Irish Times*, 5 December 1914.

47 Ibid., 7 October 1914.

48 Art Kavanagh, *The Landed Gentry & Aristocracy of Meath* (Dublin, 2005), p. 102.

49 *Meath Chronicle*, 25 December 1915.

50 *The Irish Times*, 29 November 1916.

51 IGMR, April 1917.

52 *Meath Chronicle*, 11 March 1916.

53 Ibid., 18 December 1915.

54 Ibid., 15 August 1914.

55 Ibid.

56 Ibid., 5 September 1914.

57 Ibid.

58 *Sinn Féin*, 15 August 1914, p. 5.

59 Ibid., 5 September 1914, p. 3.

60 MCPR, June 1917.

61 William Dorris to John Redmond, 8 March 1916 (NLI, Redmond papers, MS 15262/3).

62 *Meath Chronicle*, 23 September 1916.

63 Eamon Doyle, *March into Meath: In the Footsteps of 1798* (Dublin, 2011), p. 28.

64 *Notes from Ireland*, no. 3, vol. 25, 1 August 1916, p. 35.

65 Ibid., p.1.

66   R.B. Dowell, *The Irish Convention 1917–18* (London, 1970), p. 26.

67   Catherine B. Shannon, *Arthur J. Balfour and Ireland 1974–1922* (USA, 1988), p. 208.

68   *The Irish Times*, 8 July 1916. Patick Buckland, *Irish Unionism 1885–1923: A Documentary History* (Northern Ireland, 1973), p. 352.

69   Sir H. Plunkett to Redmond, 28 July 1917 (MS 15,221).

70   F.S.L. Lyons, 'The New Nationalism, 1916–18', in W.E. Vaughan (ed.), *A New History of Ireland VI: Ireland Under the Union 1870–1921* (Oxford, 2010), p. 229.

71   Sir H, Plunkett to John Redmond, 29 May 1917 (NLI, Redmond papers, MS 15,221).

72   Sir H, Plunkett to John Redmond, 18 August 1917 (NLI, Redmond papers, MS 15,221).

73   Sir H, Plunkett to John Redmond, 25 August 1917 (NLI, Redmond papers, MS 15,221).

74   Buckland, *Irish Unionism, 1885–1923*, p. 351.

75   Lyons, 'The New Nationalism, 1916–18', p. 229.

76   IGCR, June 1917.

77   Interview with Emer Mooney, 21 October 2011.

78   Mark Bence-Jones, *Twilight of the Ascendancy* (London, 1993), p. 168.

79   *Meath Chronicle*, 4 December 1915.

80   Ibid., 12 February 1916.

81   *The Irish Times*, 17 March 1917.

82   Bence-Jones, p. 182.

83   Patrick Butler to Lady Gormanston, 20 November 1914 and 1 October 1914 (NLI, Gormanston papers, Ms 44,428/3).

84   Keith Jeffery, *Ireland and the Great War* (Cambridge, 2000), p. 70.

85   Buckland, *Irish Unionism, 1885–1923*, p. 352.

86   Jeffery, *Ireland and the Great War*, p. 70.

CHAPTER 10

1   *Meath Chronicle*, 2 October 1959.

2   Interview with Noel Mahon, resident of Gate Lodge, conducted by Malachy Hand.

Bibliography

This bibliography is of various primary sources relating to the estates and Big Houses of county Meath; sources that were used in the writing of the essays in this collection. More detailed information is provided in the endnotes of each essay. While it is not definitive, it is hoped that it is comprehensive enough for the reader to delve deeper into the Big Houses and landed estates of County Meath and to have a sense of the breadth, range and location of material relating to the county. An important caveat to note for the reader is that some of the sources are individual items rather than part of a collection list. An excellent starting point for research is sources.nli.ie, which is the digitised version of Hayes' Manuscript Sources for the Study of Irish Civilisation. The online catalogue of the NLI, catalogue.nli.ie, is also an excellent resource. There are incidences, such as in relation to the Darnley papers, where there are microfilm copies of originals held outside of Ireland in the possession of the NLI. A reference starting with P. or N. indicates a microfilm copy. The 1641 Depositions are online at 1641.tcd.ie. Other excellent reference guides include Terence Dooley's *The Big Houses and Landed Estates of Ireland: A research guide* (Dublin, 2007).

This bibliography is divided into general sources and then more specific ones relating to individual estates, which are then subdivided according to which repository they are in.

GENERAL PRIMARY SOURCES

National Library of Ireland

Books of survey and distribution, County Meath MS 974
Longfield map Mount Tisdall MS 21 F 14 map 45
Longfield map Bloomsberry 1801 MS 21 F 14 map 46

National Archives of Ireland (NAI)

Distress Papers
Famine Relief Commission Papers
Outrage Papers
State of the Country Papers
Tithe Applotment Books, County Meath

Trinity College Dublin

Down Survey map of the Half Barony of Fore (Meath)
1641 Depositions 1641.tcd.ie

Registry of Deeds

Memorials

Meath County Library (MCL), Navan

Brittas Papers
Essex Papers
Pollock Papers
Russell Papers
O' Donovan, John, *Ordnance Survey field name books, Oldcastle and Moylagh parishes* (1836)
Griffith, Richard, *Valuation of the several tenements comprised in the Union of Oldcastle situated in the County of Meath* (Dublin, 1854)

Landed Estate Papers

National Library of Ireland

Darnley Papers
Domville Papers
Fingall Papers
Fowler Papers
Hamilton Papers
Hatch Papers
Map survey of the Lordship of Athboy, County Meath, the estate of the Earl of Darnley, 1767NLI, Ms. 5485
Naper Papers
Preston Papers
Pratt Papers

Tisdall Papers on microfilm n. 4704, p. 4692
Townley Hall Papers

Landed Estate Collection Lists
Gormanston Estate Papers
Headfort Estate Papers
John Sweetman Papers

Medway Archives and Local Studies Centre (MALSC)
Papers of the estates of the Earl of Darnley

Public Record Office of Northern Ireland
Meath electorate re-1807 elections. PRONI T3163/2/1
Sketch of the town of Athboy, County Meath, showing decorations erected
for the reception of the Earl and Countess of Darnley at their first visit after
becoming landlord of the estate, *c.*1850. PRONI T2851/22, NLI Microfilm
P 4571
Typescript copies of correspondence of Earl of Darnley with his sons at Eton,
1774-87. PRONI T2851/24

In Private Possession
Naper estate, rent roll 1847–53.
Naper estate accounts 1847–9.
Tisdall papers (in possession of Anthony Tisdall, Ascot, Berkshire)
Charles Tisdall's account book, 1740–51
Portrait of Michael Tisdall

Index

Also from The History Press

Irish Revolutionaries

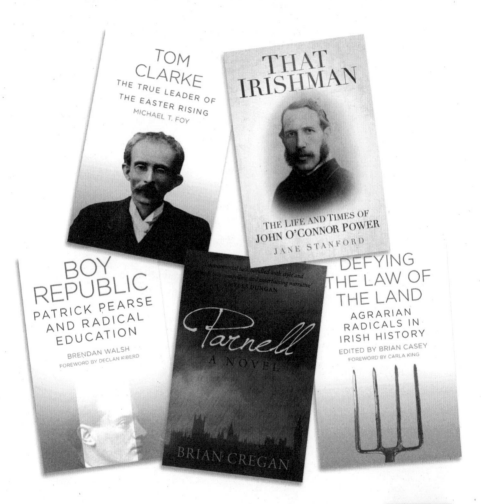

Find these titles and more at
www.thehistorypress.ie